# THE
# VEGETARIAN
# BOOK

# THE VEGETARIAN BOOK

Carla Bardi, Ting Morris
Marco Lanza

MᶜRᴀᴇ Books

This book was conceived, edited and designed by
McRae Books Srl
Borgo Santa Croce, 8,
50122 Florence, Italy
info@mcraebooks.com

Project Director: Anne McRae
Design Director: Marco Nardi
Text: Carla Bardi, Ting Morris
Photography: Marco Lanza, Walter Mericchi
Home Economist: Sara Vignozzi
Layouts: Anne McRae
Editing: Helen Farrell

ISBN: 88-88166-76-9

Color separations: Fotolito Toscana, Florence, Italy
Printed and bound in Italy

1 3 5 7 9 10 8 6 4 2

# Contents

# INTRODUCTION

There are many reasons to choose a vegetarian diet, ranging from health concerns, to ethics, and ecology. The increasing use of hormones in raising livestock is a major health worry for many, while the harsh and often unsavory conditions of modern "factory-farming" raise both health and ethical issues for others. Regardless of the reasoning behind a decision to cut down on or eliminate meat in our diets, many of us are looking for tasty, simple, and modern dishes to serve to our families and friends. With more than 400 recipes, *THE VEGETARIAN BOOK* offers a tantalizing array of vegetarian food drawn from cuisines around the world. Enjoy!

*Lemon and mint salad*
*(see page 109)*

# STARTERS

S tarters, or appetizers, should be just what their names suggests—an overture, or beginning to tantalize the palate and prepare the way for the dishes that follow. Quantities for the recipes in this chapter have been adjusted accordingly so that your family or guests will still have an appetite for the rest of the meal. That said, many of the recipes in this chapter also make wonderful snacks or even meals in themselves. In that case you should double the quantities.

*A wedge of quiche or savory pie makes the perfect starter for a family meal or a casual dinner party. Like many pies or quiches (see the recipes in the Snacks chapter for other appetizer ideas), this one can be cooked several hours in advance and either served at room temperature or reheated and brought to the table piping hot. This particular savory pie is especially good with a glass of cool, dry and fruity white wine.*

Right: Bell pepper savory pie (see page 16)
Left: Fried cabbage ravioli (see page 43)

## Tartlets with goat's cheese and sun-dried tomatoes

*Serves: 6*
*Preparation: 20 minutes + 30 minutes to rest dough*
*Cooking: 10–12 minutes*
*Recipe grading: fairly easy*

- 1$^1/_3$ cups/200 g all-purpose/plain flour
- $^1/_3$ cup/50 g finely ground almonds
- $^1/_2$ teaspoon salt
- $^1/_3$ cup/90 g butter
- 1 egg
- 2 tablespoons freshly grated Parmesan cheese
- 4 oz/125 g fresh creamy goat's cheese
- 2 tablespoons finely chopped chives
- salt and freshly ground black pepper to taste
- 6 sun-dried tomatoes, packed in oil, drained and coarsely chopped

Stir together the flour, almonds, and salt, in a medium bowl. • Cut in the butter until the mixture resembles coarse crumbs. • Add the egg and Parmesan and stir well. • Wrap the dough in plastic wrap and refrigerate for 30 minutes. • Preheat the oven to 375°F/ 190°C/ gas 5. • Butter and flour a baking sheet. • Roll the dough out on a lightly floured work surface to $^1/_8$ inch (3 mm) thick. • Use a glass or cookie cutter about 2$^1/_2$ inches (6 cm) in diameter to cut out the tartlets. • Place the tartlets on the baking sheet and bake for 10–12 minutes, or until pale golden brown. • Mix the goat's

cheese with the chives and season with salt and pepper. • Spread each tartlet with cheese mixture and top with tomato. • Serve warm.

## Rice balls with onion chutney

*Serves: 6*
*Preparation: 30 minutes*
*Cooking: 40 minutes*
*Recipe grading: fairly easy*

- 3 tablespoons extra-virgin olive oil
- 1 small onion, finely chopped
- 2 cups/400 g short-grain rice
- $^1/_2$ cup/125 ml dry white wine
- 1$^1/_4$ quarts/1.25 liters vegetable stock (bouillon cube)
- salt and freshly ground black pepper to taste
- 1 teaspoon ground saffron
- 1 tablespoon butter
- $^1/_2$ cup/60 g freshly grated Parmesan cheese
- $^1/_2$ cup/75 g all-purpose/plain flour
- 1 egg, lightly beaten
- $^1/_2$ cup/75 g fine dry bread crumbs
- 2 cups/500 ml olive oil, for frying

### Onion chutney

- 1 large onion, finely chopped
- 2 tablespoons butter
- 1 tablespoon sugar
- 1 tablespoon white wine vinegar
- salt and freshly ground black pepper to taste

Heat the oil in a large skillet (frying pan) and sauté the onion until transparent. • Add the rice and cook over high heat, stirring constantly, for 2 minutes. • Stir in the wine and when this has been absorbed, begin stirring in the stock, $^1/_2$ cup (125 ml) at a time. Cook and stir until each addition has been absorbed, until the rice is tender, about 15–18 minutes. Season with salt and pepper. • Remove from heat and stir in the saffron, butter, and Parmesan. Set aside to cool. • Prepare the onion chutney: Sauté the onion in the butter in a small saucepan over medium-low heat until golden brown and almost caramelized. Stir in the sugar and vinegar and season with salt and pepper. • Shape the cooled risotto into 24 small balls. Dredge the balls in the flour, dip in the egg, and roll in the bread crumbs. • Heat the oil in a large skillet until very hot. Fry the balls in small batches until golden brown all over. Drain on paper towels. • When all the balls are fried, place on a serving dish and spoon the onion chutney over the top.

## Mediterranean toasts

*Serves: 4*
*Preparation: 10 minutes*
*Cooking: 10 minutes*
*Recipe grading: easy*

- 4 large slices firm-textured (homestyle) bread
- 1 cup/250 ml olive oil, for frying
- 2 tablespoons white wine vinegar
- 1 tablespoon each sugar, capers, pine nuts, raisins, diced candied lemon peel
- salt and freshly ground black pepper to taste
- 2 ripe tomatoes

Heat the oil in a large skillet (frying pan) and fry the bread until golden brown. Drain on paper towels. • Bring the vinegar, sugar, and 2 tablespoons of water to a boil and stir in the capers, pine nuts, raisins, lemon peel, and tomatoes. Cook for 5 minutes. • Spread the toasts with this mixture and serve hot.

*Tartlets with goat's cheese and sun-dried tomatoes and Rice balls with onion chutney*

*Pine nuts, or kernels, are obtained from the cones of pine trees of the pinus genus. Their grey-brown shells cover small ivory-colored nuts that have a full, rich flavor and a high fat-content. Just a few tablespoons of pine nuts imparts a distinctive flavor, especially to vegetable dishes. Pine nuts can also be cold-pressed into a delicious, if expensive, oil.*

## Bell pepper savory pie

*Serves: 6–8*
*Preparation: 10 minutes*
*Cooking: 30–40 minutes*
*Recipe grading: fairly easy*

- 7 oz/200 g fresh or frozen puff pastry, thawed if frozen
- whites of 4 leeks, cut into small rounds
- 2 red bell peppers/capsicums, seeded, cored, and cut into small squares
- 3 small red chile peppers, finely chopped
- 3 tablespoons butter
- 1 tablespoon water
- 3 eggs, lightly beaten
- ³/4 cup/180 ml light/single cream
- 6 tablespoons freshly grated Parmesan cheese
- ¹/4 teaspoon paprika

Preheat the oven to 400°F/200°C/gas 6. • Butter a 10-inch (23-cm) round spring-form pan. • Unfold or unroll the puff pastry on a lightly floured work surface. Line the base and sides of the prepared baking pan, trimming the edges to fit. • Use a fork to prick the pastry all over. • Bake for 15–20 minutes, or until puffed and golden brown. • Cook the leeks, bell peppers, and chile with the butter and water in a medium saucepan over medium heat for 20 minutes. • Season with the salt and remove from heat. • Beat the eggs, cream, Parmesan, and paprika in a small bowl. Pour the beaten egg mixture into the bell pepper mixture, blending well. • Pour the mixture into the baked pastry base. • Bake for 15–20 minutes, or until firm to the touch. • Transfer to a serving plate and serve hot or at room temperature.

## Zucchini with arugula pesto, raisins, and pine nuts

*Serves: 4–6*
*Preparation: 25 minutes + 1 hour to marinate*
*Cooking: 15 minutes*
*Recipe grading: easy*

- 1¹/4 lb/600 g small, tender zucchini/courgettes
- 4 tablespoons extra-virgin olive oil
- 2 tablespoons cider vinegar
- 1 tablespoon balsamic vinegar
- 1 clove garlic, thinly sliced
- salt and freshly ground black pepper to taste
- 4 oz/125 g arugula/rocket
- 6 tablespoons pine nuts
- 4 tablespoons raisins

Rinse the zucchini thoroughly under cold running water and dry well. • Trim the ends off the zucchini and cut lengthwise in very thin slices. • Place the zucchini in a small, shallow dish. Mix 2 tablespoons of the oil, the cider vinegar, balsamic vinegar, garlic, salt, and pepper in a small bowl and beat well with a fork. Pour the mixture over the zucchini. Set aside to marinate for 1 hour. • Rinse the arugula thoroughly under cold running water, then drain and dry well. • Place 3 oz (90 g) of the arugula in a blender with 4 tablespoons of pine nuts and the remaining oil and chop until smooth. If the mixture is not liquid enough add 1–2 tablespoons hot (not boiling) water. • Drain the zucchini, setting aside the marinade. • Heat a large grill pan or skillet (frying pan) over medium heat. No fat is required. Cook the zucchini in batches for 4–5 minutes each batch, or until lightly browned. • Arrange the remaining arugula on a serving platter and arrange the zucchini on top. Sprinkle with the remaining 2 tablespoons of pine nuts and the raisins. Season with salt and pepper and drizzle with the marinade. • Serve hot or at room temperature.

## Spinach with garbanzo beans and pine nuts

*Serves: 6*
*Preparation: 30 minutes*
*Cooking: 15–20 minutes*
*Recipe grading: fairly easy*

- 2 lb/1 kg fresh spinach, stalks removed
- 1 teaspoon cumin seeds
- 6 tablespoons extra-virgin olive oil
- 1 slice white sandwich bread, crusts removed and cut in cubes
- 3 cloves garlic, thinly sliced
- 2 tablespoons pine nuts
- 1 small red chile pepper, deseeded and finely chopped
- 1 small bunch fresh oregano, roughly chopped
- 2 tablespoons red wine vinegar
- 2 tablespoons water
- two (14-oz/400-g) cans cooked garbanzo beans/chickpeas, drained, rinsed, and dried
- 1¹/₂ teaspoons sweet smoked paprika
- salt and freshly ground pepper to taste

Wash the spinach under cold running water. Do not drain but place in a saucepan and cook, with just the water clinging to its leaves, for 3 minutes. Drain, press out excess water, chop coarsely and set aside. • Crush the cumin seeds in a mortar and pestle. • Heat 4 tablespoons of the oil in a skillet (frying pan) and fry the bread until golden brown on both sides. • Add the garlic, cumin, pine nuts, chile, and oregano, and sauté for 2 minutes. • Remove from heat and chop finely in a food processor with the vinegar. • Sauté the spinach in the remaining oil. Add the garbanzo beans and bread paste, mix well and stir in a teaspoon of smoked paprika. Cook over low heat, stirring constantly, for about 3 minutes, until all the ingredients are hot and the flavors have been absorbed. Season with salt and pepper. If the mixture is too thick, add another half-tablespoon of vinegar or a little more water. Sprinkle with the remaining paprika. Serve with fried bread, or eat on its own.

---

*Marzolino is a very fresh Pecorino cheese from Tuscany. It is made in March ("Marzo," in Italian) and generally served with walnuts, pears, and honey. Combining cheese with sweet foods is an inspired Tuscan tradition, as these little pastries will attest. If you can't get Marzolino, substitute with another fresh Pecorino (ewe's milk) cheese.*

## Sweet Marzolino pastries

*Serves: 6*
*Preparation: 30 minutes*
*Cooking: 15–20 minutes*
*Recipe grading: fairly easy*

- 14 oz/400 g frozen puff pastry, thawed
- ¹/₂ cup/125 ml butter, melted
- 1¹/₄ cups/125 g Marzolino cheese, sliced
- 2 large pears, sliced
- 4 tablespoons sugar
- 1 teaspoon ground cinnamon
- 1 cup/100 g shelled walnuts, coarsely chopped
- 1 tablespoon unsweetened cocoa powder

Preheat the oven to 400°F/200°C/gas 6. • Oil and flour a baking sheet. • Roll the pastry out into thin sheets, then cut it into pieces about 3 inches (8 cm) square. Brush with half the butter. • In the center of each piece, place a slice of cheese, a slice of pear, and a teaspoon of sugar. Sprinkle with the cinnamon and walnuts. Fold the dough over the filling to form triangular pockets and pinch the edges together to seal. • Place the pastries on the baking sheet. Drizzle with the remaining butter, and sprinkle with the cocoa powder and a little extra sugar. • Bake for 15–20 minutes, or until the pastry is golden brown.

## Puff pastry vegetable parcels

*Serves: 6–8*
*Preparation: 30 minutes*
*Cooking: 15–20 minutes*
*Recipe grading: fairly easy*

- 8 oz/250 g carrots, cut in small cubes
- 2 tablespoons extra-virgin olive oil
- 10 oz/300 g zucchini/courgettes, cut in very thin slices
- white of 1 large leek, thinly sliced
- 1 medium onion, finely chopped
- 1 stalk celery, finely chopped
- salt and freshly ground black pepper to taste
- 1 teaspoon dried oregano
- 14 oz/400 g frozen puff pastry, thawed
- 4 oz/125 g Emmental or Cheddar cheese, cut in very small cubes
- 1 egg, beaten

Preheat the oven to 350°F/180°C/gas 4. • Lightly oil a baking sheet. • Cook the carrots in a large pan of lightly salted, boiling water for 5 minutes. Drain well. • Heat the oil in a large skillet (frying pan) and sauté the carrots, zucchini, leek, onion, celery, salt, pepper, and oregano for about 10 minutes. • Unroll the sheets of pastry on a lightly floured work surface. Use a sharp knife to cut into 16 rectangles measuring about 3 x 4 inches (8 x 10 cm). • Divide the vegetable filling and cheese among 8 of the rectangles, placing them in the center of each piece. Brush the edges of the pastry with the egg and cover with another rectangle of pastry, pressing down on the edges to seal well. Use the knife to make cuts in the tops of the pastries so that steam can escape during cooking. • Place the parcels on the prepared baking sheet and bake for 15–20 minutes, or until golden brown. • Serve hot or at room temperature.

Puff pastry vegetable parcels

*If you are not a vegan, eggs are an excellent source of protein. They also provide essential nutrients, such as riboflavin, folate, and vitamins B12, D, and E. Eggs yolks do contain dietary cholesterol but recent studies show that, if eaten in moderation (1–2 per week), eggs will not raise cholesterol levels in harmful ways.*

Eggs filled with zucchini and bell peppers

## Eggs filled with zucchini and bell peppers

*Serves: 4–6*
*Preparation: 30 minutes*
*Recipe grading: easy*

- 12 oz/350 g zucchini/courgettes
- 6 tablespoons extra-virgin olive oil
- 1 clove garlic
- 4 tablespoons finely chopped basil
- salt and freshly ground black pepper to taste
- 6 hard-boiled eggs, shelled
- bunch fresh salad greens
- 6 tablespoons diced mixed bell peppers/capsicums

Chop the zucchini in thin wheels. • Heat 2 tablespoons of oil in a skillet (frying pan) with the garlic, basil, salt, and pepper and sauté over medium heat for 5–7 minutes. • Scoop the yolks out of the eggs and place in a food processor or blender with the zucchini mixture and chop until smooth. • Fill the egg whites with the mixture. • Arrange the salad greens on a serving dish and place the filled eggs on top. • Scatter with the bell peppers and drizzle with the remaining oil. Season with salt and pepper and serve.

## Egg and bell pepper cream

*Serves: 4–6*
*Preparation: 50 minutes + 2 hours to chill*
*Cooking: 30 minutes*
*Recipe grading: Complicated*

- 2 lb/1 kg bell peppers/capsicums, in equal quantities of red, yellow, and green
- 6 tablespoons extra-virgin olive oil
- 1 medium onion, finely chopped
- salt and freshly ground white pepper to taste
- 1 oz/30 g gelatin
- 3 cups/750 ml milk
- 6 egg yolks
- 1³/₄ cups/430 ml heavy/double cream

Wash the bell peppers, dry, and remove the seeds and cores. Cut into small pieces, keeping the colors separate. • Place 2 tablespoons of oil in three separate saucepans, divide the onion in three parts, and sauté a third in each. • When the onion is transparent, add salt, pepper, 2 tablespoons of water, and bell peppers, keeping the colors separate in each pan. • Cover each pan and cook over medium heat for about 30 minutes, or until the bell peppers are soft and well-cooked. • Remove the pans from heat and let the mixtures cool. • Purée the contents of each pan separately in a food processor. • Soften the gelatin in a little water. • Heat the milk in a medium saucepan, but don't let it boil. • Beat the egg yolks in a bowl and add the hot milk a little at a time, stirring continuously. Season with salt and pepper. • Transfer to a saucepan and heat to just below boiling point, stirring frequently. Add the gelatin. • Remove from heat and beat with a fork so that the gelatin dissolves. • Pour equal parts of the mixture into three different bowls and let cool. • Add one color of bell pepper purée to each and stir. • Whip the cream to stiff peaks and fold in equal parts to each of the three bowls. • Moisten a rectangular mold with water and pour in the yellow mixture. Place the mold in the refrigerator for 10 minutes. • Remove and pour in the red mixture. Return the mold to the refrigerator for 10 more minutes. • Remove again and add the green mixture. • Refrigerate for at least 2 hours. • Just before serving, dip the mold for a second in hot water and invert the cream on a serving dish.

# Hard-boiled eggs with spinach cream

*Serves: 4*
*Preparation: 10 minutes*
*Cooking: 8–10 minutes*
*Recipe grading: easy*

- 4–8 slices white sandwich bread
- 2 tablespoons extra-virgin olive oil
- 8 oz/250 g fresh spinach, destalked
- $^{1}/_{2}$ cup/125 ml heavy/double cream
- 6 tablespoons freshly grated Parmesan cheese
- salt and freshly ground black pepper to taste
- 4 hard-boiled eggs, shelled
- 2 tablespoons finely chopped chives

Preheat the oven to 350°F/180°C/gas 4. • Use a small glass or cookie cutter to cut 8 disks out of the bread. Brush with the oil and place on a baking sheet. Cook for 8–10 minutes, or until nicely browned. • Wash the spinach under cold running water. Do not drain but place in a saucepan and cook, with just the water clinging to its leaves, for 3 minutes. Drain, press out excess water, and place in a food processor. • Add the cream, Parmesan, salt, and pepper and chop until smooth. • Use a teaspoon to remove the yolks from the eggs. Crumble and set aside. • Fill the eggs with the spinach cream. • Arrange the disks of toasts on a serving dish. Place half an egg, filling side up, on each and sprinkle with the yolks and chives.

Hard-boiled eggs with spinach cream

# Pecorino, pear, and walnut salad

*Serves: 6*
*Preparation: 15 minutes*
*Recipe grading: easy*

- 2–3 large eating pears
- 1 bunch arugula/rocket, washed and dried
- 10 oz/300 g Pecorino romano cheese, diced
- 1 cup/150 g walnuts, toasted
- 3 tablespoons extra-virgin olive oil
- juice of 1 small lemon
- salt and freshly ground black pepper to taste
- 1 clove garlic, lightly crushed

Wash, peel, and core the pears. Chop into $^{1}/_{2}$-inch (1-cm) dice. • Arrange the arugula in the bottom of a salad bowl and add the pears, cheese, and walnuts. • Put the oil, lemon juice, salt, pepper, and garlic in a small jar. Screw the top down and shake vigorously for 1–2 minutes. When the dressing is well mixed, remove the garlic and drizzle over the salad. • Toss carefully and serve.

# Aspargus cream

*Serves: 6–8*
*Preparation: 15 minutes*
*Cooking: 10 minutes*
*Recipe grading: easy*

- 14 oz/450 g asparagus spears, cleaned (tender green part only)
- 8 oz/250 g fresh creamy cheese (such as Philadelphia Light, Robiola, Ricotta)
- 2 tablespoons extra-virgin olive oil
- juice of 1 small lemon
- salt and freshly ground black pepper to taste
- 1 egg white

Steam the asparagus spears for 10 minutes, or until tender. • Chop in a food processor until smooth. • Stir in the cheese, oil, lemon juice, salt, and pepper. • Beat the egg white in a small bowl until stiff, then fold into the cream. Refrigerate for 30 minutes. • Serve with grissini (bread sticks) or corn or potato chips.

Filled Brussels sprouts

## Broiled bell peppers with garlic and herbs

*Serves: 4*
*Preparation: 20 minutes + 1 hour to rest*
*Cooking: 20 minutes*
*Recipe grading: fairly easy*

- 6 large bell peppers/capsicums, mixed colors
- 6 cloves garlic, thinly sliced
- 4 tablespoons pickled capers, drained
- 20 basil leaves, torn
- 15 mint leaves
- 2 tablespoons finely chopped parsley
- salt and freshly ground black pepper to taste
- 1/2 cup/125 ml extra-virgin olive oil

Place the bell peppers whole under a broiler (grill) at high heat, giving them quarter turns until their skins scorch and blacken. This will take about 20 minutes. When the peppers are black all over, wrap them in foil and set aside for 10 minutes.

When unwrapped, the skins will peel away easily. • Cut the bell peppers in half lengthwise and discard the stalks, seeds, and pulpy inner core. Rinse under cold running water to remove any remaining burnt skin and dry with paper towels. • Cut the bell peppers into strips. • Place in a serving dish and sprinkle with the garlic, capers, basil, mint, parsley, salt, pepper, and oil. • Mix carefully and set aside for at least 1 hour before serving.

## Filled Brussels sprouts

*Serves: 4–6*
*Preparation: 30 minutes*
*Cooking: 20 minutes*
*Recipe grading: fairly easy*

- 1 lb/500 g fresh or frozen Brussels sprouts
- bunch of mixed fresh herbs (parsley, dill, basil, tarragon, marjoram, etc)
- 1 tablespoon white wine vinegar
- 3 tablespoons butter
- 1 clove garlic, finely chopped
- 4 tablespoons heavy/double cream
- salt and freshly ground black pepper to taste
- 1 red bell pepper/capsicum

Cook the sprouts with the herbs and vinegar in a large pan of lightly salted, boiling water for 5–6 minutes. Drain well. • Coarsely chop one-third of the Brussels sprouts. Hollow the centers out of the remaining sprouts. • Heat half the butter in a large skillet (frying pan) and sauté the garlic for 2–3 minutes. Add all the chopped sprouts and the cream. Season with salt and pepper and cook, stirring frequently, for 10 minutes. • Place the hollow sprouts in another pan with the remaining butter. Season with salt and pepper and cook for 10 minutes. • Use a teaspoon or pastry bag to fill the sprouts. Top each sprout with a small piece of bell pepper. • Serve hot or at room temperature.

*Eggs and Parmesan make the perfect foil for the pungent, peppery, and slightly bitter flavor of the watercress. If watercress is out of season, substitute with spinach.*

## Onion feast

*Serves: 4*
*Preparation: 10 minutes*
*Cooking: 25–30 minutes*
*Recipe grading: easy*

- 3 large onions (a mixture of Spanish, brown, and red onions if available)
- salt and freshly ground black pepper to taste
- ¹/₂ cup/125 g butter
- 3–4 tablespoons red wine or balsamic vinegar
- 2 tablespoons freshly grated Parmesan cheese
- 1 tablespoon finely chopped parsley
- freshly baked bread, to serve

Peel and coarsely chop the onions. The pieces should be the thickness of your little finger. • Melt the butter in a heavy-bottomed pan and cook the onions over low heat for 25–30 minutes, or until golden brown. Stir or shake the pan every now and then. Season with salt and pepper. When the onions are very tender, pour in the wine. Turn up the heat for a minute or two so that some of the liquid bubbles away. • Sprinkle with the Parmesan and parsley. Serve hot straight from the pan. Serve with freshly baked bread.

## Baked watercress omelet

*Serves: 4*
*Preparation: 10 minutes*
*Cooking: 30 minutes*
*Recipe grading: easy*

- 1 lb/500 g fresh watercress
- 2 tablespoons extra-virgin olive oil
- 2 shallots, finely chopped
- salt and freshly ground black pepper to taste
- 5 eggs, lightly beaten
- 2 tablespoons freshly grated Parmesan cheese
- 4 tablespoons finely chopped parsley

Trim the watercress and rinse well under cold running water. Dry well. • Heat the oil in a large skillet (frying pan) and sauté the shallots until translucent. • Add the watercress, season with salt and pepper, and cook for 10 minutes, stirring frequently. • Remove from heat and chop coarsely. • Beat the eggs with a little salt and pepper until frothy. Stir in the Parmesan, parsley, and watercress mixture. • Transfer the mixture to an oiled 9-inch (24-cm) pie plate and bake for about 25 minutes, or until set. • Serve hot or at room temperature.

## Fried bean curd

Serves: 6
Preparation: 10 minutes
Cooking: 10 minutes
Recipe grading: easy

- 2 lb/1 kg bean curd, cut in $^1/_2$ -inch/ 1-cm slices
- 1 cup/150 g all-purpose/plain flour
- 1 egg, lightly beaten
- 4 tablespoons extra-virgin olive oil
- 1 tablespoon sherry
- 1 teaspoon salt
- 1 tablespoon sesame oil
- $^1/_2$ cup/125 ml vegetable stock
- 1 tablespoon finely chopped scallions/ spring onions
- 1 tablespoon finely chopped ginger root
- 2 tablespoons toasted sesame seeds

Coat the slices of bean curd with flour then dip them in the egg. • Heat 2 tablespoons of oil in a large wok and place the bean curd in it. Fry over medium heat for about 1 minute, or until golden brown. Turn over, add 2 more tablespoons of oil and fry until golden brown. • Combine the sherry, salt, sesame oil, and stock in a cup. • Sprinkle the bean curd with the scallions, ginger root, and sesame seeds and pour in the stock mixture. Pierce the bean curd with a fork. Lower the heat and cook until the liquid is absorbed by the bean curd.

Fried bean curd

## Garbanzo bean fritters

Serves: 4
Preparation: 10 minutes
Cooking: 40 minutes
Recipe grading: easy

- 2$^1/_2$ cups/375 g garbanzo bean/chickpea flour
- 1 quart/1 liter cold water
- 1 teaspoon salt
- 1 tablespoon finely chopped parsley
- 1 cup/250 ml oil, for frying

Beat the flour, water, and salt in a food processor. The mixture will be fairly thick. • Transfer to a saucepan and cook over low heat for 30 minutes, stirring constantly. • Stir in the parsley and pour onto a lightly oiled work surface. Spread with a spatula to about $^1/_4$ inch (5 mm) thick. • Let cool, then cut into diamond shapes or squares. • Heat the oil to very hot in a large skillet (frying pan). Fry the dough in batches until golden brown on both sides. Drain on paper towels, sprinkle with salt, and serve.

## Cheese eggplants

Serves: 4
Preparation: 15 minutes
Cooking: 30-40 minutes
Recipe grading: fairly easy

- 2 or 3 eggplants/aubergines
- 8 thin slices easy-to-melt cheese (French Chaumes, Italian Taleggio, Fontina or Bel Paese)
- 3 eggs, lightly beaten
- salt to taste
- 1 cup/150 g all-purpose/plain flour
- 2 cups/500 ml olive oil, for frying

Trim the eggplants and cut into 16 thin slices (about $^1/_2$ inch/1 cm thick). • Cut each cheese slice to fit the eggplant. Sandwich a slice of cheese between 2 slices of eggplant. • Beat the eggs in a shallow bowl and season with salt. Dip each eggplant sandwich in the egg and then in the flour. • Heat the oil to very hot in a large skillet (frying pan) and fry over medium heat for about 3 minutes on each side, until golden brown. Drain on paper towels. • Serve hot.

## Fried goat's cheese with caramelized onion

Serves: 4
Preparation: 20 minutes
Cooking: 40–50 minutes
Recipe grading: fairly easy

- 6 tablespoons extra-virgin olive oil
- 3 large red onions, very finely sliced
- salt to taste
- 3 tablespoons sugar
- 5 oz/150 g soft goat's cheese
- 1 egg, lightly beaten
- $^1/_2$ cup/75 g all-purpose/plain flour
- 1 tablespoon liquid honey
- 1 tablespoon pomegranate molasses
- 1 tablespoon finely chopped parsley
- 1 tablespoon finely chopped chives

Prepare the caramelized onions at least 2 hours before serving: Heat 2 tablespoons of the oil in a large skillet (frying pan) and sauté the onions with a pinch of salt over a low heat for 20–30 minutes. • When the onions are very soft, drain off the excess oil and add the sugar. Stir until the mixture has caramelized. This will take about 8 to 10 minutes. Let cool, then refrigerate. • About 30 minutes before serving, prepare the cheese. Shape the cheese into four balls, dip each into the beaten egg and the flour. Heat the remaining oil in a small skillet (frying pan) and fry the cheese balls until golden. Turn them carefully to lightly brown all over. Drain on paper towels. • Place the onions in the middle of a large serving dish and arrange the cheese balls on top. Drizzle with the honey and pomegranate molasses and sprinkle with parsley and chives. • Serve hot.

## Vegetarian spring rolls

*Serves: 6*
*Preparation: 30 minutes*
*Cooking: 20 minutes*
*Recipe grading: fairly easy*

- 2 tablespoons extra-virgin olive oil
- 1 stalk celery, finely chopped
- 4 oz/125 g mung bean sprouts
- 3 oz/90 dried black Chinese mushrooms, cut in very thin strips
- 2 oz/60 g carrots, cut in very thin strips
- 2 oz/60 g bamboo shoots
- 1 teaspoon soy sauce
- 1 teaspoon sesame oil
- $^{1}/_{2}$ teaspoon salt
- $^{1}/_{2}$ teaspoon sugar
- 12 spring roll wrappers
- 1 tablespoon all-purpose/plain flour
- 1 tablespoon water
- $1^{1}/_{2}$ quarts/1.5 liters oil, for deep frying

Heat the extra-virgin oil in a wok and sauté the celery for 2–3 minutes. Add the bean sprouts, black mushrooms, carrots, and bamboo shoots and stir-fry for 5–7 minutes. • Add the soy sauce, sesame oil, salt, and sugar to the wok. • Divide the filling into 12 equal portions. Wrap one portion of filling in each of the spring roll wrappers. • Stir the flour and water together in a cup to form a smooth paste. Use the paste to seal the spring rolls. • Heat the oil to very hot in a deep pan and deep-fry the spring rolls until golden brown all over. • Remove with a slotted spoon, drain on paper towels, and serve immediately.

## Cheese melts

*Serves: 2*
*Preparation: 5 minutes*
*Cooking: 10 minutes*
*Recipe grading: easy*

- 1 cup/100 g fresh or frozen fava/broad beans
- 1–2 tablespoons extra-virgin olive oil
- 2 teaspoons fresh lemon juice
- few sprigs dill, coarsely chopped
- salt and freshly ground black pepper to taste
- 2 thick slices crusty sourdough bread
- thin slices Camembert
- 1 clove garlic

Cook the fava beans in salted boiling water for 5 minutes, or until tender. • Drain and drizzle while still hot with the oil, lemon, dill, salt, and pepper. • Toast the bread on both sides, lightly rub with garlic. • Pile the beans on each piece of toast and cover with slices of Camembert. • Place under a hot broiler (grill) until the cheese melts. • Alternatively, serve the filling on ciabatta. Cut the loaf in half lengthways and lightly toast. Put the beans on top and cover with Taleggio, Fontina or fresh Parmesan cheese and broil (grill) until the cheese melts. • Serve hot.

Greek salads in phyllo pastry

# Camembert dip

*Serves: 4*
*Preparation: 15 minutes*
*Cooking: 10–12 minutes*
*Recipe grading: easy*

- 1 tablespoon butter
- 7 oz/200 g firm button mushrooms, very finely chopped
- 1 clove garlic, finely chopped
- 1 tablespoon finely chopped dill or chervil
- two 8 oz/250 g round Camembert cheeses
- 1 cup/250 g soft cream cheese (Philadelphia)
- 1 small chile pepper, seeded and finely chopped
- pinch of curry or cumin powder
- 1 tablespoon freshly grated Parmesan cheese

Heat the butter in a medium skillet (frying pan) and sauté the mushrooms and garlic for 3 minutes. • Add the dill or chervil (reserving some to garnish) and cook for 3–5 more minutes. • Strain, reserving the liquid. • Remove the outer crust from the Camembert and mash with a fork. Mix with the cream cheese, then stir into the mushrooms. If the mixture is too thick, add some of the mushroom liquid. • Add the Parmesan and season with the chile, curry powder (or cumin), and pepper. Refrigerate for 2 hours. Scatter with the dill just before serving. • Serve with a green salad and freshly baked bread.

# Greek salads in phyllo pastry

*Serves: 6*
*Preparation: 20 minutes*
*Cooking: 5–8 minutes*
*Recipe grading: easy*

- 4 tablespoons extra-virgin olive oil
- 6 sheets phyllo dough, cut in 3-inch/8-cm squares
- 18–20 black olives
- 1 cucumber, peeled and cubed
- 12 cherry tomatoes, cut in halves or quarters
- 4 oz/125 g Feta cheese, cubed
- 2 scallions/spring onions, finely chopped
- 1 clove garlic, finely chopped (optional)
- 6 fresh basil leaves, torn
- 6 fresh mint leaves, torn
- 1–2 tablespoons fresh lemon juice
- salt and freshly ground black pepper to taste

Preheat the oven to 350°F/180°C/gas 4. • Lightly oil 6 small tart molds. Place the phyllo dough in the molds and bake in the oven for 5–8 minutes, or until pale golden brown. Turn out carefully onto a rack to cool. • Place the olives, cucumber, tomatoes, cheese, garlic, if using, basil, and mint in a medium bowl. Season with salt and pepper and drizzle with the lemon juice and remaining oil. Toss gently. • Just before serving, fill the phyllo pastry molds with the salad.

Tomatoes filled with couscous
and grilled vegetables

## Tomatoes filled with couscous and grilled vegetables

*Serves: 4*
*Preparation: 30 minutes + 1 hour to chill*
*Cooking: 15 minutes*
*Recipe grading: easy*

- 5 oz/150 g couscous (precooked)
- 2 medium zucchini/courgettes
- 1 eggplant/aubergine
- salt and freshly ground black pepper to taste
- 4 tablespoons extra-virgin olive oil
- 1 tablespoon white wine vinegar
- 4 oz/125 g Feta cheese
- 2 tablespoons finely chopped mint
- 2 tablespoons finely chopped chives

Prepare the couscous following the instructions on the package. When tender, drain and spread out on a dish to dry a little. • Thinly slice the zucchini (lengthwise) and eggplant and cook in a nonstick grill pan. No oil is required. • Dice the grilled vegetables and season with salt, pepper, oil, and vinegar. • Place the couscous in a bowl with the vegetables, Feta, mint, and chives. Toss gently. Refrigerate for 1 hour. • Cut the tops off the tomatoes and use a teaspoon to hollow out the insides. Season the tomatoes lightly with salt and pepper and let stand upside down for 30 minutes to drain. • Fill with the couscous mixture. • Serve chilled or at room temperature.

## Summer leeks

*Serves: 6*
*Preparation: 20 minutes + 30 minutes to cool*
*Cooking: 5–7 minutes*
*Recipe grading: easy*

- 12 slim leeks, white part only, outer green layer and roots removed
- 1 tablespoon extra-virgin olive oil
- 1 red onion, finely chopped
- 3 small bell peppers/capsicums, 1 red, 1 green, 1 yellow, seeded, and with piths and stalks removed, finely chopped
- 2 small pickled gherkins, rinsed, finely chopped
- 3 tablespoons capers, rinsed, dried, and chopped
- 1 small yellow tomato, finely chopped
- 1 plum tomato, seeded and finely chopped
- 1 bunch watercress
- 3 oz/90 g arugula/rocket
- 2 oz/60 g small spinach leaves or radicchio

For the vinaigrette:
- 5 tablespoons extra-virgin olive oil
- 2 tablespoons white wine vinegar
- 1 tablespoon finely chopped parsley
- sprinkling of fresh oregano or thyme leaves
- salt and freshly ground black pepper to taste

Prepare the leeks at least an hour before serving. Rinse under cold running water. Boil in a large pan of salted water with 1 tablespoon of oil for 5–7 minutes, or until tender and slightly limp. Drain and spread out to cool. • Cut the leeks in half lengthwise. • Mix the onion, bell peppers, gherkins, capers, and tomatoes in a large bowl. • Vinaigrette: Place the oil, vinegar, parsley, and herbs in a small bowl. Season with salt and pepper. Stir well. • Just before serving, place the watercress, arugula, and spinach leaves (or radicchio) on a large serving plate. Spoon the leeks over the top and drizzle with the vinaigrette.

## Sweet and sour bell pepper rolls

*Serves: 6*
*Preparation: 30 minutes*
*Cooking: 30 minutes*
*Recipe grading: fairly easy*

- 3 large bell peppers/capsicums, 1 red, 1 green, 1 yellow
- 2 tablespoons pine nuts
- 2 tablespoons golden raisins/sultanas
- 2 tablespoons capers, rinsed, dried, and chopped
- 2 cloves garlic, finely chopped
- 2 tablespoons finely chopped parsley
- 2 cups/150 g fresh bread crumbs
- 6 tablespoons extra-virgin olive oil
- salt and freshly ground black pepper to taste

Place the bell peppers whole under a broiler (grill) at high heat, giving them quarter turns until their skins scorch and blacken. This will take about 20 minutes. When the peppers are black all over, wrap them in foil and set aside for 10 minutes. When unwrapped, the skins will peel away easily. • Cut the bell peppers in half lengthwise and discard the stalks, seeds, and pulpy inner core. Rinse under cold running water to remove any remaining burnt skin and dry with paper towels. • Cut the bell peppers into wide strips. • Preheat the oven to 350°F/180°C/gas 4. • Place the pine nuts, raisins, capers, garlic, parsley, and bread crumbs in a bowl. Add 4 tablespoons of oil and season with salt and pepper. Mix well. • Spread the filling on the pieces of bell pepper, dividing it evenly among them. Roll the peppers up and place in a baking dish

previously greased with the remaining oil. • Bake for 15 minutes. • Serve hot or at room temperature.

## Sweet and sour baby onions

*Serves: 6*
*Prep: 10 minutes*
*Cooking: 35 minutes*
*Recipes grading: easy*

- 1 lb/500 g white baby onions, cleaned
- 2 tablespoons extra-virgin olive oil
- salt and freshly ground black pepper to taste

Sweet and sour bell pepper rolls

- 1 tablespoon brown sugar
- 3 tablespoons white wine vinegar
- 1/2 cup/125 ml cold water

Heat the oil in a large skillet (frying pan) and sauté the onions for 5 minutes. • Season with salt and pepper and add the sugar. Pour in the vinegar and water. • Cook over medium-low heat for 30 minutes, or until the onions are tender and the cooking juices have almost all been absorbed. • Serve hot or at room temperature.

*Serve these delicate little soufflés with sticks of carrots and celery, flakes of Parmesan cheese, and a glass of chilled, aromatic white wine.*

## Mini pea puffs

*Serves: 4*
*Preparation: 30 minutes + 30 minutes to chill*
*Cooking: 12–15 minutes*
*Recipe grading: fairly easy*

- 6 oz/180 g fresh or frozen peas
- 2 tablespoons butter
- 2 tablespoons all-purpose/plain flour
- 1 cup/250 ml milk
- salt to taste
- 2 tablespoons freshly grated Parmesan cheese
- 6 large egg whites
- 1 tablespoon sugar

Cook the peas in a pan of salted boiling water until tender. Drain, place in a food processor, and chop until smooth. • Melt the butter in a small saucepan, then stir in the flour. Gradually stir in the milk and bring to a boil. Cook, stirring constantly over low heat for 10 minutes. Season with salt. • Stir the sauce and Parmesan into the pea mixture and let cool. Refrigerate for 30 minutes. • Preheat the oven to 400°F/ 200°C/gas 6. • Butter and flour 4 individual soufflé molds. • Beat the egg whites with a pinch of salt until stiff peaks form. Beat in the sugar. • Fold the egg whites into the pea mixture and spoon it into the prepared molds. • Bake for 12–15 minutes, or until golden brown on top. Serve hot.

Mini pea puffs

## Baked spinach crêpes

*Serves: 4–6*
*Preparation: 25 minutes + 30 minutes to rest*
*Cooking: 30 minutes*
*Recipe grading: fairly easy*

### Crêpes
- 1 cup/150 g all-purpose/plain flour
- 1 1/4 cups/310 ml milk
- 3 eggs, lightly beaten
- 1 teaspoon salt
- 4 tablespoons water
- butter, for the pan

### Filling
- 1 clove garlic, finely chopped
- 3 tablespoons extra-virgin olive oil
- 1 lb/500 g spinach, boiled and chopped
- salt and freshly ground pepper to taste
- 1/4 teaspoon ground nutmeg
- 5 oz/150 g fresh Ricotta cheese
- 4 tablespoons freshly grated Parmesan cheese

### Sauce
- 4 tablespoons extra-virgin olive oil
- 1/2 cup/75 g all-purpose/plain flour
- 2 cups/500 ml milk
- salt and freshly ground black pepper to taste
- 1/4 teaspoon ground nutmeg
- 4 tablespoons freshly grated Parmesan cheese

Crêpes: Place the flour in a large bowl and gradually pour in the milk, beating vigorously. Add the eggs, salt, and water and beat until smooth. Let stand for 30 minutes. • Preheat the oven to 400°F/200°C/gas 6. • Grease a skillet (frying pan) or crêpe pan with butter and place over medium heat. Pour in half a ladleful of the batter and tilt the pan so that the batter spreads evenly over the bottom. As soon as the crêpe sets, flip it and cook the other side. Repeat, stacking the cooked crêpes in a pile. • Filling: Sauté the garlic in the oil, add the spinach, salt, pepper, and nutmeg. Remove from heat and mix with the Ricotta and Parmesan. • Sauce: Heat the oil in a medium saucepan, then add the flour, stirring constantly. Add the milk gradually, still stirring, until the mixture boils and thickens. Add salt, pepper, nutmeg, and Parmesan. • Place a generous helping of filling on each crêpe. Roll them up loosely and arrange in an oiled oven-proof dish. Pour the sauce over the top. • Bake for a12–15 minutes, or until the top is golden. • Serve hot.

## Baked Pecorino cheese crêpes

*Serves: 2–4*
*Preparation: 25 minutes*
*Cooking: 8–10 minutes*
*Recipe grading: fairly easy*

- 6 eggs, lightly beaten
- 6 tablespoons milk
- 4 tablespoons all-purpose/plain flour
- salt and freshly ground black pepper to taste
- 1/2 cup/125 g butter
- 4 oz/125 g Pecorino romano cheese, in flakes or shavings
- 6 fresh sage leaves, torn

Preheat the oven to 350°F/180°C/gas 4. • Beat the eggs in a bowl with a whisk. Add the milk, then gradually stir in the flour, salt, and pepper to make a smooth batter. • Grease a crêpe pan with a little of the butter. Pour in half a ladleful of the batter and tilt the pan so that the batter spreads evenly over the bottom. Cook until light golden brown on one side then flip and brown the other side. Repeat until all the batter is used up. • Sprinkle each crêpe with cheese and roll it very loosely. Arrange the crêpes in an ovenproof baking dish. • Melt the remaining butter and pour over the top. Sprinkle with the sage and bake for 10 minutes, or until browned. • Serve hot.

## Puff pastry cheese appetizers

*Serves: 4–6*
*Preparation: 25 minutes*
*Cooking: 25–30 minutes*
*Recipe grading: fairly easy*

- 4 oz/125 g Fontina or Cheddar cheese, cut in small cubes
- 1 tablespoon finely chopped parsley
- 2/3 cup/80 g freshly grated Parmesan cheese

- 3 eggs, lightly beaten
- freshly ground black pepper to taste
- 1 lb/500 g frozen puff pastry, thawed
- 4 tablespoons butter, melted

Preheat the oven to 400°F/200°C/gas 6. • Butter a baking sheet. • Mix the Fontina or Cheddar, parsley, Parmesan, eggs, and pepper together in a large mixing bowl. • Unroll the pastry on a lightly floured work surface. Use a sharp knife to cut into 4-inch (10-cm) squares. • Brush with half the melted butter. In the center of each pastry square, place one tablespoon of the cheese mixture and fold the dough over it to form a triangular shape. Pinch the edges to seal. • Place on the baking sheet and brush with the remaining butter. Bake for 25–30 minutes, or until the pastry is golden brown. • Serve hot.

Spicy peanut fritters with coconut milk

# Spicy peanut fritters with coconut milk

*Serves: 6*
*Preparation: 30 minutes*
*Cooking: 30 minutes*
*Recipe grading: fairly easy*

- 1¼ cups/200 g raw peanuts
- 1 teaspoon coriander seeds
- ½ tablespoon finely chopped ginger root
- 2 cloves garlic
- ½ teaspoon turmeric
- 1 teaspoon salt
- 1 teaspoon red pepper flakes (or 2 crumbled dried chilies)
- 1 cup/150 g rice flour
- ⅔ cup/100 g all-purpose/plain flour
- 1 cup/250 ml coconut milk
- 2 cups/500 ml oil, for frying

Place the peanuts in a wok and dry fry over low heat for 5 minutes. Rub to remove the skins and chop coarsely. • Chop the coriander seeds, ginger, garlic, turmeric, salt, and red pepper flakes in a food processor until smooth. • Place both flours in a bowl and stir in the spice mixture and the coconut milk, blending well. Add the peanuts. • Heat half the oil in a wok to very hot and drop in a tablespoonful of batter at a time, frying until golden brown. Drain on paper towels and repeat until all the mixture is fried. Add more oil as required as you fry. • Serve hot or at room temperature.

# Fava bean fritters with yogurt and cucumber sauce

*Serves: 6*
*Preparation: 15 minutes*
*Cooking: 30 minutes*
*Recipe grading: easy*

- 2 cups/400 g cooked fava/broad beans (either dried, soaked, and precooked, or canned), drained
- 1 medium onion, finely grated
- 2 cloves garlic, finely chopped
- ½ teaspoon ground cumin seeds
- 2 tablespoons finely chopped parsley
- 2 tablespoons finely chopped marjoram
- 1 egg, lightly beaten
- 2 tablespoons all-purpose/plain flour
- salt and freshly ground black pepper to taste
- about ½ cup/125 ml tablespoons sesame oil

Yogurt sauce:
- 1½ cups/375 ml Greek yogurt
- 2 tablespoons sour cream
- 1 medium cucumber, peeled and diced
- 2 tablespoons finely chopped mint
- salt and freshly ground black pepper to taste

Mash the fava beans in a medium bowl. Add the onion, garlic, cumin, parsley, marjoram, egg, and flour and mix well. Season with salt and pepper. • Scoop up spoonfuls of the mixture and shape into flattened fritters. • Heat the oil in a medium skillet (frying pan) until very hot and fry the fritters in batches until golden brown all over. Add more oil if required while frying. • Drain on paper towels. • Yogurt sauce: Place the yogurt in a small bowl with the sour cream. Stir in the cucumber and mint. Season with salt and pepper. • Arrange the fritters on a serving platter and either spoon the sauce over the top, or serve separately in a bowl.

# Curried onion appetizers

*Serves: 8*
*Preparation: 20 minutes*
*Cooking: 30–40 minutes*
*Recipe grading: fairly easy*

Crisp mini rösti

- 16 slices soft white or whole-wheat sandwich bread
- 4 tablespoons extra-virgin olive oil
- 4 medium white onions, chopped
- 2 cloves garlic, finely chopped
- 1 teaspoon curry powder
- $^1/_2$ teaspoon ground cumin seeds
- 2 tablespoons golden raisins/sultanas
- 2 tablespoons all-purpose/plain flour
- 2 tablespoons finely chopped parsley
- salt and freshly ground black pepper to taste
- 2 tablespoons slivered almonds

Preheat the oven to 350°F/180°C/gas 4. • Butter 16 muffin tins. • Use a glass or cookie cutter to cut out 3-inch (8-cm) disks from the bread. Press each disk into a muffin tin and bake for 12–15 minutes, or until golden brown. • Turn out onto a rack to cool. • Turn the oven up to 400°F/200°C/gas 6. • Heat the oil in a large skillet (frying pan) and sauté the onions and garlic until translucent, about 10 minutes. • Add the curry powder, cumin, raisins, flour, and parsley. Season with salt and pepper. Cook, stirring frequently, for another 10–15 minutes more, or until the onions are very tender. • Spoon the filling into the toasted bread molds and sprinkle each one with a few slivered almonds. • Bake for 10–15 minutes, or until the almonds are lightly browned. • Serve hot or at room temperature.

## Hash brownies

*Serves: 4–6*
*Preparation: 15 minutes*
*Cooking: 30 minutes*
*Recipe grading: easy*

- $1^1/_2$ lb/750 g potatoes
- 2–4 tablespoons butter or extra-virgin olive oil
- 1 small onion, finely chopped
- salt and freshly ground white pepper to taste

Cook the potatoes in a large pan of lightly salted, boiling water for 15 minutes. They should only be partly cooked. • Drain and let cool (this part of the recipe can be done several hours ahead — the night before, if serving this classic American breakfast dish in the morning). • Remove the skins from the potatoes and grate coarsely. • Heat the butter or oil in a large skillet (frying pan) and sauté the onion for about 5 minutes, or until translucent. • Add the potato. Season with salt and pepper, stir well, and press down on the brownies as they cook, to make them more compact. Cook until golden brown on one side, about 5 minutes, then turn and cook on the other side. • Serve piping hot.

## Crisp mini rösti

*Serves: 4–6*
*Preparation: 15 minutes*
*Cooking: 20 minutes*
*Recipe grading: easy*

- 4 large potatoes
- 2–3 tablespoons extra-virgin olive oil
- salt and freshly ground black pepper to taste

Peel the potatoes and cut into very thin strips. • Place the potatoes on a clean cloth and gently squeeze out as much moisture as possible. The more moisture you remove, the crispier the finished rösti will be. • Heat $^1/_2$ tablespoon of oil in a medium skillet (frying pan) and add a quarter of the potato to the pan. Press down on the potato is it cooks with a metal spatula so that the bottom turns crisp and golden brown. Flip the rösti and cook the other side. • Season the cooked rösti with salt and pepper and serve hot.

Garbanzo bean flat bread with summertime topping

## Garbanzo bean flat bread with summertime topping

*Serves: 4–6*
*Preparation: 20 minutes + 30 minutes to rest*
*Cooks: 20–25 minutes*
*Recipe grading: easy*

- 1¹/₃ cups/200 g garbanzo bean/chickpea flour
- 4 bay leaves
- 2 cups/500 ml cold water
- ¹/₂ cup/125 ml extra-virgin olive oil
- salt and freshly ground black pepper to taste
- 1 bunch arugula/rocket, washed and coarsely chopped
- 6 oz/180 g cherry tomatoes, cut in halves or quarters
- 2 oz/60 g Parmesan cheese, in flakes

Place the garbanzo bean flour in a medium bowl with the bay leaves and gradually stir in the water. When it has all been absorbed, stir in the oil. Season with salt and set aside for 30 minutes. • Preheat the oven to 400°F/200°C/gas 6. • Oil a 9-inch (23-cm) square baking dish. • Remove the bay leaves from the garbanzo bean mixture and spoon it into the baking dish. • Bake for 20–25 minutes, or until pale golden brown. • Cool on a rack for 10 minutes in the pan then turn out onto the rack to cool completely. • Cut into 4 or 6 squares and top with the arugula, tomatoes, and Parmesan. Season lightly with salt and pepper and drizzle with the remaining oil.

## Sweet and sour phyllo rolls

*Serves: 6–8*
*Preparation: 30 minutes*
*Cooking: 15–20 minutes*
*Recipe grading: easy*

- 4 tablespoons butter, melted
- 3 tablespoons extra-virgin olive oil
- 1 large onion, finely chopped
- 4 cloves garlic, finely chopped
- ¹/₂ small Savoy cabbage
- 6 tablespoons apple cider (or apple juice)
- 2 medium Granny Smith apples, peeled, cored, and finely chopped
- 4 tablespoons golden raisins/sultanas
- ¹/₂ teaspoon freshly ground cumin seeds
- 1 teaspoon dried oregano
- 1 teaspoon curry powder
- salt and freshly ground black pepper to taste
- 8 sheets frozen phyllo dough, thawed
- 6 tablespoons butter, melted

Preheat the oven to 400°F/200°C/gas 6. • Butter a baking sheet. • Heat the oil in a large skillet (frying pan) and sauté the onion and garlic for 5 minutes, or until translucent. • Add the cabbage and apple cider and cook for 5 more minutes, or until the cabbage is wilted. • Add the apples, raisins, cumin, oregano, and curry powder and cook until the apples are tender. Season with salt and pepper. Set aside to cool. • Place a sheet of phyllo pastry on a clean kitchen towel and brush with a little butter. Cover with another sheet and brush with butter. Repeat with two more sheets of phyllo. • Spoon half the cabbage mixture along the short edge of the phyllo, leaving a 1-inch (2.5-cm) border at the ends. Roll up from the short edge and place seam-side down on the baking sheet. Repeat with the remaining filling and phyllo. • Brush the tops of the rolls with the remaining butter and bake for 15–20 minutes, or until golden brown. • Serve, in thick slices, hot or at room temperature.

# Baked cheese and polenta balls

*Serves: 6–8*
*Preparation: 30 minutes*
*Cooking: 10–15 minutes*
*Recipe grading: fairly easy*

- 2 quarts/2 liters cold water
- 1 teaspoon salt
- 1 lb/500 g polenta (finely ground yellow cornmeal)
- $^1/_2$ teaspoon ground nutmeg
- 1 cloves garlic, finely chopped
- 10 oz/300 g Fontina or tasty Cheddar cheese
- 4 tablespoons freshly grated Parmesan cheese

Bring the water and salt to a boil in a large saucepan (or polenta pan). Pour in the polenta and stir until the polenta is thick and coming away from the sides of the pan as you stir, about 60 minutes. (Alternatively, this dish can also be made with precooked polenta that will be ready in 10–15 minutes. Follow the instructions on the package ). • Stir the nutmeg and garlic into the polenta. • Spread the polenta out on a marble bench top or polenta board and let cool. • Preheat the oven to 400°F/200°C/gas 6. • Butter a large baking dish. • Dice the Fontina (or Cheddar) cheese into cubes about $^1/_4$-inch (5-mm) square. • Shape table-spoonfuls of the polenta into rounds about the size of a golf ball and use your index finger to press 2-3 pieces of cheese into each one. • Place in the baking dish and sprinkle with the Parmesan. • Bake for 10–15 minutes, or until the Parmesan is browned and the cheese inside the balls is melted. • Serve hot straight from the oven.

# Savory Bolognese fritters

*Serves: 8–10*
*Preparation: 30 minutes + 1 hour to rest the dough*
*Cooking: 20 minutes*
*Recipe grading: fairly easy*

- $1^1/_2$ oz/45 g fresh yeast or 3 ($^1/_4$ -oz/7-g) packages active dry yeast
- 1 cup/250 ml warm water
- $3^1/_3$ cups/500 g all-purpose/plain flour
- $^1/_2$ teaspoon salt
- 4 tablespoons extra virgin-olive oil
- 2 cups/500 ml vegetable oil, for frying

Dissolve the yeast in the warm water and set aside for 10 minutes, or until foaming. • Sift the flour and salt into a large bowl. Make a well in the center and pour in the oil and yeast mixture. Stir with a fork, gradually working in the flour, adding a little more water if needed. • Transfer to a floured work surface and knead until the dough is smooth and elastic, about 10 minutes. • Shape into a ball and place in an oiled bowl. Cover with a clean cloth and let rise for about 1 hour, or until doubled in bulk. • Punch the dough down and knead quickly on a lightly floured work surface. • Roll out the dough into $^1/_8$-inch (3-mm) thick sheets. Cut into diamonds or rectangles about 2 inches (5 cm) long. • Heat the oil in a large skillet (frying pan) to very hot and fry the fritters in batches of 6–8 until golden brown all over. • Drain on paper towels. • Serve very hot with a platter of fresh creamy cheeses.

Baked cheese and polenta balls

## Artichoke caponata

*Serves: 4*
*Preparation: 15 minutes*
*Cooking: 35–40 minutes*
*Recipe grading: easy*

- 8 very young, fresh artichokes
- 2¹/₂ tablespoons all-purpose/plain flour
- 6 tablespoons extra-virgin olive oil
- 3 tablespoons finely chopped onion
- 1 tablespoon capers, rinsed
- 12 green olives, pitted and chopped
- 1 small carrot, diced
- 2 tender stalks celery, trimmed and thinly sliced
- salt and freshly ground black pepper to taste
- ¹/₂ cup/125 ml hot water
- 4 medium tomatoes
- 2 teaspoons sugar
- 4 tablespoons Italian wine vinegar

Clean the artichokes by stripping off the tough outer leaves, cutting off the top third of the leaves, and trimming the stalk. Cut in half and use a sharp knife to remove any fuzzy choke. Cut each artichoke lengthwise into six sections. • Coat the artichokes lightly with flour and fry in the oil in a flameproof casserole over a fairly high heat for 2–3 minutes, turning once or twice. • Remove the artichokes, letting the excess oil drain back into the casserole. • Add the onion, capers, olives, carrot, celery, salt, pepper, and hot water and simmer over medium heat for about 10 minutes. • Stir in the tomatoes and then add the artichokes. Cover and simmer over a low heat for 20–25 minutes. • Mix the sugar with the vinegar and stir into the vegetables. Cook for 4–5 minutes more. • Serve hot or at room temperature.

*Caponata is a classic Sicilian appetizer. Originally the dish included seafood, especially octopus and scorpion, or capone, fish, from which it is believed to have taken its name. Among the poor, who could not afford fish, it was made with vegetables, and this is the version that we are most familiar with today.*

## Classic caponata

*Serves: 4–6*
*Preparation: 1 hour + 6 hours to stand*
*Cooking: 50 minutes*
*Recipe grading: easy*

- 2 lb/1 kg eggplants/aubergine, cut into ¹/₂-inch/1 cm cubes
- coarse sea salt
- ¹/₂ cup/125 ml extra-virgin olive oil
- 4 tender stalks celery, trimmed and cut into ³/₄-inch/2-cm lengths
- 1 large onion, thinly sliced
- 2 cups/500 g sieved (canned or fresh) tomatoes
- 12 fresh basil leaves, torn
- 1 small, firm pear, peeled, cored, and diced
- 2 tablespoons capers, rinsed, drained, and dried
- 20 green or black olives, pitted and chopped
- 3 tablespoons pine nuts
- 2 tablespoons sugar
- 4 tablespoons white wine vinegar
- 4 tablespoons coarsely chopped toasted almonds

Place the eggplants in a colander, sprinkle with coarse salt, and let drain for at least 1 hour. Drain well and pat dry with paper towels. • Heat about two-thirds of the oil in a skillet (frying pan) and sauté the eggplant over medium heat for 10 minutes. Set aside. • Blanch the celery in salted, boiling water for 5 minutes. Drain and set aside. • Sauté the onion in the remaining oil until pale golden brown and add the tomatoes and half the basil. Cook for 10 minutes and then add the celery, pear, capers, olives, pine nuts, sugar, and vinegar. • Simmer for 20 minutes, stirring now and then. • Add the eggplant and the remaining basil. Cook, stirring occasionally, for 10 more minutes. • Remove from heat and when the mixture is just warm, transfer to a serving dish, heaping it up into a mound. The eggplant should have absorbed most of the moisture. • Let stand for at least 6 hours or overnight. • Serve at room temperature, adding a few fresh basil leaves and sprinkling with the almonds (or bread crumbs). • Caponata keeps well for 3–4 days if refrigerated in a tightly closed container.

Classic caponata

Stuffed baked tomatoes

*Lentils have been cultivated since ancient times. Next to soya beans, they have the highest protein content of all vegetables. Each plant pod contains two seeds, and these come in various sizes and colors. India is the chief lentil producer, but this topping uses French Puy lentils. Their dark green colour and nutty taste are due to the volcanic soil in Le Puy, where they are grown.*

## Lentil crostini

*Serves: 4*
*Preparation: 15 minutes*
*Cooking: 40 minutes*
*Recipe grading: easy*

- 1$^1$/$_2$ cups/200 g Puy lentils, rinsed under cold running water
- 2$^1$/$_2$ cups/625 ml cold vegetable stock
- 4 tablespoons extra-virgin olive oil
- 1 large onion, finely chopped
- 4 plum tomatoes, washed, deseeded and finely diced
- 14 oz/450 g fresh spinach, washed and destalked
- 2 tablespoons balsamic vinegar
- 4 large slices French bread, toasted
- salt and freshly ground black pepper to taste
- 1 clove garlic (optional)

Place the lentils and vegetable stock in a saucepan, bring to the boil, cover and simmer for 30 minutes, or until the lentils are just tender. Drain and set aside. • In a large saucepan, heat 2 tablespoons of olive oil and fry the onion with a pinch of salt for 4–5 minutes. • Stir in the tomatoes and lentils, and sauté for 3 or 4 minutes more. Add the spinach and cook for 1–2 minutes, or until the spinach leaves have almost wilted. • Whisk together the vinegar and remaining oil to make a dressing. Season with salt and pepper. • Lightly rub the garlic clove over the toast and divide the leafy lentils evenly among the 4 slices of toast. • Drizzle with the dressing and serve.

## Stuffed baked tomatoes

*Serves: 4*
*Preparation: 10 minutes*
*Cooking: 35–40 minutes*
*Recipe grading: easy*

- 8 medium-large ripe tomatoes
- salt to taste
- freshly ground black pepper to taste
- 2 medium onions, finely chopped
- 2 cloves garlic, finely chopped
- 2 tablespoons extra-virgin olive oil
- 4 tablespoons bread crumbs
- 8 black olives, pitted and chopped
- 1 tablespoon pine nuts
- 1 tablespoon raisins
- 1 tablespoon capers, rinsed

Preheat the oven to 350°F/180°C/gas 4. • Rinse the tomatoes under cold running water and pat dry with paper towels. • Cut the tough pithy core from the top of each tomato. Use a teaspoon to scoop out the flesh and juice and place in a bowl. Sprinkle the whole tomatoes with salt and pepper. • Sauté the onion and garlic in the oil until transparent, then add the tomato flesh and juice and cook for 5 minutes, or until it reduces a little. • Remove from the heat and stir in the bread crumbs, olives, pine nuts, raisins, and capers. • Spoon the mixture into the tomatoes and place in an oiled ovenproof dish. • Bake for 25–30 minutes, or until browned on top. • Serve hot or at room temperature.

# Tomato and bell pepper loaf

*Serves: 4*
*Preparation: 45 minutes + 4 hours to chill*
*Cooking: 40–50 minutes*
*Recipe grading: fairly easy*

- 1 1/2 lb/750 g ripe tomatoes
- 2 tablespoons extra-virgin olive oil
- 2 large red bell peppers
- 2 eggs + 3 egg yolks
- 6 leaves fresh basil
- salt and freshly ground black pepper to taste

Plunge the tomatoes into a large pan of boiling water. Blanch for 1 minute, then drain well. Slip off the skins and chop coarsely. • Heat the oil in a large skillet (frying pan) and cook the tomatoes over medium heat for 10 minutes. Set aside to cool. • Place the bell peppers whole under a broiler (grill) at high heat, giving them quarter turns until their skins scorch and blacken. This will take about 20 minutes. When the peppers are black all over, wrap them in foil and set aside for 10 minutes. When unwrapped, the skins will peel away easily. • Cut the bell peppers in half lengthwise and discard the stalks, seeds, and pulpy inner core. Rinse under cold running water to remove any remaining burnt skin and dry with paper towels. • Preheat the oven to 350°F/180°C/gas 4. • Oil a loaf pan. • Chop the tomatoes and bell peppers in a food processor together with the eggs, yolks, basil, salt, and pepper. • Pour the mixture into the loaf pan and bake for 30–40 minutes, or until firm. • Set aside to cool. Refrigerate for at least 4 hours before serving.

# Provençal baked tomatoes

*Serves: 4*
*Preparation: 30 minutes*
*Cooking: 35 minutes*
*Recipe grading: fairly easy*

- 4 large, ripe tomatoes
- salt and freshly ground black pepper to taste
- 5 cloves garlic, finely chopped
- 1 cup/30 g finely chopped parsley
- 1/2 cup/60 g dry bread crumbs
- 1/2 cup/60 g freshly grated Parmesan cheese
- 1/2 cup/125 ml extra-virgin olive oil

Preheat the oven to 350°F/180°C/gas 4. • Cut the tomatoes in half, remove the seeds, sprinkle with a little salt, and place upside down in a colander for 20 minutes. • Mix the garlic and parsley together in a bowl, add the bread crumbs and Parmesan, and, using a fork, work the oil in little by little. Season with salt and pepper. • Using a teaspoon, push the filling mixture into the tomato halves. Press it down with your fingers so that it sticks to the inside of the tomatoes (it will swell slightly in the oven and could overflow). • Place the filled tomatoes in a greased ovenproof dish and bake for 35 minutes, or until the topping is crisp and the tomatoes are tender.

Tomato and bell pepper loaf

Mushroom and truffle toasts

## Tomato and jalapeno peppers salsa

*Serves: 6*
*Preparation: 15 minutes + 1 hour to rest*
*Recipe grading: easy*

- 2 large ripe tomatoes or 5 plum tomatoes, finely chopped
- 1 large red onion, peeled and finely chopped
- 2 cloves garlic, finely sliced
- 2 tinned jalapeno peppers, rinsed and finely chopped
- $^1/_4$ teaspoon red pepper flakes, or 1 small jalapeno chile finely chopped
- 2 tablespoons fresh cilantro/coriander, finely chopped
- juice of 1 fresh lime
- salt and freshly ground black pepper to taste

Combine all the ingredients in a large bowl and mix well. • Leave the salsa to rest and absorb the flavors for at least 1 hour before serving with corn chips.

## Mushroom and truffle toasts

*Serves 6*
*Preparation: 30 minutes*
*Cooking: 20 minutes*
*Recipe grading: easy*

- 10 oz/300 g fresh mushrooms (porcini, or white cultivated mushrooms, or a mixture of the two)
- 4 tablespoons butter
- 1 tablespoon brandy
- scant 1 cup/200 ml light/single cream
- $3^1/_2$ oz /100 g semi-soft melting cheese (Stracchino, Robiola, or similar)
- 1 small white truffle, fresh if possible, grated
- 12 slices French bread, toasted

Clean the mushrooms thoroughly and chop coarsely. • Melt the butter in a skillet (frying pan) and add the mushrooms a few at a time (giving the moisture produced a chance to evaporate). Cook, stirring at intervals, until tender, about 10 minutes. • Drizzle with the brandy and cook until it has evaporated. • Heat the cream separately in a small saucepan. Add the cheese and let melt over low heat while stirring. • When the cheese is completely blended with the cream, remove from the heat and stir in the mushrooms and the truffle. • Spread this mixture on the pieces of toast and serve hot.

## Black beans and mango relish

*Serves: 6–8*
*Preparation: 20 minutes + 2 hours to soak beans*
*Cooking: 60–90 minute*
*Recipe grading: easy*

- $2^1/_2$ cups/250 g dried black beans
- 1 quart/1 liter boiling water
- 4 fresh bay leaves, crushed
- 10 oz/300 g mango, peeled and cubed
- 1 tablespoon fresh lemon juice
- 1 tablespoon orange juice
- 1 tablespoon maple syrup
- 3 tablespoons fresh cilantro/coriander leaves and stalks, chopped
- $^1/_2$ tablespoon fresh lime juice
- salt and freshly ground black pepper to taste

Wash the beans in cold water, and drain well. Place them in a large saucepan and cover with boiling water. Bring to a boil, then turn off the heat. Cover and leave to soak for at least 2 hours. • Drain, then add the 1 quart (1 liter) of boiling water and the bay leaves. Simmer for 60–90 minutes, or until just tender. • Drain, remove the bay leaves, and leave to cool. • Place the mango, lemon juice, orange juice, maple syrup, and cilantro in a large bowl. Season with salt, pepper, and lime juice. Refrigerate until ready to use. • Serve with freshly made tortillas.

## Piquant marinated olives

*Serves: 4*
*Preparation: 15 minutes + time to stand*
*Recipe grading: easy*

- 2 cups, tightly packed/300 g mild green olives, in brine, drained
- 1–2 cloves garlic, thinly sliced
- 1 small chile pepper, seeded and finely chopped
- 4 tablespoons extra-virgin olive oil
- 1 tablespoon white wine vinegar
- 2 teaspoons finely chopped oregano

Pit the olives and press them with the back of a kitchen knife to crush slightly. • Place them in a bowl and add all the remaining ingredients. • Stir well, then let stand for several hours before serving to let the flavors penetrate. • The olives will keep for up to a week if stored in a tightly closed container in the refrigerator. • For a slightly different but equally delicious dish, add 1 tablespoon of capers, a handful of chopped mint leaves, and a finely chopped heart of crisp green celery.

## Black olives in herb marinade

*Serves: 4–6*
*Preparation: 15 minutes + time to stand*
*Recipe grading: easy*

Piquant marinated lives

- 2 cups, tightly packed/300 g black olives, in brine, drained
- 3 cloves garlic, lightly crushed
- 1 small chile pepper, seeded and finely chopped
- 1 tablespoon extra-virgin olive oil
- 4 tablespoons red wine vinegar
- $1/2$ teaspoon freshly ground cumin seeds
- $1/2$ teaspoon dried oregano
- 1 tablespoon finely chopped marjoram
- 1 tablespoon finely chopped parsley

Pit the olives and press them with the back of a kitchen knife to crush slightly. • Place the olives in a jar in which they will fit tightly and add the garlic, chile pepper, oil, vinegar, cumin, oregano, marjoram, and parsley. Top the jar up with water and screw on the lid. Shake well to blend the ingredients thoroughly. • Leave overnight at room temperature, then store in the refrigerator. The olives will keep for up to a month. Bring to room temperature to serve.

## Stuffed fried zucchini flowers

*Serves: 4*
*Preparation: 10 minutes*
*Cooking: 15 minutes*
*Recipe grading: fairly easy*

- 20 fresh zucchini/courgette flowers
- 6 tablespoons freshly grated Parmesan cheese
- 1 cup/150 g fine dry bread crumbs
- 1 tablespoon finely chopped parsley
- 3 eggs
- salt and freshly ground black pepper to taste
- 1 cup/150 g all-purpose/plain flour
- 1–2 cups/250–500 ml olive oil, for frying

Rinse the flowers carefully under cold running water. Trim the stalks and dry the flowers carefully with paper towels. • Mix the Parmesan with the bread crumbs in a bowl. Add the parsley, 1 egg, salt, and pepper. Mix well. • Use this mixture to carefully stuff the flowers. • Beat the remaining eggs and place them in a small bowl. Place the flour in a small bowl and dip the stuffed flowers first in the flour, then in the egg. • Heat the oil in a large skillet (frying pan) until very hot. Fry the flowers in batches of 5–6 at a time. Turn them so that they brown all over. Drain on paper towels. Repeat until all the flowers are cooked. Sprinkle with a little salt, if liked. • Serve hot.

## Simple fried zucchini flowers

*Serves: 4*
*Preparation 10 minutes*
*Cooking: 25 minutes*
*Recipe grading: fairly easy*

- 20 very fresh zucchini/courgette flowers
- 1 cup/150 g all-purpose/plain flour
- $^1/_2$ teaspoon salt
- 1 cup/250 ml extra-virgin olive oil
- 1–2 tablespoons cold water

Remove the pistil (the bright yellow center) and calyx (the green leaflets at the base) from each flower, rinse carefully in cold water, and gently pat dry with paper towels. • Sift the flour into a medium bowl, make a well in the center and add the salt, and 1 tablespoon each of oil and water. • Gradually mix into the flour, adding enough extra water to make a batter with a thick pouring consistency that will cling to the flowers. • Heat the remaining oil in a large skillet (frying pan) until very hot. • Dip 4–6 flowers in the batter and fry until golden brown on both sides. Drain on paper towels. Fry all the flowers in the same way. • Serve immediately.

## Fried cabbage ravioli

*Serves: 6*
*Preparation: 35 minutes*
*Cooking: 30 minutes*
*Recipe grading: fairly easy*

Pastry
- 1 cup/150 g all-purpose/plain flour
- $^1/_3$ cup/90 ml cold water
- 2 tablespoons extra-virgin olive oil
- $^1/_4$ teaspoon salt

Filling
- $^1/_2$ small Savoy cabbage
- 2 tablespoons butter
- 2 leeks, white part only, finely chopped
- salt and freshly ground black pepper to taste
- 7 oz/200 g Ricotta cheese
- 1$^1/_2$ cups/375 ml oil, for frying

Pastry: Mix the flour, water, oil, and salt in a medium bowl and mix with a wooden spoon until smooth. • Transfer to a lightly floured work surface and knead for 4–5 minutes. Wrap in plastic wrap and set aside to rest for 30 minutes. • Filling: Clean the cabbage and coarsely chop. • Plunge the cabbage into a large pan of boiling water. Leave for 1 minute, then drain. • Heat the butter in a large skillet (frying pan) and sauté the leeks for 5 minutes. Add the cabbage and cook for 10 minutes. Season with salt and pepper. • Remove from heat and stir in the Ricotta. • Roll out the pastry (by hand or with a pasta machine). Cut out disks about 3 inches (8 cm) in diameter. • Place about 2 tablespoons of the filling mixture on one half of each disk then fold over in a classic half-moon ravioli shape. • Heat the oil in a large skillet and fry the ravioli in small batches until golden brown on both sides. Drain on paper towels. • Serve immediately.

Stuffed fried zucchini flowers

*Quark is a high-protein, skimmed-milk soft cheese with a smooth texture and creamy taste. It was traditionally made by draining warm soured milk in cotton sacks. As it is Germany's most popular cheese, the curds are now produced by more modern methods. Quark does not separate when heated and can also be used in cooking and baking. Mixed with fresh herbs, vegetables, other cheeses, and spices, it makes a versatile topping for hot dishes. It is also an excellent base for dips. If your local supermarket or cheese shop does not stock Quark, substitute with a mixture of half Ricotta and half cream cheese.*

## Pepper and paprika quark

*Serves: 4*
*Preparation: 15 minutes + 1 hour to chill*
*Cooking: 20 minutes*
*Recipe grading: easy*

- 2 tablespoons extra-virgin olive oil
- 1 small onion, finely chopped
- 3 small bell peppers/capsicums, 1 red, 1 yellow, 1 green, cored, seeded, and finely chopped
- 1 clove garlic, finely chopped
- 1 teaspoon ground paprika
- 8 oz/250 g Quark cheese
- salt and freshly ground white pepper to taste

Heat the oil in a large skillet (frying pan) and sauté the onion for 3–4 minutes. • Add the bell peppers and garlic, and cook for 5 more minutes. Stir in the paprika and cook for 1–2 minutes. The vegetables should be soft. Set aside to cool. • Place the Quark in a bowl and stir in the vegetable mixture. Season with salt and pepper, cover the bowl, and refrigerate for at least 1 hour. • Serve with an extra sprinkling of paprika, and crackers, potato chips, corn chips, or fresh, sliced fruit and vegetables, such as carrots, radishes, bell peppers, green onions, apples, pears, etc.

## Herb quark

*Serves: 2–4*
*Preparation: 5 minutes + 1 hour to chill*
*Recipe grading: easy*

- 8 oz/250 g Quark cheese
- 1 tablespoon finely chopped chives
- 1 tablespoon finely chopped parsley
- 1 tablespoon finely chopped dill
- salt and freshly ground black pepper to taste

Place the Quark in a bowl and stir in the herbs. You may vary the herbs according to what you have on hand. • Season with salt and pepper, cover, and refrigerate for at least 1 hour. • Serve with crackers, potato chips, corn chips, or fresh, sliced fruit and vegetables (carrots, radishes, bell peppers, green onions, apples, pears, etc).

## Gherkin quark

*Serves: 2–4*
*Preparation: 5 minutes + 1 hour to chill*
*Recipe grading: easy*

- 8 oz/250 g Quark cheese
- 4 oz/125 g sweet Gorgonzola, or other soft, blue cheese
- 2 finely chopped pickled gherkins
- 1 shallot, finely chopped
- salt and freshly ground black pepper to taste

Place the Quark in a bowl and stir in the blue cheese, gherkins, and shallot. • Season with salt and pepper, cover the bowl, and refrigerate for at least 1 hour. • Serve with crackers, potato chips, corn chips, or fresh, sliced fruit and vegetables, such as carrots, radishes, bell peppers, green onions, apples, pears, etc.

## Horseradish quark

*Serves: 2–4*
*Preparation: 5 minutes + 1 hour to chill*
*Recipe grading: easy*

- 8 oz/250 g Quark cheese
- 1 tablespoon finely grated horseradish root
- 1 tablespoon finely grated carrot
- ¹/₂ teaspoon sugar
- salt and freshly ground black pepper to taste

Place the Quark in a bowl and stir in the horseradish, carrot, and sugar. • Season with salt and pepper, cover the bowl, and refrigerate for at least 1 hour. • Serve with crackers, potato chips, corn chips, or fresh, sliced vegetables, such as carrots, radishes, bell peppers, green onions, etc.

# Spicy Gorgonzola quark

*Serves: 4*
*Preparation: 10 minutes + 1 hour to chill*
*Recipe grading: easy*

- 3 tablespoons butter, at room temperature
- 5 oz/150 g Quark cheese
- 4 oz/125 g Gorgonzola cheese, mashed
- 1–2 tablespoons heavy/double cream
- salt and paprika to taste

Beat the butter into the Quark, then beat in the Gorgonzola and cream. Whisk until smooth. Add more cream if the mixture needs thinning. • Season with salt and paprika, cover the bowl, and refrigerate for at least 1 hour. • Serve with boiled potatoes.

# Cheese and mushroom dip

*Serves: 4–6*
*Preparation: 20 minutes + 2 hours to chill*
*Recipe grading: easy*

- 2 cups/500 ml sour cream
- 3 oz/90 g Cheddar cheese, grated
- 1 (¹/₂ oz/45 g) package dry mushroom soup mix
- freshly ground white pepper to taste

Place the sour cream and cheese in a medium bowl. • Add the soup mix and stir until smooth. Season with the pepper. • Cover the bowl and refrigerate for 2 hours. • Serve with potato chips, crackers, or raw vegetables.

# Roasted eggplant dip

*Serves: 4*
*Preparation: 20 minutes + 1 hour to stand*
*Cooking: 30–40 minutes*
*Recipe grading: easy*

- 1 lb/500 g eggplant/aubergine
- 4 cloves garlic, finely chopped
- 2 tablespoons finely chopped parsley
- 4 tablespoons extra-virgin olive oil
- salt and freshly ground white pepper to taste

Preheat the oven to 400°F/200°C/gas 6. • Rinse the eggplants thoroughly and bake for 30–40 minutes, or until tender. • Cool to room temperature, then remove the skins. Chop the flesh coarsely and place in a bowl. • Stir in the garlic, parsley, and oil. Season with salt and pepper. Set aside for at least 1 hour. • Serve with pita bread, fresh French bread, or toast.

# Olive paste

*Serves: 4*
*Preparation: 10 minutes*
*Recipe grading: easy*

- 5 oz/150 g large, fleshy black olives, pitted
- 2 tablespoons capers, rinsed and dried
- 2 cloves garlic
- ¹/₂ teaspoon dried oregano
- 2 tablespoons extra-virgin olive oil
- freshly ground white pepper to taste

Place the olives, capers, garlic, and oregano in a food processor and chop until smooth. Add the oil as you chop. • Season with pepper. • Serve spread on fresh bread, toast, or hard-boiled eggs.

Cheese and mushroom dip

# SOUPS

Light and nutritious, soups are enormously adaptable. Hearty, chunky minestrones and soups with bread, pasta, rice, or other cereals are delicious, and healthy, dishes to serve at family or informal meals. When entertaining, try some of the more sophisticated creamy concoctions, such as *Cool cantaloupe soup* (see page 48), *Mushroom cream with sherry* (see page 56), or *Cream of scallion soup* (see page 61). Summertime soups include the Andalucían classic—Gazpacho—and many others too!

*This fabulous creamy soup should only be made at the height of summer when zucchinis and their flowers are at their tastiest. The subtle flavor of the zucchini flowers adds an extra dimension to the finished dish. For a special flourish, serve each bowl of soup with a well-rinsed zucchini flower floating on the top.*

Right: Cream of zucchini and zucchini flower soup (see page 52)
Left: Spinach rice soup (see page 61)

46

*Like all bright orange or yellow vegetables, pumpkin is a good source of vitamin A and beta carotene. It is also rich in vitamin C and potassium. A dieter's friend, pumpkin is low in carbohydrates and is a good source of dietary fiber, which not only promotes regularity but also helps control calorie intake.*

## Cream of pumpkin soup

*Serves: 4*
*Preparation: 15 minutes*
*Cooking: 50 minutes*
*Recipe grading: fairly easy*

- 1 lb/500 g pumpkin flesh, cut into small cubes
- 2 fennel bulbs, finely chopped
- 1 onion, finely chopped
- 2 quarts/2 liters vegetable stock (bouillon cube)
- $^{1}/_{4}$ teaspoon ground cumin seeds
- 1 small chile pepper, seeded and finely chopped
- 2 tablespoons finely chopped thyme
- salt and freshly ground black pepper to taste
- 1 tablespoon extra-virgin olive oil
- 1 tablespoon cornstarch/cornflour, dissolved in 4 tablespoons water

Cook the pumpkin, fennel, onion, and 1 cup (250 ml) vegetable stock in a large saucepan over medium heat for 15 minutes, or until the pumpkin has softened slightly. • Pour in the remaining stock and add the cumin, chile, and thyme. Season with salt and pepper. • Cook over medium-low heat for 30 minutes. • Add the oil and transfer to a food processor or blender. Process until smooth. • Return the mixture to the saucepan over low heat and stir in the cornstarch mixture. Cook for 5 minutes, or until the soup begins to thicken. • Serve hot.

## Spiced spinach soup

*Serves: 4–6*
*Preparation: 30 minutes*
*Cooking: 35 minutes*
*Recipe grading: fairly easy*

- 2 red onions, finely chopped
- 2 cloves garlic, peeled and finely chopped
- 1 small red chile pepper, seeded and finely chopped
- 2 medium potatoes, cut into small cubes
- 2 tablespoons extra-virgin olive oil
- 1 teaspoon cumin seeds
- seeds of 3 green cardamom pods
- 4 black peppercorns
- 1 quart/1 liter vegetable stock (bouillon cube)
- $^{3}/_{4}$ cup/180 ml coconut milk
- 1 bunch parsley, finely chopped
- 1 tablespoon finely chopped mint
- 14 oz/400 g fresh spinach leaves, stalks removed and shredded
- 1 tablespoon fresh lime juice
- salt and freshly ground black pepper to taste
- 1 tablespoon plain yogurt

Sauté the onions, garlic, chile, and potatoes in the oil in a large saucepan over medium heat. Cook, covered, for 5 minutes. • Use a pestle and mortar to finely grind the cumin seeds, cardamom, and peppercorns. • Add the spice mixture to the vegetables and cook for 5 minutes more, stirring constantly. • Pour in the vegetable stock and bring to a boil. Simmer, covered, for 20 minutes. • Stir in the coconut, half the parsley, and mint. Remove from heat and add the spinach and lime juice. • Stir until the spinach has wilted and the soup has cooled slightly. Transfer to a food processor or blender and process until puréed. • Return the mixture to the saucepan over low heat and season with the salt and pepper. • Serve hot, garnished with yogurt and sprinkled with the remaining parsley.

## Cool cantaloupe soup

*Serves: 4*
*Preparation: 20 minutes + 1 hour to chill*
*Recipe grading: easy*

- 2 small cantaloupe/rock melons, weighing about 2 lb/1 kg each
- seeds of 6 cardamom pods
- 2 leaves fresh basil, torn
- 1 small chile pepper, seeded and finely chopped
- $^{1}/_{2}$ clove garlic
- 1 bunch fresh dill or chervil, finely chopped
- 1 tablespoon extra-virgin olive oil
- $^{1}/_{2}$ teaspoon salt
- 1 tablespoon fresh lemon juice
- 1 teaspoon Worcestershire sauce

Cut the melons in half horizontally. Scoop out the flesh with a spoon, leaving a $^{1}/_{2}$-inch (1-cm) border. Place the flesh in a bowl. Reserve the shells. • Chop the cardamom, basil, chile, garlic, and dill in a food processor until they form a smooth pesto (sauce). • Place the melon flesh, pesto, oil, and salt in a food processor or blender and process until smooth. • Add the lemon juice and Worcestershire sauce and stir until well blended. • Spoon the soup into the melon shells and chill in the refrigerator for 1 hour before serving.

*Cool cantaloupe soup*

*Tomatoes are an excellent, low calorie, no-cholesterol, health food. Eaten raw, they are rich in vitamins A and C, and also contain traces of a wide variety of minerals. When cooked, they release an antioxidant that is believed to help lower cholesterol levels, prevent heart disease, and provide protection against many forms of cancer.*

## Spicy Tuscan bread soup

*Serves: 4*
*Preparation: 15 minutes*
*Cooking: 25 minutes*
*Recipe grading: fairly easy*

- 2 lb/1 kg firm-ripe tomatoes
- 3 cloves garlic, peeled and finely chopped
- 2 bay leaves
- 1 dried chile pepper, crumbled
- 6 tablespoons extra-virgin olive oil
- 1 lb/500 g day-old firm-textured bread, cut in 1-inch/2.5-cm cubes
- 2 cups/500 ml water
- salt and freshly ground black pepper to taste
- 8–10 leaves fresh basil, torn

Blanch the tomatoes in a large pot of salted, boiling water for 1 minute. Drain, run under cold water, and peel. Cut in half horizontally, squeezing gently to remove the seeds. Chop the flesh into small pieces. • Sauté the garlic, bay leaves, and chilies in 3 tablespoons of oil in a large saucepan until aromatic. • Add the bread and cook over medium heat for 3–4 minutes, stirring often. • Stir in the tomatoes and pour in the water. Season with the salt and pepper. • Cook for 15 minutes, stirring often. If the soup becomes too thick, add a little more water (it should be about the same consistency as porridge). • Drizzle with the remaining oil, sprinkle with the basil, and serve.

## Tomato and yogurt soup

*Serves: 4*
*Preparation: 15 minutes*
*Cooking: 15 minutes*
*Recipe grading: fairly easy*

- 2 lb/1 kg firm-ripe tomatoes
- salt and freshly ground black pepper to taste
- 1/2 teaspoon dried oregano
- 2 cups/500 ml plain yogurt
- 4 leaves fresh basil, torn

Blanch the tomatoes in a large pot of salted boiling water for 1 minute. Drain, run under cold water, and peel. Run through a vegetable mill or chop with a knife. • Place the tomato purée in a medium saucepan over medium heat. Bring to a boil and season with the salt and pepper. Add the oregano. • Stir in the yogurt until well blended, reserving 1 tablespoon to garnish. • Bring to a boil and cook over low heat for 8 minutes. • Sprinkle with 2 leaves basil and cook for 2 minutes more. • Serve in individual soup bowls, garnished with the remaining basil and dotted with the yogurt. • Serve with freshly baked bread or warm toast.

## Tomato and orange soup

*Serves: 4*
*Preparation: 15 minutes*
*Cooking: 25–35 minutes*
*Recipe grading: easy*

- 2 lb/1 kg firm-ripe tomatoes
- 1 onion, finely chopped
- 2 cups/500 ml vegetable stock (bouillon cube)
- salt and freshly ground black pepper to taste
- grated zest and juice of 1 orange
- 1 tablespoon butter
- 1 tablespoon all-purpose/plain flour
- 2 tablespoons tomato concentrate/purée

Cut the tomatoes in half and strain the juice. Cut the tomato flesh into cubes. • Place the tomato flesh and strained juice and onion in a large saucepan over low heat. Pour in the stock and season with the salt and pepper. • Add the orange zest and bring to a boil. Simmer, covered, for 25–35 minutes over low heat, or until the tomatoes have softened. • Strain. • Stir the butter and flour in a small bowl until smooth. Add the roux to the soup and stir until well blended. • Stir in the tomato concentrate and return to a boil, stirring constantly. Drizzle with the orange juice, blending well. • Pour into individual soup bowls and serve hot.

Tomato and yogurt soup

## Cream of zucchini and zucchini flower soup

Serves: 4
Preparation: 10 minutes
Cooking: 20 minutes
Recipe grading: easy

- 14 oz/400 g potatoes, peeled and finely chopped
- 1 onion, finely chopped
- 2 tablespoons butter
- 2 cups/500 ml vegetable stock (bouillon cube)
- 1¹/₂ lb/650 g zucchini/courgettes, cut in thin wheels
- 10 oz/300 g zucchini/courgette flowers, washed carefully and cut in half
- 2 tablespoons extra-virgin olive oil
- salt and freshly ground black pepper to taste
- 1 tablespoon plain yogurt
- 4 leaves fresh basil, torn

Sauté the potatoes and onion in the butter in a skillet (frying pan) until lightly browned. • Add 1 cup (250 ml) stock and let it reduce. • Cook the zucchini and zucchini flowers in a large saucepan with the oil and the remaining 1 cup (250 ml) stock for 10 minutes. • Season with the salt and pepper. Transfer the cooked potato mixture and the zucchini mixture to a food processor or blender. Process until smooth. • Return to the saucepan and cook for 5 minutes more. • Swirl with the yogurt and garnish with the basil. Serve hot.

## Spelt and lentil soup

Serves: 4
Preparation: 15 minutes
Cooking: 40–50 minutes
Recipe grading: easy

- ¹/₂ onion, finely chopped
- ¹/₂ stalk celery, finely chopped
- ¹/₂ carrot, finely chopped
- 4 tablespoons extra-virgin olive oil
- ¹/₂ cup/100 g short-grain rice
- 2 cups/200 g spelt
- 1 cup/100 g red lentils
- 1 cup/100 g cannellini beans, soaked overnight and drained
- ³/₄ cup/90 g peas
- 8 cherry tomatoes
- salt and freshly ground black pepper to taste

Sauté the onion, celery, and carrot in the oil in a skillet (frying pan) until the onion is lightly browned. • Stir in the rice and toast it. Add the spelt, lentils, beans, peas, and tomatoes. • Cook, stirring occasionally, over medium heat for 30–40 minutes, or until the pulses are tender. • Season with the salt and pepper and serve.

## Cream of asparagus soup

Serves: 4
Preparation: 10 minutes
Cooking: 20–25 minutes
Recipe grading: easy

- 4 tablespoons butter
- ²/₃ cup/100 g all-purpose/plain flour
- 2 cups/500 ml milk
- 2 cups/500 ml vegetable stock (bouillon cube)
- 2 lb/1 kg asparagus, trimmed and coarsely chopped
- salt and freshly ground white pepper to taste
- 3 egg yolks
- 1 cup/125 g freshly grated Parmesan cheese
- ¹/₂ cup/125 ml light/single cream

Melt 2 tablespoons of butter in a small saucepan and add the flour, stirring constantly. • Pour in the milk and stock. • Bring to a boil, add the asparagus, and season with the salt and pepper. • Cook for 15–20 minutes, or until thick. • Chop in a food processor and return to medium heat. • Beat the egg yolks, remaining butter, Parmesan, and cream in a small bowl. • Pour the beaten egg mixture into the asparagus, blending well. • Serve hot.

## Spelt and vegetable soup

Serves: 4
Preparation: 30 minutes
Cooking: 1 hour 10–20 minutes
Recipe grading: fairly easy

- 2 cups/200 g cannellini or white kidney beans, soaked overnight and drained
- 4 cloves garlic, 2 lightly crushed, 2 finely chopped
- 4 leaves fresh sage
- salt and freshly ground black pepper to taste
- 6 tablespoons extra-virgin olive oil
- 1 onion, finely chopped
- 1 stalk celery, finely chopped
- 1 carrot, finely chopped
- 2 quarts/2 liters vegetable stock (bouillon cube)
- 6 tomatoes, peeled and finely chopped
- 8 oz/250 g Swiss chard, shredded
- 2¹/₂ cups/250 g spelt

Place the beans in a large pot of salted, boiling water with the lightly crushed garlic and sage. Bring to a boil and simmer for 30–40 minutes, or until the beans are tender. • Discard the garlic and sage and season with salt. • Drain the beans, reserving the cooking liquid. Place half the beans in a food processor and chop until smooth. • Sauté the chopped garlic in 4 tablespoons of oil in a large saucepan over medium heat for 2–3 minutes. Add the onion, celery, and carrot and sauté until softened. • Pour in the stock, add the tomatoes and Swiss chard. Season with the salt and pepper. Cover and simmer over medium heat for 30 minutes. • Add the spelt and cook for 20 minutes. Stir in the bean purée and reserved whole beans and cooking liquid. Season with the salt and pepper and simmer for 20 minutes more. • Drizzle with the remaining oil and serve hot.

Spelt and vegetable soup

MIxed bean and spelt soup in bread rolls

## Mixed bean and spelt soup in bread rolls

*Serves: 4–6*
*Preparation: 40 minutes*
*Cooking: 50 minutes*
*Recipe grading: easy*

- 1 onion, finely chopped
- 1 carrot, finely chopped
- 1 stalk celery, finely chopped
- 1 tablespoon extra-virgin olive oil
- $^3/_4$ cup/75 g spelt
- 2 cups/500 ml vegetable stock (bouillon cube)
- 6 round bread rolls
- 8 oz/250 g mixed pulses, such as cannellini beans, borlotti beans, black beans, and lentils, soaked overnight
- 2 cloves garlic, finely chopped
- 1 teaspoon finely chopped rosemary
- 1 teaspoon finely chopped sage
- 4 cherry tomatoes

Sauté the onion, carrot, and celery in the oil in a heavy-bottomed pressure cooker until the onion is lightly browned. • Add the spelt and pour in the vegetable stock.

Cook, with the pressure cooker lid attached, for 12 minutes. • Cut the tops off the bread rolls and remove the bread interior. Cut the interior into small cubes. • Toast the bread cubes in a dry skillet (frying pan) until lightly browned. • Release the pressure valve and lid and stir in the mixed pulses, garlic, rosemary, sage, and tomatoes. • Return to the heat and cook for 30–40 minutes, or until the pulses are tender. • Spoon the soup into the rolls and serve.

## Tortilla soup

*Serves: 4*
*Preparation: 20 minutes*
*Cooking: 35 minutes*
*Recipe grading: easy*

- $^1/_2$ onion, finely chopped
- 2 cloves garlic, peeled and finely chopped
- 1 stalk celery, finely chopped
- 2 zucchini/courgettes, finely chopped
- 2 tablespoons vegetable oil
- 2 cups/500 g chopped tomatoes
- 1 cup/250 ml water
- 2 cups/500 ml vegetable stock (bouillon cube)
- 8 oz/250 g canned corn/sweetcorn
- $^1/_2$ teaspoon ground cumin
- 1 avocado, thinly sliced
- 8 oz/250 g tortilla chips

Sauté the onion, garlic, celery, and zucchini in the oil in a large saucepan over low heat until the vegetables have softened. • Stir in the tomatoes, water, vegetable stock, corn, and cumin until well blended. • Simmer, stirring often, over low heat for 30 minutes. • Pour into individual serving bowls and garnish with slices of avocado and tortilla chips.

## Ukrainian borsch

*Serves: 4–6*
*Preparation: 40 minutes*
*Cooking: 1 hour*
*Recipe grading: fairly easy*

- 1 lb/500 g raw beets/red beet, peeled and cut in thin strips, reserving $^1/_4$ beet to grate
- 2 carrots, cut into thin strips

- $^1/_2$ medium turnip, cut in thin strips
- $^1/_2$ medium parsnip, cut in thin strips
- $3^1/_2$ oz/100 g celeriac or swede, cut in thin strips
- 1 potato, cut into thin strips
- 1 lb/500 g white cabbage, shredded
- whites of 2 leeks, finely chopped
- 1 red onion, finely chopped
- $2^1/_4$ quarts/2.25 liters vegetable stock (bouillon cube)
- 2 tablespoons tomato concentrate/purée
- 6 peppercorns
- 1 bay leaf
- 3 tablespoons balsamic vinegar
- 1 teaspoon sugar
- 2 tablespoons finely chopped parsley
- $^2/_3$ cup/150 ml sour cream

Place the chopped beets, carrots, turnip, parsnip, celeriac, potato, cabbage, leeks, and onion in a large saucepan with the vegetable stock. • Bring to a boil. Cover and simmer for 35 minutes. • Stir in the tomato concentrate, peppercorns, bay leaf, vinegar, and sugar. • Simmer for 20 minutes more, or until the vegetables are tender. • Grate in the reserved beet and cook for 5 minutes more. • Ladle into individual soup bowls and garnish with the parsley and a swirl of sour cream.

# Fava bean and pasta soup

*Serves: 4*
*Preparation: 35 minutes*
*Cooking: 50–60 minutes*
*Recipe grading: easy*

- 2 cups/200 g fava/broad beans
- 1 onion, finely chopped
- 2 cloves garlic, peeled and finely chopped
- 4 tablespoons extra-virgin olive oil
- 2 medium potatoes, peeled and cut in small cubes
- 10 oz/300 g small penne pasta
- 1 teaspoon tomato concentrate/purée dissolved in 2 cups/500 ml vegetable stock (bouillon cube)
- salt and freshly ground black pepper to taste

Blanch the fava beans in a large pot of salted boiling water for 1 minute. • Drain well and rub off the skins. • Sauté the onion and garlic in the oil in a medium saucepan until lightly browned. • Add the potatoes and pasta. Cook, stirring constantly, for 1 minute. • Pour in the vegetable stock. Cook over medium heat, stirring constantly, until the pasta is tender. • Add the fava beans and cook for 30–40 minutes, or until tender. • Season with the salt and pepper. The soup should be very thick.

# Leek, potato, and pearl barley soup

*Serves: 6*
*Preparation: 25 minutes*
*Cooking: 1 hour 10 minutes*
*Recipe grading: fairly easy*

- white of 1 leek, finely chopped
- 2 quarts/2 liters vegetable stock (bouillon cube)
- 1 lb/500 g floury potatoes, peeled and cut in small cubes
- $^1/_2$ cup/75 g pearl barley
- 2 tablespoons butter
- 4 tablespoons freshly grated Parmesan cheese
- 1 tablespoon finely chopped parsley
- $^1/_4$ teaspoon ground nutmeg

Cook the leek in a large saucepan filled with the vegetable stock over medium heat. • Bring to a boil and simmer for 10 minutes. • Add the potatoes and cook for 15 minutes. • Add the pearl barley, stirring constantly, and cook for 45 minutes. • Stir in the butter. Sprinkle with the Parmesan, parsley, and nutmeg. Serve hot.

Fava bean and pasta soup

Mushroom soup
with sherry

## Mushroom cream with sherry

*Serves: 4*
*Preparation: 35 minutes*
*Cooking: 30 minutes*
*Recipe grading: complicated*

Béchamel sauce
• 3 tablespoons butter
• 3 tablespoons all-purpose/plain flour
• 3 cups/750 ml milk
• salt and freshly ground black pepper to taste
• $^1/_2$ teaspoon ground nutmeg

• 4 tablespoons butter
• 8 oz/250 g white mushrooms, cleaned and cut in small cubes
• 8 oz/250 g wild mushrooms, cleaned and finely chopped
• 2 cloves garlic, finely chopped
• 3 tablespoons finely chopped parsley

• 1 cup/250 ml dry sherry
• salt and freshly ground black pepper to taste
• $1^1/_3$ cups/330 ml vegetable stock (bouillon cube)

Béchamel sauce: Melt the butter in a medium heavy-bottomed saucepan over low heat. Add the flour and cook for 3 minutes, stirring constantly. Gradually pour in the milk, a little at a time, beating vigorously to prevent lumps from forming. Season with the salt and pepper and add the nutmeg. • Bring to a boil and cook for 5–10 minutes, stirring constantly. If lumps do form, beat with a wire whisk until smooth. • Melt the 4 tablespoons of butter in a large saucepan over low heat. Stir in the white and wild mushrooms and cook for 10 minutes, stirring often. • Add the garlic, parsley, and sherry. Season with the salt and pepper. • Cook for 3 minutes, then stir in the Béchamel sauce and half the vegetable

stock. The soup should be thick and creamy. Add more stock if it is too thick. • Cook for 3 more minutes and serve hot.

## Mushroom and chestnut soup

*Serves: 4*
*Preparation: 40 minutes*
*Cooking: 30 minutes*
*Recipe grading: fairly easy*

• 7 oz/200 g tagliatelle
• $3^1/_2$ oz/100 g dried porcini mushrooms
• 2 cups/500 ml warm water
• 3 oz/90 g fresh or frozen chestnuts, thawed if frozen
• 1 onion, finely chopped
• 3 tablespoons extra-virgin olive oil
• 2 tablespoons butter

- 1 tablespoon all-purpose/plain flour
- 1 quart/1 liter vegetable stock (bouillon cube)
- 1 tablespoon finely chopped thyme
- salt and freshly ground black pepper to taste
- 2 tablespoons finely chopped parsley

If using fresh tagliatelle, chop into short lengths. If using dry tagliatelle, break into short pieces. • Soak the porcini mushrooms in the water for 20 minutes. • Drain well and pat dry with paper towels. • If using fresh chestnuts, preheat the oven to 350°F/180°C/gas 4. • Place the chestnuts on a large baking sheet. Toast for 10 minutes. Remove from the oven, let cool a little, and peel. • Coarsely chop the chestnuts. • Sauté the onion in the oil and butter in a large saucepan over low heat until softened. • Drain the mushrooms. and sprinkle with the flour. • Pour in the vegetable stock, stirring constantly. Add the chestnuts and thyme and cook for 20 minutes over low heat. • Add the pasta and cook for 5 minutes, or until the pasta is cooked *al dente*. Season with the salt and pepper. • Pour into individual soup bowls and garnish with the parsley.

## Creamy fennel soup

*Serves: 4*
*Preparation: 40 minutes*
*Cooking: 1 hour*
*Recipe grading: fairly easy*

- 10 oz/300 g fennel bulbs, finely chopped
- white of 1 leek, finely chopped
- 1 stalk celery, finely chopped
- 1 large potato, peeled and cut into small cubes
- 4 tablespoons butter
- 2 cups/500 ml vegetable stock (bouillon cube)
- 2 cups/500 ml milk
- 2 eggs, lightly beaten
- 4 tablespoons freshly grated Parmesan cheese

Sauté the fennel, leek, celery, and potato in the butter in a large saucepan over low heat

*Fennel is a cleansing vegetable, restorative for the digestive, urinary, and respiratory systems. Its mildly aniseed taste gives an interesting twist to many salads and is wonderful when baked in a gratin of cheese.*

until the vegetables have softened. • Heat the vegetable stock and milk in separate saucepans. • Pour the milk into the vegetable mixture and cook for 15 minutes, stirring often. • Pour in the stock and cook for 40 minutes, or until the vegetables begin to break down. • Remove from heat and let cool for 15 minutes. • Transfer to a food processor or blender and process until smooth. • Season with the salt and pepper. Return the mixture to the saucepan over low heat and bring to a boil. • Add the eggs, beating until just blended. Cook for 3 minutes. • Sprinkle with the Parmesan and pour into individual soup bowls. Serve hot.

## Fennel miso

*Serves: 4–6*
*Preparation: 20 minutes*
*Cooking: 35 minutes*
*Recipe grading: easy*

- 14 oz/400 g fennel bulbs, cut into wedges and finely sliced
- 1 carrot, cut into very thin strips
- whites of 2 leeks, washed and cut into 1/2-inch/ 1-cm rounds
- 2 potatoes, peeled and cut into small cubes

- 2 tablespoons extra-virgin oil
- one 1-inch/2.5-cm piece root ginger, peeled and finely chopped
- 1 clove garlic, finely chopped
- 1/2 small green chile pepper, seeded and finely chopped
- 1 small red chile pepper, seeded and finely chopped
- 1 teaspoon fennel seeds
- salt to taste
- 1 1/2 quarts/1.5 liters water
- 3 tablespoons barley miso
- 3 1/2 oz/100 g watercress, stems removed and coarsely chopped, reserving some leaves to garnish
- 5 sugar snaps, broken in half (optional)
- 1 tablespoon fresh lemon juice
- 1 tablespoon finely chopped parsley

Sauté the fennel, carrot, leeks, and potatoes in the oil in a large saucepan for 10 minutes. • Stir in the ginger, garlic, chilies, and fennel seeds. Season with the salt and sauté over low heat for 10 more minutes. • Pour in the water and bring to a boil. • Stir in the miso and simmer for 15–20 minutes, or until tender. • Add the watercress, sugar snaps, and lemon juice. Simmer for 3 minutes more. • Serve hot, garnished with the parsley and watercress.

## Smooth bean soup

*Serves: 6*
*Preparation: 20 minutes*
*Cooking: 2 hours 15 minutes*
*Recipe grading: fairly easy*

- 2 lb/1 kg borlotti beans, soaked overnight and drained
- salt and freshly ground black pepper to taste
- 1 onion, finely chopped
- 4 tablespoons extra-virgin olive oil
- 4 quarts/4 liters water
- 2 teaspoons tomato concentrate/purée
- 5–6 leaves fresh sage

Cook the beans in a large pan of salted, boiling water for 50 minutes, or until tender. Season with salt. • Sauté the onion in 2 tablespoons of oil in a large saucepan until lightly browned. • Drain the beans. Add to the pan and cook for 3 minutes. • Pour in the water, partially cover, and cook for 75 minutes over medium-low heat. • Remove from heat and run through a vegetable mill or chop in a food processor until smooth. • Return the mixture to the saucepan and stir in the tomato concentrate. Cook for 5 minutes more. • Season with the salt and pepper and stir in the remaining oil. • Garnish with the sage and serve hot.

Smooth bean soup

## Celery soup

*Serves: 6*
*Preparation: 15 minutes*
*Cooking: 45 minutes*
*Recipe grading: easy*

- 1 head celery, leaves removed and coarsely chopped
- 1 onion, finely chopped
- 4 tablespoons butter
- 3 cups/750 ml vegetable stock (bouillon cube)
- 1 bay leaf
- 1 tablespoon cornstarch/cornflour
- 1 cup/250 ml milk
- 1/2 cup/125 ml sour cream

Sauté the celery and onion in the butter in a large saucepan over medium heat for 10 minutes. • Pour in the vegetable stock and add the bay leaf. Season with the salt and pepper. • Cover and simmer for 30 minutes over low heat. • Discard the bay leaf and remove from heat. • Transfer to a food processor or blender and process until smooth. • Place the cornstarch in a cup with 2 tablespoons of milk and stir until smooth. • Place the remaining milk and the soup in a large saucepan and stir in the cornstarch mixture. Bring to a boil and cook for 5 minutes, stirring constantly. • Stir in the sour cream and serve hot.

## Watercress and potato soup

*Serves: 4*
*Preparation: 20 minutes*
*Cooking: 40 minutes*
*Recipe grading: easy*

- 1 onion, finely chopped
- white of 1 leek, finely chopped
- 2 tablespoons butter
- 1 quart/1 liter vegetable stock (bouillon cube)
- 1 lb/500 g potatoes, peeled and thinly sliced
- 1 bunch watercress, coarsely chopped, reserving a few leaves to garnish
- 1 bay leaf

- salt and freshly ground black pepper to taste
- 1 tablespoon finely chopped parsley

Sauté the onion and leek in the butter in a large saucepan over low heat for 7 minutes. • Pour in the stock and add the potatoes, watercress, and bay leaf. Season with the salt and pepper. • Bring to a boil and simmer for 30 minutes. • Discard the bay leaf and transfer to a food processor or blender and process until smooth. • Return the mixture to the saucepan and bring to a boil. • Ladle the soup into individual soup bowls. Serve hot, garnished with the parsley and reserved watercress leaves.

## Celery and almond soup

*Serves: 4*
*Preparation: 20 minutes*
*Cooking: 1 hour 15 minutes*
*Recipe grading: easy*

- 1 head celery, leaves removed and coarsely chopped
- 1/2 onion, finely chopped
- 4 tablespoons almonds, peeled
- 4 tablespoons butter
- 1 quart/1 liter vegetable stock (bouillon cube)
- 2 tablespoons all-purpose/plain flour
- 2/3 cup/150 ml milk
- salt and freshly ground black pepper to taste
- 2 tablespoons finely ground almonds

Sauté the celery, onion, and almonds in 2 tablespoons butter in a large saucepan over medium heat for 10 minutes. • Pour in the vegetable stock and simmer over low heat for 1 hour. • Transfer to a food processor or blender and process until smooth. • Melt the remaining butter in a medium saucepan and stir in the flour. • Pour in the milk, stirring constantly, and cook over low heat for 2–3 minutes. • Add the celery and almond mixture and season with the salt and pepper and cook for 5 minutes. • Ladle into individual soup bowls. Serve hot, sprinkled with the ground almonds.

Smooth herb soup

## Smooth herb soup

*Serves: 4*
*Preparation: 20 minutes*
*Cooking: 40 minutes*
*Recipe grading: fairly easy*

• 1 onion, finely chopped
• ²/₃ cup/150 g butter
• 3 oz/90 g celery stalks, coarsely chopped
• 3 oz/90 g watercress, coarsely chopped
• 1 bunch parsley
• 1 quart/1 liter water
• salt and freshly ground black pepper to taste
• 2 lb/1 kg potatoes, peeled and cut in small cubes
• 2–4 fresh basil leaves, torn

Sauté the onion in 6 tablespoons butter in a large saucepan over low heat until lightly browned. • Add the celery, watercress, and parsley. Cover and cook over low heat for 5 minutes. • Pour in the water and season with salt. • Add the potatoes and cook for 30 minutes, or until the potatoes are tender. • Run through a vegetable mill or chop in a food processor until smooth. • Return to the saucepan over low heat and stir in the remaining butter. • Serve in individual bowls garnished with freshly ground black pepper and the basil.

## Egg and lemon soup

*Serves: 4*
*Preparation: 10 minutes*
*Cooking: 10–15 minutes*
*Recipe grading: fairly easy*

• 1 onion, finely chopped
• 2 tablespoons butter
• 2 tablespoons all-purpose/plain flour
• 1 quart/1 liter vegetable stock (bouillon stock)
• grated zest and juice of 1 lemon
• salt and freshly ground black pepper to taste
• 2 eggs, lightly beaten
• 4 tablespoons light/single cream
• 1 tablespoon finely chopped parsley

Sauté the onion in the butter in a large saucepan over low heat until softened. • Remove from heat and stir in the flour. Pour in the vegetable stock, stirring constantly. • Add the lemon zest and juice and season with the salt and pepper. • Bring to a boil, cover, and simmer over low heat for 20 minutes. • Transfer to a food processor and chop until smooth. • Beat the eggs and cream in a medium bowl. • Pour the soup into the egg mixture, blending well. • Return to the saucepan over medium heat and bring to a boil, stirring constantly. • Serve hot, garnished with the parsley.

Cream of scallion soup

# Cream of scallion soup

*Serves: 4*
*Preparation: 20 minutes*
*Cooking: 40 minutes*
*Recipe grading: easy*

- 8 scallions/spring onions, very thinly sliced
- 1 tablespoon butter
- 3 cups/750 ml vegetable stock (bouillon cube)
- 1 cup/250 ml milk
- 1 tablespoon cornstarch/cornflour
- salt to taste
- $1/2$ teaspoon ground nutmeg
- 1 tablespoon finely chopped parsley
- 4 tablespoons freshly grated Parmesan cheese
- 2 egg yolks, lightly beaten

Sauté the scallions in the butter in a large saucepan over low heat until softened. • Heat the vegetable stock and milk in separate saucepans. • Sprinkle the scallions with the cornstarch. • Gradually pour in the stock, alternating with the milk, stirring constantly. • Season with salt and nutmeg. • Cook for 20 minutes over low heat, stirring often. • Add the parsley, Parmesan, and egg yolks, beating until just blended. • Cook for 5 minutes more and serve hot.

# Spinach and rice soup

*Serves: 4*
*Preparation: 10 minutes*
*Cooking: 20–25 minutes*
*Recipe grading: easy*

- 12 oz/350 g fresh spinach leaves, stalks removed
- 2 tablespoons butter
- salt and freshly ground white pepper to taste
- 1 quart/1 liter vegetable stock (bouillon cube)
- 1 cup/200 g short-grain rice
- 1 egg, lightly beaten
- 3 tablespoons freshly grated Parmesan cheese

Wash the spinach under cold running water. Do not drain, but place in a saucepan and cook, with just the water clinging to its leaves, for 3 minutes. Drain, press out excess water, chop coarsely, and set aside. • Sauté the spinach in the butter in a medium saucepan over medium heat for 3 minutes. • Season with salt. • Pour the vegetable stock into a large saucepan and bring to a boil. • Stir in the rice and cook for 12–15 minutes, or until tender. • Add the spinach. • Beat the egg and Parmesan in a small bowl. Season with salt and pepper. • Pour the beaten egg mixture into the soup and stir until well blended. • Pour into individual soup bowls and serve hot.

## Cauliflower soup

*Serves: 4*
*Preparation: 15 minutes*
*Cooking: 30 minutes*
*Recipe grading: easy*

- 1 medium cauliflower, leaves removed
- 2 cups/500 ml milk
- $1/2$ onion, finely chopped
- 4 tablespoons butter
- 4 tablespoons all-purpose/plain flour
- $1/8$ teaspoon paprika
- salt and freshly ground black pepper to taste
- 2 tablespoons freshly grated Cheddar cheese

Cook the cauliflower in salted, boiling water for 10–15 minutes, or until tender. • Drain well and chop in a food processor until smooth. • Sauté the onion in the butter in a large saucepan over medium heat until transparent. • Stir in the flour and paprika and season with salt and pepper. • Gradually add the cauliflower and milk, stirring until well blended. Cook for 5 minutes. • Ladle into individual soup bowls, sprinkle with the cheese, and serve hot.

## Cream of tomato soup

*Serves: 4*
*Preparation: 20 minutes*
*Cooking: 20 minutes*
*Recipe grading: easy*

- 1 cup/250 ml peeled and chopped tomatoes
- 3 tablespoons butter
- 1 quart/1 liter vegetable stock (bouillon cube)
- $1/2$ quantity Béchamel sauce (see recipe Mushroom soup with sherry, page 56)
- 1 tablespoon finely chopped thyme

Cook the tomatoes and butter in a medium saucepan over medium heat for 10 minutes. • Add the vegetable stock then gradually stir in the Béchamel sauce. Cook for 10 minutes more, stirring often. • Serve very hot, garnished with the thyme.

Cream of tomato soup

## Simple veggie soup

*Serves: 4*
*Preparation: 15 minutes*
*Cooking: 1 hour*
*Recipe grading: easy*

- 8 oz/250 g onions, finely chopped
- 8 oz/250 g carrots, thinly sliced
- 4 stalks celery, finely chopped
- 1 tablespoon butter
- 1 cup/250 g chopped tomatoes
- 3 cups/750 ml vegetable stock (bouillon cube)
- salt and freshly ground black pepper to taste

Sauté the onions, carrots, and celery in the butter in a large saucepan over low heat until softened. • Add the tomatoes and pour in the vegetable stock. Season with the salt and pepper. • Bring to a boil and simmer, covered, for 1 hour, or until the vegetables are tender.

# Carrot and cilantro soup

*Serves: 6*
*Preparation: 20 minutes*
*Cooking: 40 minutes*
*Recipe grading: easy*

- 1 large onion, finely chopped
- 1 lb/500 g carrots, coarsely chopped
- 3 potatoes, coarsely chopped
- 1 stalk celery, finely chopped
- 1 tablespoon finely chopped parsley
- 1 clove garlic, finely chopped
- 1 bunch cilantro/coriander, finely chopped, reserving a few sprigs to garnish
- 4 tablespoons extra-virgin olive oil
- 1½ quarts/1.5 liters vegetable stock (bouillon cube)
- salt and freshly ground black pepper to taste
- 2 tablespoons heavy/double cream

Sauté the onion, carrots, potatoes, celery, parsley, garlic, and half the cilantro in the oil in a large saucepan over medium heat for 10 minutes. • Add the vegetable stock. • Simmer for 25–35 minutes, or until the vegetables are tender. Transfer to a food processor or blender and process until smooth. • Return the mixture to the saucepan over medium heat and bring to a boil. Season with salt and pepper. Stir in the cream and remaining cilantro. • Garnish with a few cilantro sprigs and serve hot.

# Cool pea consommé

*Serves: 4*
*Preparation: 30 minutes*
*Cooking: 35 minutes*
*Recipe grading: fairly easy*

- 1 scallion/spring onion, finely chopped
- 2 tablespoons extra-virgin olive oil
- 3 cups/375 g peas, shelled
- 1 quart/1 liter vegetable stock (bouillon cube)
- salt and freshly ground black pepper to taste
- ½ cup/125 ml light/single cream
- 1 tablespoon cornstarch/cornflour dissolved in 2 tablespoons water
- 4 leaves fresh basil, finely chopped

Cool pea consommé

Egg croutons
- 2 eggs, lightly beaten
- 6 tablespoons light/single cream
- salt and freshly ground black pepper to taste

Sauté the scallion in the oil in a large saucepan over medium heat until softened. • Add the peas and pour in the stock. Season with the salt and pepper. • Bring to a boil, cover, and cook for 15 minutes. • Stir in the cream and cornstarch mixture. Return to a boil and cook for 2 minutes. • Add the basil and stir well. Remove from heat and set aside. • Egg croutons: Preheat the oven to 400°F/ 200°C/gas 6. • Butter a small square baking pan. • Beat the eggs and cream in a small bowl. Season with salt and pepper. • Pour into the prepared baking pan. • Bake for 12–15 minutes, or until set. • Cut into cubes. • Sprinkle the egg croutons into individual soup bowls and ladle the soup over.

Gazpacho comes from the
Andalucía region of Spain
where it is prepared in
many different ways. This
classic recipe includes
tomatoes, but the origins
of the dish date back to
Roman times, long before
tomatoes were imported
from America.

## Gazpacho

*Serves: 4*
*Preparation: 30 minutes + 2 hours to chill*
*Recipe grading: easy*

- 6 oz/180 g day-old white bread
- $^1/_2$ cup/125 ml extra-virgin olive oil
- 3 cloves garlic, peeled
- $1^3/_4$ lb/800 g firm-ripe tomatoes, peeled and cut into small cubes
- 1 cucumber, peeled and cut into cubes
- 1 green bell pepper/capsicum, seeded, cored, and cut into cubes (reserve a few cubes to garnish)
- 1 cup/250 ml water
- 2 tablespoons red wine vinegar
- salt and freshly ground black pepper to taste

Crumble 5 oz/150 g of the bread into a large bowl. Pour in the oil and add the garlic. Set aside for 20 minutes. • Place the tomatoes, cucumber, and bell pepper in a food processor or blender along with the soaked bread mixture. Process until very finely chopped. Transfer to a large bowl. • Pour in the water and vinegar. Season with the salt and pepper. • Refrigerate for at least 2 hours, or until well chilled. • Cut the remaining bread into cubes. • Garnish with the bread and reserved tomatoes just before serving.

*Garlic is believed to stimulate the immune system, helping to protect against many illnesses, including heart disease, cancer, and arthritis. Clinical studies also suggest that garlic can act as an anticoagulant, preventing and dissolving blood clots.*

## Vichyssoise

Serves: 4
Preparation: 30 minutes + 2 hours to chill
Cooking: 30 minutes
Recipe grading: fairly easy

- 1 onion, finely chopped
- white of 1 leek, finely chopped
- 2 tablespoons butter
- 1 quart/1 liter vegetable stock (bouillon cube)
- 1 lb/500 g potatoes, peeled and thinly sliced
- 1 bay leaf
- salt and freshly ground black pepper to taste
- $^1/_2$ cup/125 ml light/single cream
- 1 tablespoon finely chopped parsley
- 1 tablespoon finely chopped chives

Sauté the onion and leek in the butter in a large saucepan over low heat until softened. • Pour in the vegetable stock and add the potatoes and bay leaf. Season with the salt and pepper. Bring to a boil and simmer for 30 minutes. • Discard the bay leaf and skim off any foam. • Transfer to a food processor or blender and process until smooth. • Season with the salt and pepper and stir in the cream until well blended. • Refrigerate for at least 2 hours. • Serve chilled, garnished with the parsley and chives.

## Chilled cucumber and mint soup

Serves: 4
Preparation: 20 minutes + 2 hours to chill
Cooking: 30 minutes
Recipe grading: easy

- 1 large cucumber, coarsely chopped
- 12 leaves fresh mint
- 2 cups/500 ml vegetable stock (bouillon cube)
- 1 cup/250 ml milk
- 1 tablespoon fresh lemon juice
- salt and freshly ground black pepper to taste

Place the cucumber, mint, and vegetable stock in a large saucepan over medium heat. • Bring to a boil, cover, and simmer, for 15 minutes. • Transfer to a food processor or blender and process until smooth. • Pour in the milk and lemon juice until well blended. Season with the salt and pepper. • Return the mixture to the saucepan over medium heat and cook for 5 minutes. • Remove from heat and pour into a large bowl. Let cool completely and refrigerate for 2 hours before serving.

## Chilled garlic soup

Serves: 4–6
Preparation: 20 minutes
Recipe grading: easy

- 1 cup/150 g almonds, peeled
- 2 cloves garlic
- salt to taste
- 2 cups/120 g fresh bread crumbs, soaked in 4 tablespoons water
- 1 cup/250 ml extra-virgin olive oil
- $^1/_2$ cup/125 ml vinegar
- 1 quart/1 liter water
- 8 oz/250 g seedless white grapes

Place the almonds and garlic in a food processor or blender and process until smooth. Season with the salt. • Add the bread crumbs and pour in the oil. Process until the mixture is smooth. • Pour in the vinegar and water and process until well blended. • Season with the salt. • Pour into individual serving bowls and garnish with the grapes.

## Chilled bell pepper soup

Serves: 4
Preparation: 25 minutes + 2 hours to chill
Cooking: 20 minutes
Recipe grading: fairly easy

- 3 red bell peppers/capsicums, seeded, cored, and cut in 4
- 1 onion, finely chopped
- 1 small red chile pepper, finely chopped
- 1 clove garlic, peeled and finely chopped
- 1 tablespoon extra-virgin olive oil
- 1 cup/250 ml tomato juice
- 2 cups/500 ml vegetable stock (bouillon cube)
- $^1/_4$ teaspoon dried thyme
- salt and freshly ground black pepper to taste

Turn on the broiler (grill). Roast the bell peppers 4–6 inches (10–15 cm) from the heat source, turning often until blackened all over. Wrap in foil and set aside for 10 minutes. When unwrapped, the skins will peel away easily. Rinse off any remaining pieces of charred skin. • Sauté the onion, chile, and garlic in the oil in a large saucepan over low heat for 5 minutes. • Transfer the onion mixture, bell peppers, and tomato juice to a food processor and process until smooth. • Return to the saucepan over medium heat. • Pour in the vegetable stock and thyme. Bring to a boil, cover and simmer for 20 minutes. Season with the salt and pepper. • Remove from heat and pour into a large bowl. Let cool completely and refrigerate for 2 hours before serving.

*Celery has been used for centuries in traditional Asian medicines to lower blood pressure. According to these ideas, just two stalks of celery every day could be enough to normalize blood pressure. The Ancient Romans believed that celery could ward off a hangover, while one Dutch researcher has claimed that it acts as an aphrodisiac. Whatever its health values, celery certainly adds zip and flavor to a wide range of salads, soups, and sauces.*

## Kidney bean soup with pasta

*Serves: 4–6*
*Preparation: 30 minutes + 1 hour to rest the pasta*
*Cooking: 1 hour 30 minutes*
*Recipe grading: fairly easy*

- 8 oz/250 g fresh maltagliati pasta
- 3 cups/300 g dried borlotti or red kidney beans, soaked overnight and drained
- 1 onion, finely chopped
- 1 carrot, finely chopped
- 1 stalk celery, finely chopped
- salt to taste
- 1 clove garlic, lightly crushed
- $^1/_2$ cup/125 ml extra-virgin olive oil
- 1 tablespoon finely chopped parsley
- scant 1 cup/200 g chopped tomatoes
- 2 tablespoons freshly grated Parmesan cheese

Maltagliati pasta is a fresh, egg-based pasta cut into uneven shapes. In Italian the name *maltagliati* means "badly cut." Replace with tagliatelle or fettuccine chopped into short lengths if preferred. • Cook the beans in a large deep saucepan with enough cold water to cover. Add the onion, carrot, and celery. • Bring to a boil, cover, and simmer for about 1 hour, or until the beans are

tender. Drain half the beans and chop in a food processor until smooth. Season with the salt. • Reserve the remaining beans and cooking liquid. • Sauté the garlic in the oil in a large saucepan until pale gold. Discard the garlic. • Add the parsley and tomatoes. Cook for 10 minutes, or until the tomatoes have reduced. • Stir in the bean purée, the reserved beans, and the cooking liquid. • Bring to a boil, then add the pasta. Cook for 3–4 minutes, or until the pasta is cooked *al dente*. • Serve hot, sprinkled with the Parmesan.

## Bean and spaghetti soup

*Serves: 4*
*Preparation: 25 minutes*
*Cooking: 1 hour 20 minutes*
*Recipe grading: easy*

- 1 quart/1 liter vegetable stock (bouillon cube)
- 3 tablespoons tomato concentrate/purée
- 4 cups/400 g borlotti beans, soaked overnight and drained
- 2 cloves garlic, finely chopped
- 4 leaves fresh sage, finely chopped
- 1 tablespoon finely chopped rosemary
- 1 tablespoon finely chopped basil
- 1 tablespoon finely chopped parsley
- 2 tablespoons extra-virgin olive oil
- 5 oz/150 g spaghetti, broken into short lengths
- salt and freshly ground black pepper to taste

Heat the vegetable stock in a large saucepan and stir in the tomato concentrate. • Add the beans and cook for about 1 hour, or until tender. • Remove from heat and transfer to a food processor or blender. Process until smooth. Return the mixture to the saucepan over medium heat. • Sauté the garlic, sage, rosemary, basil, and parsley in the oil in a skillet (frying pan) over low heat for 5 minutes. • Stir the garlic mixture into the soup and mix well. • Bring to a boil and add the spaghetti. Cook for 10–12 minutes, or until the pasta is *al dente*. • Season with the salt and pepper. Serve hot.

## Vegetable stock and egg

*Serves: 4*
*Preparation: 10 minutes*
*Cooking: 10 minutes*
*Recipe grading: easy*

- 4 eggs
- 4 tablespoons freshly grated Parmesan cheese
- $^1/_4$ teaspoon freshly grated nutmeg
- salt and freshly ground white pepper to taste
- 1 quart/1 liter boiling vegetable stock (bouillon cube)

Beat the eggs, Parmesan, nutmeg, salt, and pepper in a medium bowl. • Pour into a large saucepan filled with the vegetable stock over medium heat. Use a wire whisk to beat the mixture. • Bring to a boil, and serve immediately.

Kidney bean soup with pasta

# Cream of mushroom soup

*Serves: 4*
*Preparation: 30 minutes*
*Cooking: 35 minutes*
*Recipe grading: easy*

• $^3/_4$ oz/25 g dried porcini mushrooms
• 2 cups/500 ml warm water
• 1 onion, finely chopped
• 4 tablespoons extra-virgin olive oil
• 1 lb/500 g white mushrooms
• 1 quart/1 liter vegetable stock (bouillon cube)
• 4 tablespoons heavy/double cream
• salt and freshly ground black pepper to taste

Place the dried porcini mushrooms and warm water in a medium bowl. Soak for 20 minutes. • Sauté the onion in the oil in a large skillet (frying pan) over medium heat until lightly browned. • Add the white mushrooms and sauté for 5 minutes. • Pour in the vegetable stock, dried mushrooms, and their liquid. • Bring to a boil, then simmer for 30 minutes. • Remove from heat and transfer to a food processor or blender. Process until smooth. • Return the mixture to the saucepan. Add the cream and season with the salt and pepper. • Serve hot.

# Minestrone

*Serves: 6*
*Preparation: 30 minutes*
*Cooking: 1 hour 40 minutes*
*Recipe grading: easy*

• 1 onion, finely chopped
• 2 cloves garlic, finely chopped
• 4 tablespoons extra-virgin olive oil
• 1 stalk celery, finely chopped
• 2 carrots, cut into small cubes
• 2 zucchini/courgettes, cut into small cubes
• 1 cup/125 g peas
• 2 cups/200 g borlotti beans, soaked overnight and drained
• $2^1/_2$ quarts/2.5 liters vegetable stock (bouillon cube)
• 10 oz/300 g potatoes, peeled and cut into small cubes
• 8 oz/250 g firm-ripe tomatoes, cut into small cubes
• salt and freshly ground black pepper to taste
• 4 tablespoons freshly grated Parmesan cheese

Sauté the onion and garlic in the oil in a large saucepan over medium heat until the onion is transparent. • Add the celery, carrots, zucchini, peas, and beans. Cook for 3 minutes. • Pour in the vegetable stock and add the potatoes and tomatoes. Season with the salt and pepper. • Bring to a boil, cover and cook for 1 hour and 30 minutes. • Ladle into individual soup bowls and sprinkle with the Parmesan. Serve hot.

# Leghorn-style minestrone

*Serves: 6–8*
*Preparation: 35 minutes*
*Cooking: 3 hours 30 minutes*
*Recipe grading: fairly easy*

- 1 lb/500 g fresh borlotti beans
- 10 oz/300 g fresh spinach, stalks removed and shredded
- 3 oz/90 g Swiss chard, stalks removed and shredded
- ½ small Savoy cabbage, shredded
- 2 cloves garlic, finely chopped
- 2 tablespoons finely chopped parsley
- 2 tablespoons finely chopped basil
- 6 tablespoons extra-virgin olive oil
- 1 onion, coarsely chopped
- 1 carrot, coarsely chopped
- 2 stalks celery, coarsely chopped
- 2 zucchini/courgettes, coarsely chopped
- 2 waxy potatoes, coarsely chopped
- 2 quarts/2 liters vegetable stock (bouillon cube)
- salt and freshly ground black pepper to taste
- 1½ cups/300 g short-grain rice
- 1 cup/125 g freshly grated Parmesan cheese

Boil the beans in a large pot of salted, boiling water for 30 minutes, or until tender. • Wash the spinach under cold running water. Do not drain but place in a saucepan and cook, with just the water clinging to its leaves, for 3 minutes. Drain, press out excess water, chop finely, and set aside. • Repeat with the Swiss chard and cabbage. • Sauté the garlic, parsley, and basil in the oil in a large saucepan until aromatic. • Add the onion, carrot, celery, zucchini, potatoes, beans and their cooking liquid, spinach, Swiss chard, and cabbage, stirring well. • Pour in the vegetable stock. Season with the salt and pepper. • Cover and simmer over low heat for 2½ hours. • Add the rice and cook for 20 minutes more. • Serve hot, sprinkled with the Parmesan.

Leghorn-style minestrone

Egg and vegetable soup

choke. Cut each artichoke into eight pieces. • Sauté the onion in the butter in a large saucepan over low heat. • Add the artichokes. Pour in the wine and cook until evaporated, about 4 minutes. • Pour 1 quart (1 liter) of stock into the artichoke mixture. • Place the flour in a small bowl and stir in enough of the remaining stock to obtain a smooth paste. • Add this mixture and the remaining stock to the artichoke mixture, stirring constantly to prevent lumps from forming. • Add the peas and season with salt. • Cook over low heat, stirring occasionally, for 1 hour. • Use a ladle to remove and set aside a quarter of the artichokes and peas in a small bowl. • Transfer the rest of the soup to a food processor and process until smooth. • Return to the saucepan over medium heat and add the egg yolks, beating until just blended. Cook for 3 minutes. • Return the reserved artichokes and peas to the soup and serve hot.

## Egg and vegetable soup

*Serves: 4*
*Preparation: 30 minutes*
*Cooking: 1 hour*
*Recipe grading: fairly easy*

- 2 onions, finely chopped
- 2¹/₂ cups/300 g fresh or frozen peas
- 2 cups/200 g fresh fava/broad beans
- 1 carrot, thinly sliced
- 1 stalk celery, thinly sliced
- 1 dried chile pepper, crumbled
- 4 tablespoons extra-virgin olive oil
- salt and freshly ground black pepper to taste
- 12 oz/300 g Swiss chard or fresh spinach leaves, stalks removed and shredded
- 1 cup/250 g chopped tomatoes
- 1¹/₂ quarts/1.5 liters boiling water
- 4 eggs
- ¹/₂ cup/60 g freshly grated Parmesan cheese
- 4 slices day-old firm-textured bread, toasted
- 1 clove garlic

## Artichoke and pea soup

*Serves: 4*
*Preparation: 40 minutes*
*Cooking: 1 hour*
*Recipe grading: fairly easy*

- 3 artichokes
- 1 lemon
- 1 onion, finely chopped
- 6 tablespoons butter
- ¹/₂ cup/125 ml dry white wine

- 1¹/₂ quarts/1.5 liters boiling vegetable stock (bouillon cube)
- 4 tablespoons all-purpose/plain flour
- 1¹/₄ cups/150 g peas
- salt to taste
- 2 egg yolks

Clean the artichokes by pulling the tough outer leaves down and snapping them off at the base. Cut off the top third of the leaves and trim the stem. Cut the artichokes in half and use a sharp knife to remove any fuzzy

Sauté the onions, peas, fava beans, carrot, celery, and chile pepper in the oil in a large saucepan for 10 minutes. • Season with salt and pepper. Add the Swiss chard and tomatoes and simmer for 15 minutes. • Pour in the water and simmer for 40 minutes. • Beat the eggs and Parmesan in a small bowl. Season with the salt and pepper. • Rub the toast with the garlic. • Place the toast in individual soup bowls and cover with a quarter of the beaten egg mixture. Ladle the soup over the top. • Serve immediately.

## Leek and potato soup

*Serves: 4–6*
*Preparation: 20 minutes*
*Cooking: 20 minutes*
*Recipe grading: easy*

- 1 large onion, finely chopped
- 1 bunch parsley, finely chopped
- 1 clove garlic, finely chopped
- 1 carrot, finely chopped
- 1 stalk celery, finely chopped
- 4 tablespoons extra-virgin olive oil
- whites of 6 leeks, finely chopped
- 6 large potatoes, peeled and cut into small cubes
- 1 quart/1 liter water
- 6 leaves fresh basil
- salt and freshly ground black pepper to taste

Sauté the onion, parsley, garlic, carrot, and celery in the oil in a large saucepan over low heat until the vegetables have softened. • Add the leeks and cook for 10 minutes. • Add the potatoes and pour in the water. Season with the salt and pepper and add the basil. Cook for 10 minutes more, or until the potatoes are very tender. • Remove from heat and serve hot.

## Fava bean soup

*Serves: 4*
*Preparation: 10 minutes*
*Cooking: 1 hour 45 minutes*
*Recipe grading: fairly easy*

Fava bean soup

- 3¹/₂ cups/350 g dried fava/broad beans, soaked overnight and drained
- 1 onion, finely chopped
- 1 stalk celery, finely chopped
- 1 carrot, finely chopped
- 2 tablespoons finely chopped marjoram
- 4 tablespoons extra-virgin olive oil
- ³/₄ cup/200 g chopped tomatoes
- salt and freshly ground black pepper to taste
- 1 cup/250 ml boiling water
- 4 slices day-old firm-textured bread, toasted

Cook the beans in a large pot of salted boiling water for 1 hour, or until tender. • Sauté the onion, celery, carrot, and marjoram in the oil in a large saucepan over low heat until the vegetables have softened. • Add the tomatoes and cook over medium heat for 15 minutes. • Season with salt and pepper. Add the beans and pour in the water. • Cook for 10 minutes, stirring often. • Place a slice of toast in each of 4 individual soup bowls. Ladle the soup over the top, and serve hot.

## Winter cabbage soup

Serves: 4
Preparation: 15 minutes
Cooking: 1 hour
Recipe grading: easy

- 3 cloves garlic, finely chopped
- 2 tablespoons extra-virgin olive oil
- 1³/₄ lb/800 g Savoy cabbage, shredded
- 1 quart/1 liter vegetable stock (bouillon cube)
- salt and freshly ground black pepper to taste
- 4–8 slices of day-old firm-textured bread, toasted
- 8 tablespoons freshly grated Parmesan cheese

Sauté the garlic in the oil in a large saucepan over low heat until pale gold. • Add the cabbage and cook, stirring often, until it has wilted. • Pour in the vegetable stock and simmer for 40 minutes. Season with the salt and pepper. • Preheat the oven to 350°F/180°C/gas 4. • Place a layer of toasted bread in a casserole pot. Sprinkle with the Parmesan and pour in 1¹/₂ cups (375 ml) of the soup. Repeat until all the ingredients are in the casserole. • Bake for 10 minutes and serve piping hot.

## Cabbage and cornmeal soup

Serves: 8
Preparation: 20 minutes
Cooking: 1 hour
Recipe grading: fairly easy

Winter cabbage soup

- 3 cups/400 g finely shredded green cabbage
- 2 red onions, finely chopped
- ¹/₂ cup/125 ml extra-virgin olive oil
- 1¹/₂ quarts/1.5 liters vegetable stock (bouillon cube)
- ³/₄ cup/125 g finely ground yellow cornmeal
- salt and freshly ground black pepper to taste

Blanch the cabbage in a large pot of salted, boiling water for 3 minutes. • Drain well and set aside. • Sauté the onions in the oil in a large deep skillet (frying pan) over medium heat until lightly browned. • Stir in the cabbage and cook, stirring often, for 8 minutes. • Bring the stock to a boil in a large saucepan. Gradually add the cornmeal, stirring constantly to prevent lumps from forming. • Lower the heat and continue cooking for 20–30 minutes, or until thick and smooth. • Add the cabbage mixture and cook for 10 minutes more. • Season with the salt and pepper. • Serve hot.

## Onion soup

Serves: 6
Preparation: 15 minutes
Cooking: 45 minutes
Recipe grading: fairly easy

- 1¹/₂ lb/750 g onions, finely chopped
- 2 cloves garlic, finely chopped
- 2 tablespoons extra-virgin olive oil
- 1 teaspoon sugar

- 1¹/₂ quarts/1.5 liters vegetable stock (bouillon cube)
- 2 bay leaves
- salt and freshly ground white pepper to taste
- 1 cup/125 g freshly grated Emmental cheese

Sauté the onions and garlic in the oil in a large saucepan over low heat until pale gold. • Sprinkle with the sugar and continue cooking until the onions are lightly browned. • Pour in the vegetable stock and add the bay leaves. Bring to a boil, cover, and simmer for 30 minutes. • Discard the bay leaves and season with the salt and pepper. • Pour into individual soup bowls and sprinkle generously with the cheese.

## Cheese and onion soup

Serves: 4
Preparation: 15 minutes
Cooking: 30 minutes
Recipe grading: easy

- 1 lb/500 g onions, finely chopped
- 2 tablespoons extra-virgin olive oil
- 2 tablespoons butter
- 2 tablespoons all-purpose/plain flour
- 3 cups/750 ml vegetable stock (bouillon cube)
- 1 bay leaf
- salt and freshly ground black pepper to taste
- 1 cup/125 g freshly grated Cheddar cheese
- 4 slices day-old firm-textured bread, toasted

Sauté the onions in the oil and butter in a large saucepan over medium heat until transparent. • Add the flour and stir for 2–3 minutes. • Pour in the vegetable stock and add the bay leaf. Bring to a boil, stirring constantly. • Season with the salt and pepper, turn heat down to low, and simmer for 30 minutes. • Add the cheese and cook until melted, about 5 minutes. • Place a slice of toast in each of 4 individual soup bowls and ladle the soup over the top. • Serve hot.

*Broccoli is an excellent source of vitamin C and a good source of vitamin A. It provides dietary fiber, is low in calories, and is believed to prevent stroke and cancer. However, broccoli's nutritional value decreases quickly after it has been harvested, so try to eat it as fresh as possible.*

## Tofu and miso soup

*Serves: 4*
*Preparation: 25 minutes*
*Cooking: 30 minutes*
*Recipe grading: easy*

- 1 quart/1 liter vegetable stock (bouillon cube)
- 1 carrot, cut into thin strips
- 8 radishes, thinly sliced
- 4 tablespoons barley miso
- 4 white mushrooms, finely chopped
- 8 oz/250 g tofu, cut into small cubes
- 1 teaspoon soy sauce

Bring the vegetable stock to a boil in a large saucepan and add the carrot and radishes. • Dissolve the miso in 4 tablespoons of hot stock in a small bowl. • Stir the miso mixture into the stock. • Add the mushrooms and tofu, and cook for 10–15 minutes. • Remove from heat and drizzle with the soy sauce. Serve hot.

## Cream of pea soup

*Serves: 4*
*Preparation: 10 minutes*
*Cooking: 20–25 minutes*
*Recipe grading: easy*

- 1 onion, finely chopped
- 2 tablespoons butter
- 4 cups/500 g peas
- 1 quart/1 liter vegetable stock (bouillon cube)
- 1 quantity Béchamel sauce (see recipe Mushroom soup with sherry, page 56)
- salt to taste

Sauté the onion in the butter in a large saucepan over low heat until softened. • Add the peas and cook for 2 minutes. • Add two-thirds of the vegetable stock and cook for 15–20 minutes, or until the peas are tender. • Transfer to a food processor or blender and process until smooth. • Stir in the Béchamel sauce. If the soup seems too dense, add some of the remaining stock. Season with the salt. • Return to the heat and cook for 5 minutes, or until piping hot.

## Smooth broccoli soup

*Serves: 4*
*Preparation: 25 minutes*
*Cooking: 30 minutes*
*Recipe grading: easy*

- 1 onion, finely chopped
- 2 cloves garlic, finely chopped
- 1 tablespoon extra-virgin olive oil
- 2 lb/1 kg broccoli, cut into small cubes
- 1 tablespoon finely chopped thyme
- $^{1}/_{4}$ teaspoon ground nutmeg
- 1 quart/1 liter vegetable stock (bouillon cube)
- $^{3}/_{4}$ cup/180 ml light/single cream
- salt and freshly ground black pepper to taste

Sauté the onion and garlic in the oil in a large saucepan over low heat until softened. • Add the broccoli, thyme, and nutmeg and cook for 2 minutes. • Pour in the vegetable stock and bring to a boil. Cover and simmer for 20 minutes, or until the broccoli is very tender. • Transfer to a food processor or blender and process until smooth. • Return the mixture to the saucepan over low heat and pour in the cream, blending well. • Season with the salt and pepper. • Pour into individual soup bowls and serve hot.

## Smooth lettuce soup

*Serves: 4*
*Preparation: 25 minutes*
*Cooking: 20 minutes*
*Recipe grading: easy*

- $1^{1}/_{2}$ lb/750 g lettuce, shredded
- 1 onion, finely chopped
- 1 carrot, finely chopped
- 7 oz/200 g potatoes, peeled
- $2^{1}/_{4}$ cups/310 ml vegetable stock (bouillon cube)
- $^{1}/_{4}$ cup/50 g short-grain rice
- 6 tablespoons milk
- 1 tablespoon butter

Place the lettuce, onion, carrot, and potatoes in a pressure cooker over medium heat. Pour in the vegetable stock and add the rice. • Cook, with the pressure cooker lid attached, for 7 minutes. • Release the pressure valve and lid. • Heat the milk in a small saucepan over low heat. • Transfer the soup to a food processor or blender and pour in the hot milk. Process until smooth. • Return the mixture to the saucepan and cook for 5 minutes. • Serve hot.

This recipe comes from Tuscany, a region of central Italy famous for its bread soups. There are many variations—some cooks add 2 bays leaves during cooking, discarding them before they serve. In another variation, red pepper flakes are added for a fiery dish.

## Tuscan tomato and bread soup

*Serves: 4*
*Preparation: 15 minutes*
*Cooking: 25 minutes*
*Recipe grading: easy*

- 1¹/₂ lb/750 g firm-ripe tomatoes
- 2–3 cloves garlic, finely chopped
- 8–10 leaves fresh basil, torn
- 6 tablespoons extra-virgin olive oil
- 8 oz/250 g day-old firm-textured white bread, coarsely chopped
- salt and freshly ground black pepper to taste
- 1¹/₄ cups/310 ml vegetable stock (bouillon cube)

Blanch the tomatoes in a large pot of salted boiling water for 1 minute. Drain well, rinse in cold water, and then skin. Cut in half, gently squeeze out as many seeds as possible, and chop into small pieces. • Sauté the garlic and basil in the oil in a large saucepan over low heat for 2–3 minutes. Add the bread. • Increase the heat to medium and cook, stirring constantly, for 2 minutes. Season with the salt and pepper. • Cook for 2 minutes, then add the tomatoes and pour the stock. • Cook for 15 minutes, stirring often. Season with the salt and pepper, adding more stock if the soup becomes too thick. • Ladle into individual soup bowls and serve hot.

Tuscan tomato and bread soup

# SNACKS

This chapter is brimming with healthy ideas for after-school snacks for hungry children, treats to fill a picnic hamper, and casual food to satisfy unexpected visitors. Many of the pizza, quiche, and bread recipes can be prepared in advance and frozen until required. Other recipes, such as the bruschetta, toasts, and omelets can be thrown together quickly with ingredients such as eggs, cheese, and bread that are always on hand.

*Once you master the dough-making process, pizzas are surprisingly easy to make. They are not even very time-consuming; it takes just a few minutes to mix the dough and knead it, then it can be put aside until you prepare the topping and bake. An added bonus is that children usually love to help with the mixing and kneading—the feel of the dough squishing through their fingers is irresistible! This pizza, made with whole wheat (wholemeal) flour, is a healthy alternative to a white flour base. All the pizzas in this chapter can be made with whole wheat flour, or a mixture of the two.*

Mixed vegetable pizza (see page 78)
Eggplant and cheese sandwiches
(see page 90)

76

*Widely available, easy to prepare, and delicious, walnuts are a fabulous health food. They are especially rich in polyunsaturated fatty acids which are believed to lower cholesterol and fight heart disease. Walnuts also contain a host of vitamins, minerals, protein, and antioxidants that bring all-round health benefits.*

## Mixed vegetable pizza

*Serves: 4*
*Preparation: 30 minutes + 1 hour 30 minutes to rise*
*Cooking: 25–30 minutes*
*Recipe grading: fairly easy*

Base
- 1 oz/30 g fresh yeast or 2 packages ($^1$/$_4$ oz/7 g) active dry yeast
- 1$^1$/$_3$ cups/310 ml warm water + more if needed
- 1 teaspoon sugar
- 2 cups/300 g unbleached flour
- 1 cup/150 g all-purpose/plain flour
- 1 cup/150 g whole-wheat/wholemeal flour
- 1 teaspoon salt

Topping
- 1 eggplant/aubergine, cut in small cubes
- 1 clove garlic, finely chopped
- 1 tablespoon finely chopped parsley
- 6 tablespoons extra-virgin olive oil
- 5 oz/150 g zucchini/courgettes, cut in small cubes
- 20 green olives, pitted
- 5 oz/150 g Pecorino cheese, cut into small cubes
- 12 cherry tomatoes, cut in half

Base: Mix the yeast, $^1$/$_2$ cup (125 ml) of the water, and sugar in a small bowl. Set aside for 10 minutes, or until foamy. • Sift the flours and salt into a large bowl and make a well in the center. • Stir in the yeast mixture and as much of the remaining water as required to obtain a firm dough. • Knead for 5–7 minutes, or until smooth and elastic. • Shape into a ball, place in an oiled bowl, and cover with a clean cloth. Let rise in a warm place for 45 minutes. • Turn out onto a lightly floured work surface and knead for 10 minutes. • Return to the bowl, cover with a clean cloth, and let rise for 45 minutes, or until doubled in bulk. • Preheat the oven to 375°F/190°C/gas 5. • Grease a 13-inch (32-cm) round pizza pan with oil. • Topping: Sauté the eggplant, garlic, and parsley in 4 tablespoons of oil in a skillet (frying pan) over medium heat until the eggplant is lightly browned. • Add the zucchini and cook for 7 minutes. • Place the risen pizza dough in the prepared pan, pushing it outward with your fingertips to cover the bottom of the pan in an even layer. • Sprinkle the vegetable mixture, olives, Pecorino, and tomatoes on top. Drizzle with the remaining oil. • Bake for 25–30 minutes, or until the dough is cooked and the vegetables are tender. • Serve hot or at room temperature.

## Pancakes with walnuts, Pecorino cheese, and apple

*Serves: 4*
*Preparation: 10 minutes*
*Cooking: 20 minutes*
*Recipe grading: easy*

- 1$^1$/$_3$ cups/200 g all-purpose/plain flour
- 1 cup/150 g whole-wheat/wholemeal flour
- 2 teaspoons baking powder
- $^1$/$_2$ teaspoon salt
- 2 large eggs, lightly beaten
- salt and freshly ground black pepper
- 4 tablespoons butter, melted
- 1$^1$/$_2$ cups/375 ml milk
- salt and freshly ground black pepper
- 1–2 Granny Smith apples, cored and thinly sliced
- 5 oz/150 g Pecorino romano cheese, thinly sliced
- 4 tablespoons honey, warmed
- 1 cup/125 g walnuts, hulled and lightly toasted

Sift both flours, the baking powder, and salt into a medium bowl. • Add the eggs, butter, and milk and beat until smooth and creamy. Season with salt and pepper. • Heat a lightly small oiled griddle or small skillet (frying pan) and add 4 tablespoons of batter, tilting the pan so that the batter covers the bottom in an even layer. • Cook on one side until the bubbles that form in the pancake look dry. Use a spatula to turn the pancake and cook until the other side is golden brown. • Place the pancake in a warm oven and cook the rest of the batter. You should get 12 pancakes. • To assemble: Place a pancake on a serving dish and cover with a layer of apple, walnuts, and cheese. Drizzle with $^1$/$_2$ tablespoon of honey and cover with another pancake. Repeat the layering process and top with a third pancake. Decorate the top with cheese and walnuts. • Serve immediately.

Pancakes with walnuts,
Pecorino cheese, and apple

*Zucchini, or courgettes, are a member of the gourd family. They can grow to a large size, but the smaller zucchini are the most flavorful. They are a source of vitamin C, which is vital for one's health.*

## Zucchini and artichoke quiche

*Serves: 4*
*Preparation: 30 minutes*
*Cooking: 25–30 minutes*
*Recipe grading: fairly easy*

- 1 lb/500 g fresh or frozen puff pastry, thawed if frozen
- 1 clove garlic, lightly crushed
- 3 tender artichoke hearts, thinly sliced
- 3 zucchini/courgettes, thinly sliced
- 3 tablespoons extra-virgin olive oil
- 2 tablespoons water
- 6 tablespoons fresh, creamy goat's cheese
- 4 tablespoons Ricotta cheese
- 3 eggs, lightly beaten
- $^2/_3$ cup/150 ml milk
- 4 tablespoons light/single cream
- $^1/_4$ teaspoon salt

Preheat the oven to 350°F/180°C/gas 4. • Butter a 10 inch (26 cm) quiche or pie pan. • Unfold or unroll the puff pastry on a lightly floured work surface. Line the base and sides of prepared pan, trimming the edges to fit. • Use a fork to prick the pastry all over. • Sauté the garlic, artichokes, and zucchini in the oil in a skillet (frying pan) over low heat until the zucchini are lightly browned. • Add the water and cook over low heat until the vegetables are tender. • Discard the garlic. • Spoon the goat's cheese and Ricotta into the pastry base. Sprinkle the vegetable mixture on top. • Beat the eggs, milk, cream, and salt in a small bowl. • Pour the mixture over the vegetables. • Bake for 25–30 minutes, or until set. • Serve hot or at room temperature.

## Bell pepper and zucchini quiche

*Serves: 6*
*Preparation: 30 minutes*
*Cooking: 30–35 minutes*
*Recipe grading: fairly easy*

- 1 lb/500 g fresh or frozen puff pastry, thawed if frozen
- 2 yellow bell peppers/capsicums, seeded, cored, and cut into thin slices
- 10 oz/300 g zucchini/courgettes, cut into long strips
- 12 cherry tomatoes, cut in half
- salt and freshly ground black pepper to taste
- 1$^1/_2$ cups/180 g freshly grated Fontina cheese
- 2 tablespoons extra-virgin olive oil

Preheat the oven to 400°F/200°C/gas 6. • Butter a 10 inch (26 cm) quiche or pie pan. • Unfold or unroll the puff pastry on a lightly floured work surface. Line the base and sides of prepared pan, trimming the edges to fit. • Use a fork to prick the pastry all over. • Heat a grill pan and cook the bell peppers and zucchini in batches until tender. • Remove from heat and set aside. • Arrange the bell peppers, zucchini, and tomatoes in alternating layers in the pastry base. Season each layer with salt and pepper. Sprinkle with the Fontina and drizzle with the oil. • Bake for 30–35 minutes, or until lightly browned and the cheese is bubbling. • Serve hot or at room temperature.

## Pumpkin and artichoke quiche

*Serves: 4*
*Preparation: 30 minutes*
*Cooking: 15–20 minutes*
*Recipe grading: fairly easy*

- 1 lb/500 g fresh or frozen puff pastry, thawed if frozen
- 3 large onions, finely chopped
- 1 lb/500 g pumpkin flesh, cut into small cubes
- 8 tender artichoke hearts, thinly sliced
- 4 tablespoons extra-virgin olive oil
- salt and freshly ground black pepper to taste
- 1 tablespoon water
- 5 oz/150 g Mozzarella cheese, thinly sliced

Preheat the oven to 400°F/200°C/gas 6. • Butter a 10 inch (26 cm) quiche or pie pan. • Unfold or unroll the puff pastry on a lightly floured work surface. Line the base and sides of prepared pan, trimming the edges to fit. • Use a fork to prick the pastry all over. • Sauté the onions, pumpkin, and artichokes in 2 tablespoons of oil in a skillet (frying pan) over medium heat until lightly browned. • Season with salt and pepper and add the water. • Spoon the pumpkin mixture into the pastry base. • Lay the Mozzarella on top and drizzle with the remaining oil. • Bake for 15–20 minutes, or until lightly browned and the cheese is bubbling. • Serve hot or at room temperature.

Zucchini and artichoke quiche

## Onion rings with basil

*Serves: 4*
*Preparation: 20 minutes + 30 minutes to soak the onions*
*Cooking: 15–20 minutes*
*Recipe grading: easy*

- 2 large onions, cut into 1-inch/2.5-cm rings
- 1²/₃ cups/250 g all-purpose/plain flour
- ¹/₃ cup/50 g cornstarch/cornflour
- 2 tablespoons finely chopped parsley
- 3 tablespoons finely chopped basil
- salt and freshly ground black pepper to taste
- 1 cup/250 ml milk
- 2 cups/500 ml olive oil, for frying

Soak the onion rings in a large bowl of cold water for 30 minutes. • Drain well and pat dry with paper towels. • Sift 1 cup (150 g) of flour into a large bowl. Stir in the cornstarch, parsley, and basil. Season with salt and pepper. • Sift the remaining flour into a small bowl. Dip the onion rings first in the plain flour, then in the milk, followed by the seasoned flour mixture. • Heat the oil in a deep fryer or skillet (frying pan) to very hot. • Fry the onion rings in batches for 5–7 minutes, or until golden brown and crispy. • Drain well on paper towels. • Serve hot.

## Fried potato fritters

*Serves: 4*
*Preparation: 20 minutes*
*Cooking: 20–30 minutes*
*Recipe grading: easy*

- 1¹/₄ lb/575 g potatoes, peeled and grated
- 2 eggs, lightly beaten
- 2 tablespoons all-purpose/plain flour
- salt and freshly ground black pepper to taste
- 2 cups/500 ml olive oil, for frying

Rinse the grated potatoes under cold running water, drain well, squeezing out excess moisture. Spread out on a clean

## Fried Mozzarella sandwiches

*Serves: 4*
*Preparation: 20 minutes + 1 hour to rest*
*Cooking: 5–7 minutes*
*Recipe grading: easy*

- 4 large, thin slices white sandwich bread, crusts removed and cut in half
- salt and freshly ground black pepper to taste
- 12 oz/350 g Mozzarella cheese, thinly sliced
- scant 1 cup/200 ml milk
- 1 cup/150 g all-purpose/plain flour
- 2 eggs
- 1–2 cups/250–500 ml olive oil, for frying

Season the bread with salt and pepper. • Cover half the bread with the Mozzarella slices. Place the remaining slices of bread on top to make sandwiches. • Pour the milk into a small bowl. Dip the sandwiches briefly in the milk. Sprinkle with the flour. Arrange the sandwiches on a large deep plate. • Beat the eggs until frothy and season with pepper. Pour the beaten egg over the sandwiches. Set aside for 1 hour, or until the egg has been absorbed. • Heat the oil in a large deep skillet (frying pan) to very hot. • Fry the sandwiches 2–4 at a time for about 5 minutes, or until golden brown on one side. Turn and cook on the other side too. • Drain well on paper towels. • Serve hot.

cloth to dry. • Beat the eggs and flour in a small bowl until frothy. Season with salt and pepper. Add the potatoes, mixing well. • Heat the oil in a deep fryer or skillet (frying pan) to very hot. • Drop 6 tablespoonfuls of the mixture into the oil and fry for about 4–5 minutes, or until the fritters are golden brown on one side. • Use a slotted spoon to turn the fritters and fry until golden brown on the other side. • Drain well on paper towels. • Serve hot.

## Fried Parmesan balls

*Serves: 6*
*Preparation: 20 minutes*
*Cooking: 20–30 minutes*
*Recipe grading: easy*

- 1 cup/250 ml water
- 3 tablespoons butter
- 1 teaspoon salt
- 1 cup/150 g all-purpose/plain flour
- 4 eggs
- 1 cup/125 g freshly grated Parmesan cheese
- ¹/₂ cup/60 g freshly grated Emmental cheese
- ¹/₄ teaspoon ground nutmeg
- 2 cups/500 ml olive oil, for frying

Bring the water, butter, and salt to a boil in a small saucepan. • Add the flour all at once, remove from heat, and stir with a wooden spoon. • When the mixture is smooth, return the saucepan to the heat and cook until the mixture pulls away from the sides of the pan. Set aside to cool. • Add the eggs, beating until just blended. • Stir in the Parmesan, Emmental, and nutmeg. • Shape into small balls. • Heat the oil in a deep fryer or skillet (frying pan) to very hot. • Fry the puffs a few at a time for 5–7 minutes, or until golden brown all over. • Drain well on paper towels. • Serve hot.

Fried Mozzarella sandwiches

*For successful bruschetta, always use the highest quality extra-virgin olive oil. It should be dark green in color and translucent. Be sure to check the expiry date on the bottle.*

## Bruschette

*Serves: 4*
*Preparation: 5 minutes*
*Recipe grading: easy*

• 4–8 slices day-old, firm-textured bread
• 4 cloves garlic
• 4–6 tablespoons extra-virgin olive oil
• salt and freshly ground black pepper to taste

Turn on the broiler (grill). Toast the bread until golden brown on both sides. • Rub the garlic evenly over each slice. • Drizzle with the oil and season with the salt and pepper. • Serve warm.

## Eggplant tortilla wraps

*Serves: 4*
*Preparation: 20 minutes*
*Cooking: 8 minutes*
*Recipe grading: fairly easy*

• 1 large or 2 medium-sized eggplants/aubergines, cut in 4
• 4 tablespoons extra-virgin olive oil
• salt and freshly ground black pepper to taste
• 4 large tortilla wraps
• 4 tablespoons tomato chile sauce (homemade or store-bought)
• 8 oz/250 g Mozzarella cheese, thinly sliced
• 2 firm-ripe tomatoes, sliced
• 1 bunch basil
• 7 oz/200 g salad leaves (curly endive or crisp cos)

Brush the eggplant slices with the oil and season with the salt and pepper. Turn on the broiler (grill). Broil the eggplants for 3–5 minutes all over, or until they are golden brown and tender. • Flatten the tortilla wraps out and place an eggplant slice in the center. • Spread with the tomato chile sauce and top with Mozzarella, tomatoes, and basil. • Fold the sides of the tortillas inward until the filling is enclosed. • Grease a grill pan with oil and cook 2 wraps at a time, seam-side down, for 2 minutes. Turn over and cook for 2 minutes more, or until the tortillas are crispy and well-warmed. • Transfer to a heated serving plate and cover with a plate to keep warm. • Repeat with the remaining wraps. • Serve hot on a bed of salad leaves.

## Robiola and olive toasts

*Serves: 4*
*Preparation: 5 minutes*
*Recipe grading: easy*

• 6 tablespoons Robiola or other fresh, creamy cheese
• 1 tablespoon finely chopped chives
• $^1/_2$ cup/50 g black olives, pitted
• 1 teaspoon capers in vinegar, rinsed
• 2 tablespoons extra-virgin olive oil
• 8 slices whole-wheat/wholemeal bread, crusts removed, cut into small squares, and toasted

Mix the cheese and chives in a small bowl. • Finely chop the olives, capers, and oil in a food processor or blender. • Spread the cheese mixture over the toast and top with a teaspoonful of the olive mixture.

## Bruschette with tomato and basil

*Serves: 4*
*Preparation: 25 minutes*
*Recipe grading: easy*

- 4 slices firm-textured bread
- 2 cloves garlic
- salt and freshly ground black pepper to taste
- $^1/_2$ cup/125 ml extra-virgin olive oil
- 6 firm-ripe tomatoes
- 8–12 leaves fresh basil, torn

Toast the bread and rub each slice with the garlic. Season with the salt and pepper and drizzle with 4 tablespoons of oil. • Cut the tomatoes in half. Squeeze out the seeds, sprinkle with salt, and set upside-down in a colander for 20 minutes to drain. • Chop the tomatoes into small cubes. Arrange them on the toasts and sprinkle with the basil. • Drizzle with the remaining oil and serve.

## Four-cheese crostini

*Serves: 4*
*Preparation: 10 minutes*
*Cooking: 8–10 minutes*
*Recipe grading: easy*

- $^1/_2$ cup/125 g fresh, creamy goat's cheese
- $^1/_2$ cup/60 g freshly grated Parmesan cheese
- 4 oz/125 g Gorgonzola cheese, cut in small cubes
- 4 oz/125 g freshly grated Fontina cheese
- 2 tablespoons extra-virgin olive oil
- salt and freshly ground black pepper to taste
- $^1/_2$ teaspoon dried oregano
- $^1/_4$ teaspoon dried marjoram
- 8 large slices firm-textured bread

Preheat the oven to 375°F/190°C/gas 5. • Mix the cheeses and oil in a medium bowl. Season with salt and pepper and sprinkle with the oregano and marjoram. • Use a fork to mash the cheeses until well blended. If the mixture is too thick, add more oil. • Spread the cheese mixture over the bread and season with the pepper. • Arrange the bread on a large baking sheet. • Bake for 8–10 minutes, or until the cheese is bubbling.

## Garbanzo bean flatbread

*Serves: 6*
*Preparation: 5 minutes*
*Cooking: 8–10 minutes*
*Recipe grading: easy*

- 4 cups/600 g garbanzo bean/chickpea flour
- 2 quarts/2 liters water
- $^3/_4$ cup/180 ml extra-virgin olive oil
- salt and freshly ground black pepper to taste

Preheat the oven to 400°F/200°C/gas 6. • Set out a large nonstick roasting pan. • Sift the flour into a large bowl and make a well in the center. Use a wooden spoon to gradually stir in enough water to form a thick pouring batter. • Add the oil and a season with salt. • Pour the batter into the pan, filling to a depth of $^1/_4$ inch (6 mm). • Bake for 8–10 minutes, or until a thin crust forms on the surface. • Transfer to a serving dish and season with the pepper. • Serve hot.

## Bruschette with white beans

*Serves: 4*
*Preparation: 10 minutes*
*Recipe grading: easy*

- 4 slices firm-textured bread
- 2 cloves garlic, peeled and lightly crushed
- salt and freshly ground black pepper to taste
- 5 tablespoons extra-virgin olive oil
- 1 can (15 oz) white beans, drained

Toast the bread and rub it with the garlic. Season with salt and pepper and drizzle with 4 tablespoons of oil. • Heat the beans in a small saucepan. Season with salt. • Spoon the hot beans over the bruschette. • Drizzle with the remaining oil. • Season with pepper and serve hot.

Garbanzo bean flatbread

Fresh cheese and zucchini baguette

## Boat-shaped shells

*Serves: 6*
*Preparation: 15 minutes*
    *+ 30 minutes to chill*
*Cooking: 15 minutes*
*Recipe grading: easy*

- 2 cups/300 g all-purpose/plain flour
- ¹/₄ teaspoon salt
- ²/₃ cup/150 g butter
- 2–3 tablespoons cold water

Preheat the oven to 350°F/180°C/gas 4. •
Sift the flour and salt into a large bowl. •
Use your fingertips to rub in the butter
until the mixture resembles coarse
crumbs. • Make a well in the center and
gradually add the water, stirring with a
wooden spoon to obtain a firm dough. •
Shape into a ball, wrap in waxed paper,
and refrigerate for 30 minutes. • Roll the
dough out on a lightly floured work
surface to about ¹/₈-inch (3-mm) thick. •
Line about 18 small boat-shaped molds
with the dough and prick all over with a
fork. Cover with aluminum foil and fill
with dried beans. • Bake for 15 minutes,
or until pale golden brown. • Remove the
foil with the beans, invert the molds
carefully onto a wire rack, and let cool. •
Fill the shells with mayonnaise or soft
fresh cheeses.

## Fresh cheese and zucchini baguette

*Serves: 2*
*Preparation: 15 minutes*
*Cooking: 15 minutes*
*Recipe grading: easy*

- ¹/₂ zucchini/courgette, thinly sliced lengthwise
- 1 tablespoon extra-virgin olive oil
- salt and freshly ground black pepper to taste
- 1 long French-style baguette
- ¹/₂ cup/125 g fresh creamy goat's cheese
- 2 tomatoes, thinly sliced
- 6 oz/180 g smoked Provolone cheese or
  Mozzarella cheese, thinly sliced

Heat a grill pan over medium heat and
arrange the zucchini slices on top. Season
with salt and pepper. Cook until the
zucchini are tender on both sides, about 10
minutes. • Cut the baguette lengthwise in
half. • Place the baguette halves on the grill
pan until lightly toasted. • Spread with the
goat's cheese and arrange the tomatoes,
Provolone cheese, and zucchini on top.
Season with salt and pepper. • Press the
two halves of the baguette together to make
a sandwich. • Serve immediately.

# Rice and zucchini tartlets

*Serves: 6*
*Preparation: 35 minutes*
*Cooking: 15–20 minutes*
*Recipe grading: fairly easy*

### Dough
- 1¹/₃ cups/200 g all-purpose/plain flour
- ¹/₈ teaspoon salt
- 6 tablespoons milk
- 3 tablespoons water + more if needed
- 3 tablespoons extra-virgin olive oil

### Filling
- 1 quart/1 liter milk
- ¹/₄ teaspoon salt
- ³/₄ cup/150 g short-grain rice
- 1 shallot, finely chopped
- 2 tablespoons extra-virgin olive oil
- 4 zucchini/courgettes, cut into small rounds
- salt and freshly ground black pepper to taste
- 6 zucchini flowers, carefully washed
- 2 eggs, lightly beaten
- ²/₃ cup/80 g freshly grated Parmesan cheese
- ¹/₂ teaspoon dried marjoram
- ¹/₄ teaspoon freshly ground nutmeg
- 1 tablespoon butter, cut up

Preheat the oven to 350°F/180°C/gas 4. • Grease six 2¹/₂-inch (6-cm) tartlet pans with oil. • Dough: Sift the flour and salt into a large bowl and make a well in the center. Use a wooden spoon to mix in the milk, water, and oil until a smooth dough has formed, adding more water if needed. • Shape into a ball, cover with a damp clean cloth, and set aside. • Filling: Bring the milk and salt to a boil in a large saucepan. • Add the rice and cook over low heat for 12–15 minutes, stirring often, until the rice is tender and has absorbed the milk. • Remove from heat and set aside. • Sauté the shallot in the oil in a skillet (frying pan) over medium heat until softened. • Add the zucchini and cook for 5 minutes. Season with salt. • Blanch the zucchini flowers in a large pot of salted boiling water for 5 seconds. Drain well and pat dry with paper towels. • Stir the zucchini mixture into the rice and add the eggs, beating until just blended. Stir in the Parmesan, marjoram, and nutmeg. Season with pepper. • Roll the dough out on a lightly floured work surface to ¹/₈ inch (3 mm) thick. • Use a cookie cutter or glass to stamp out rounds to line the pans. Spoon in the rice mixture and place a zucchini flower in the center. Dot with the butter. • Bake for 15–20 minutes, or until lightly browned. • Cool the tartlets in the pans for 15 minutes. Turn out onto serving plates and serve warm.

# Tomato and Mozzarella pizza

*Serves: 2–4*
*Preparation: 15 minutes + 1 hour to rest*
*Cooking: 25–30 minutes*
*Recipe grading: fairly easy*

### Dough
- 1 oz/30 g fresh yeast or 2 packages ($^1/_4$ oz/ 7 g) active dry yeast
- 1 cup/250 ml warm water
- 1 teaspoon sugar
- 4 cups/600 g all-purpose/plain flour
- 2 tablespoons extra-virgin olive oil
- 1 teaspoon salt

### Topping
- 2 cups/500 g chopped tomatoes
- 1 tablespoon capers
- 1 clove garlic, finely chopped
- 1 onion, finely chopped
- $^1/_4$ teaspoon dried oregano
- salt and freshly ground black pepper to taste
- 5 oz/150 g Mozzarella cheese, cut up

Dough: Mix the yeast, $^1/_2$ cup (125 ml) warm water, and sugar in a small bowl. Set aside for 5 minutes, or until foamy. • Sift 1 cup (150 g) of flour into a large bowl and make a well in the center. Stir in the yeast mixture and oil. • Stir in the remaining flour and salt, adding enough water to obtain a firm dough. • Knead for 5–7 minutes, or until smooth and elastic. • Shape into a ball, place in an oiled bowl, and cover with a clean cloth. Let rest for about 1 hour, or until doubled in bulk. • Preheat the oven to 400°F/200°C/ gas 6. • Grease a large baking sheet with oil. • Topping: Mix the tomatoes, capers, garlic, onion, and oregano in a medium bowl. Season with the salt and pepper. • Break the dough into four and shape into small pizzas. Place on the baking sheet. • Spread with the topping. • Bake for 20–25 minutes, or until the dough is almost cooked. • Remove from the oven and dot with the Mozzarella. Bake for 5 more minutes, or until the cheese has melted.

# Eggplant calzone

*Serves: 4*
*Preparation: 15 minutes*
 *+ 1 hour to rest*
*Cooking: 20–25 minutes*
*Recipe grading: fairly easy*

- 1 quantity pizza dough (see recipe left)

### Filling
- 1 lb/500 g eggplant/aubergine, cut into small cubes
- $^1/_2$ cup/125 ml extra-virgin olive oil
- 3 tablespoons finely chopped marjoram
- 1 clove garlic, peeled and finely chopped
- $^1/_4$ teaspoon salt
- scant 1 cup/200 g chopped tomatoes
- 2 teaspoons finely chopped parsley
- 6 leaves fresh basil, torn
- 5 oz/150 g Pecorino cheese, cut into small cubes

Prepare the pizza dough. • Preheat the oven to 450°F/ 230°C/gas 7. • Grease two baking sheets with oil. • Knead the dough for 1 minute on a lightly floured surface. • Divide the dough into 4 small balls, flattening slightly. • Press the dough out, stretching it, until each piece is about 9-inches (23-cm) in diameter. • Filling: Sauté the eggplant in the oil in a skillet (frying pan) over medium heat for 8–10 minutes. Add the marjoram, garlic, and salt. Cook for 3 minutes more. • Stir in the tomatoes, parsley, basil, and Pecorino. Stir for 1 minute, then remove from heat. • Spread the filling on one half of each calzone, leaving a 1-inch (2.5-cm) border. Fold the other half of the dough over the top, pressing down firmly on the edges to seal.

Tomato and Mozzarella pizza

• Brush the calzoni with the remaining oil and arrange on the baking sheets. • Bake for 20–25 minutes, or until lightly browned. • Serve warm.

# Swiss chard calzone

*Serves: 4*
*Preparation: 15 minutes*
 *+ 1 hour to rest*
*Cooking: 20–25 minutes*
*Recipe grading: fairly easy*

- 1 quantity pizza dough (see recipe left)

### Filling
- $1^3/_4$ lb/800 g Swiss chard, shredded
- 4 tablespoons extra-virgin olive oil
- 2 cloves garlic, peeled and thinly sliced
- 1 teaspoon red pepper flakes (or to taste)
- salt to taste
- 1 cup/100 g black olives, pitted and coarsely chopped

Prepare the pizza dough. • Preheat the oven to 450°F/ 230°C/gas 7. • Grease two baking sheets with oil. • Place the Swiss chard in a large saucepan with 2 tablespoons of oil, garlic, and red pepper flakes. Season with salt. Cook over medium heat, for 10 minutes, stirring occasionally, until the Swiss chard is tender. • Add the olives and cook for 5 minutes more. • Remove from heat and set aside. • Knead the dough for 1 minute on a lightly floured surface. • Divide the dough into 4 small balls, flattening slightly. • Press the dough out, stretching it, until each piece is about 9-inches (23-cm) in diameter. • Spread the filling on one half of each calzone, leaving a 1-inch (2.5-cm) border. Fold the other half of the dough over the top, pressing down firmly on the edges to seal. • Brush the calzoni with the remaining oil and arrange on the baking sheets. • Bake for 20–25 minutes, or until lightly browned. • Serve warm.

on a lightly floured surface to a thickness of $^1/_8$ inch (3 mm). • Line the bottom and sides of the pan with the dough, trimming the edges to fit. • Cover with aluminum foil and fill with dried beans or pie weights. • Bake for 15 minutes. • Remove from the oven and remove the foil with the beans or pie weights. • Beat the egg and cream in a large bowl. Season with salt. Stir in the cooked cauliflower until well mixed. • Spoon the cauliflower mixture into the baked pastry. • Bake for 15–18 minutes, or until set and lightly browned. • Serve hot or at room temperature.

## Eggplant and cheese sandwiches

*Serves: 4*
*Preparation: 20 minutes + 1 hour to drain the eggplants*
*Cooking: 30 minutes*
*Recipe grading: easy*

- 4 medium eggplants/aubergines, cut into $^1/_4$-inch/6-mm slices
- 1 tablespoon coarse sea salt
- 2 eggs, lightly beaten
- 4 oz/125 g Pecorino cheese, cut into thin strips
- 15–20 leaves fresh basil, torn
- $^1/_2$ cup/60 g fine dry bread crumbs
- 2 cups/500 ml olive oil, for frying

Place the eggplant slices in a colander, sprinkle with salt, and let drain for 1 hour. • Season the eggs with salt and pepper in a small bowl. • Fill two eggplant slices with the

## Cauliflower quiche

*Serves: 4*
*Preparation: 50 minutes + 30 minutes to chill*
*Cooking: 15–18 minutes*
*Recipe grading: fairly easy*

- $^3/_4$ cup/125 g all-purpose/plain flour
- 6 tablespoons butter
- $^1/_2$ cup/50 g finely chopped almonds
- 2 tablespoons freshly grated Parmesan cheese
- 1 teaspoon ground cinnamon
- 1 egg + 1 egg white, lightly beaten
- 12 oz/350 g cauliflower florets

- 6 tablespoons light/single cream
- $^1/_8$ teaspoon salt

Sift the flour into a large bowl and make a well in the center. • Use a wooden spoon to stir in the butter, almonds, Parmesan, and cinnamon. Add 1 egg white and stir until a smooth dough has formed. • Shape into a ball, wrap in plastic wrap, and refrigerate for 30 minutes. • Cook the cauliflower in a large pot of salted, boiling water for 15 minutes. • Drain well. • Preheat the oven to 350°F/180°C/gas 4. • Oil a 10-inch (25-cm) quiche or pie pan. • Roll the dough out

Pecorino and basil. • Press the slices together firmly. Dip them first in the egg, then in the bread crumbs, pressing the edges together. • Heat the oil in a large deep skillet (frying pan) to very hot. • Fry the sandwiches a few at a time for 10 minutes, or until golden brown on both sides. • Serve hot.

## Tomato and bread omelet

*Serves: 4*
*Preparation: 15 minutes*
*Cooking: 15–20 minutes*
*Recipe grading: easy*

- 2 tablespoons butter, melted
- 5 firm-ripe tomatoes, thinly sliced
- 2 slices firm-textured bread, cut into small cubes
- 1 cup/125 g freshly grated Emmental cheese
- 5 eggs, lightly beaten
- $^2/_3$ cup/150 ml milk
- salt and freshly ground black pepper to taste
- 1 tablespoon finely chopped basil

Preheat the oven to 400°F/200°C/gas 6. • Place a 9-inch (23-cm) round nonstick baking pan in the oven until warmed. • Drizzle with the butter. • Place the tomatoes, bread cubes, and Emmental in the pan. • Beat the eggs and milk in a medium bowl. Season with the salt and pepper. • Pour the beaten egg mixture into the pan. • Bake for 15–20 minutes, or until set. • Turn the omelet out onto a serving plate and cut into wedges. • Garnish with the basil and serve hot or at room temperature.

## Baked potato frittata

*Serves: 4*
*Preparation: 20 minutes*
*Cooking: 30 minutes*
*Recipe grading: fairly easy*

- 10 oz/300 g potatoes, peeled and very thinly sliced
- 1 large red onion, coarsely chopped
- 2 tablespoons extra-virgin olive oil
- salt to taste
- 4 eggs
- 1 tablespoon freshly grated Parmesan cheese

Preheat the oven to 375°F/190°C/gas 5. • Grease a 9-inch (23-cm) round nonstick baking pan with oil. • Cook the potato slices in a large pot of salted, boiling water for 10 minutes, or until tender. • Drain well and set aside. • Sauté the onion in the oil in a skillet (frying pan) over medium heat for 10 minutes, or until lightly browned. Season with the salt. • Beat the eggs in a medium bowl until frothy. Add the potatoes and onions. Stir in the Parmesan. • Pour the mixture into the prepared pan. • Bake for 12–15 minutes, or until golden brown. • Serve hot or at room temperature.

## Olive and rosemary bread

*Serves: 6*

*Preparation: 30 minutes + 1 hour 15 minutes to rise*

*Cooking: 25–35 minutes*

*Recipe grading: fairly easy*

- 1 oz/30 g fresh yeast or 2 packages ($^1/_4$ oz/7 g) active dry yeast
- about 1$^1/_2$ cups/310 ml warm water
- 2 teaspoons salt
- 5$^1/_3$ cups/800 g all-purpose/plain flour
- 1$^1/_3$ cups/200 g whole-wheat/wholemeal flour
- $^1/_2$ cup/125 ml extra-virgin olive oil
- 2 cups/200 g black olives, pitted
- 3 tablespoons finely chopped rosemary

Mix the yeast, $^1/_2$ cup (125 ml) of water, and salt in a small bowl. Set aside for 5 minutes, or until foamy. • Sift the flours into a large bowl and make a well in the center. • Stir in the yeast mixture and enough of the remaining water to obtain a firm dough. • Knead the dough for 5–7 minutes, or until smooth and elastic. • Shape into a ball, place in an oiled bowl, and cover with a clean cloth. Let rest for 45 minutes in a warm place. • Grease a large ring baking pan with oil. • Knead the dough again, working in the olives and rosemary. • Place in the prepared baking pan. Cover with a clean cloth and let rest for 30 minutes, or until doubled in bulk. • Preheat the oven to 350°F/180°C/gas 4. • Bake for 25–35 minutes, or until lightly browned. • Cool the bread for 15 minutes in the pan. • Turn out onto a rack and let cool completely.

Olive and rosemary bread

## Spinach flatbread

*Serves: 10*
*Preparation: 30 minutes + 45 minutes to rest*
*Cooking: 20–25 minutes*
*Recipe grading: fairly easy*

- $^1/_2$ oz/15 g fresh yeast or 1 package ($^1/_4$ oz/7 g) active dry yeast
- about 1$^1/_2$ cups/310 ml warm water
- 1 tablespoon granulated sugar
- 3 cups/450 g all-purpose/plain flour
- 1$^1/_2$ cups/225 g whole-wheat flour
- 1 teaspoon salt
- 2 teaspoons finely chopped rosemary
- 3 cloves garlic, peeled and finely chopped
- 2 tablespoons extra-virgin olive oil
- 7 oz/200 g fresh spinach leaves, stalks removed and shredded
- 3 oz/90 g freshly grated Mozzarella cheese
- 2 tablespoons freshly grated Parmesan cheese

Mix the yeast, $^1/_2$ cup (125 ml) of water, and sugar in a small bowl. Set aside for 5 minutes, or until foamy. • Sift the flours and salt into a large bowl and make a well in the center. • Stir in the yeast mixture, rosemary, and enough of the remaining water to obtain a firm dough. • Knead the dough for 5–7 minutes, or until smooth and elastic. • Shape into a ball, place in an oiled bowl, and cover with a clean cloth. Let rest for 45 minutes in a warm place, or until doubled in bulk. • Preheat the oven to 350°F/ 180°C/gas 4. • Butter a large baking sheet. • Spread the dough into a round shape on the prepared baking sheet. • Bake for 15–20 minutes, or until risen and lightly browned. • Sauté the garlic in the oil in a skillet (frying pan) over medium heat until pale gold. • Add the spinach and cook for 5 minutes, or until wilted. • Remove from heat and set aside. • Spread the spinach mixture over the baked bread and sprinkle with the Mozzarella and Parmesan. • Bake for 5 minutes more, or until the cheese is lightly browned. • Cut into slices and serve warm.

## Raisin bread rolls

*Serves: 8*
*Preparation: 30 minutes + 1 hour 15 minutes to rise*
*Cooking: 15–20 minutes*
*Recipe grading: fairly easy*

- 1 oz/30 g fresh yeast or 2 packages ($^1/_4$ oz/7 g) active dry yeast
- about 1 cup/250 ml warm water
- 2 tablespoons sugar
- 3 cups/450 g unbleached flour
- 1 teaspoon salt
- 1$^1/_3$ cups/240 g golden raisins/sultanas
- 3 tablespoons butter, cut up

Mix the yeast, $^1/_2$ cup (125 ml) of water, and sugar in a small bowl. Set aside for 5 minutes, or until foamy. • Sift the flour and salt into a large bowl and make a well in the center. Stir in the yeast mixture and enough of the remaining water to obtain a firm dough. • Knead the dough for 5–7 minutes, or until smooth and elastic. • Shape into a ball, place in an oiled bowl, and cover with a clean cloth. Let rest for 45 minutes, or until doubled in bulk. • Soak the raisins in 2 cups (500 ml) warm water. Drain well and pat dry with paper towels. • Knead the raisins and butter into the dough until well combined. • Preheat the

oven to 400°F/200°C/gas 6. • Grease a large baking sheet with oil. • Divide the dough into 8 equal portions, sprinkle with flour, and shape into long rolls. • Place on the prepared baking sheet, spacing well apart. Cover with a clean cloth and let rise for 30 minutes. • Bake for 15–20 minutes, or until golden brown. • Serve warm.

## Corn bread

*Serves: 8*
*Preparation: 30 minutes + 1 hour 15 minutes to rise*
*Cooking: 25– 30 minutes*
*Recipe grading: fairly easy*

- 1$^1/_2$ oz/45 g fresh yeast or 3 packages ($^1/_4$ oz/ 7 g) active dry yeast
- about 1 cup/250 ml warm milk
- 1 teaspoon sugar
- 2 cups/300 g unbleached flour
- 2 cups/300 g finely ground cornmeal
- 4 teaspoons salt
- 1 egg

Mix the yeast, $^1/_2$ cup (125 ml) milk, and sugar in a small bowl. Set aside for 5 minutes, or until foamy. • Sift the flour, cornmeal, and salt onto a surface and make a well in the center. Stir in the yeast mixture, the egg, and enough of the remaining milk to obtain a firm dough. • Knead the dough for 5–7 minutes, or until smooth and elastic. • Shape into a ball, place in an oiled bowl, and cover with a clean cloth. Let rest in a warm place for 45 minutes, or until doubled in bulk. • Preheat the oven to 400°F/200°C/ gas 6. • Grease a large baking sheet with oil. • Divide the dough in half and shape into two round loaves. Sprinkle with flour and transfer to the prepared baking sheet. • Cover with a clean cloth and let rest for 30 minutes. • Bake for 25–30 minutes, or until risen and lightly browned. • Transfer to racks and let cool completely.

# SALADS

Salads nourish us as few other foods do. The crisp, raw (or lightly steamed) vegetables are packed full of vitamins and minerals undamaged by extensive cooking. However, this makes it even more essential that the ingredients you use are fresh and of the highest quality. Many supermarkets and stores now have a wide selection of vegetables grown without the use of pesticides or herbicides. In any case, always rinse salad vegetables thoroughly before use.

*Traditional Javanese Salad, or Gado Gado, is more of a concept than a strictly-to-be-followed recipe. The idea is to lightly boil or steam some fresh, in-season vegetables, arrange them with crisp salad greens, onion rings, bean sprouts, sliced tomatoes, and fruit (if liked) in a bowl or platter, then sprinkle them all with fragrant herbs. This is topped by fried eggs, cut into strips or dice, then drizzled with spicy peanut sauce. There are endless variations and you should follow own inclinations.*

Gado gado (see page 117)
Spinach and Feta salad (see page 96)

*Golden yellow corn, or sweetcorn, is a versatile vegetable that can be boiled, baked, or grilled. It is also available in handy vacuum-packed cans and makes a delicious addition to a variety of salads.*

## Arugula, corn, and kiwifruit salad

*Serves: 4*
*Preparation: 10 minutes*
*Recipe grading: easy*

- 2 bunches arugula/rocket
- 3–4 kiwifruit, peeled and thinly sliced
- 7 oz/200 g canned/sweetcorn corn
- 2 cloves garlic, finely chopped
- 1 red chile pepper, finely chopped (optional)
- salt and freshly ground black pepper to taste
- 3–4 tablespoons white wine vinegar
- 6 tablespoons extra-virgin olive oil

Rinse the arugula thoroughly under cold running water and dry well. Place around the outer edge of a large salad bowl. • Arrange the kiwifruit at the base of the arugula in a decorative manner. • Spoon the corn into the center. • Add the garlic and chile, if using. • Season with the salt and pepper. • Drizzle with the vinegar and oil and serve.

## Greek salad

*Serves: 4–6*
*Preparation: 10 minutes*
*Recipe grading: easy*

- 2 bunches arugula/rocket
- 7 oz/200 g Feta cheese, cut into small cubes
- 4–6 salad tomatoes, sliced
- 1 red onion, finely chopped
- 1 1/2 cups/150 g black olives, pitted
- 8 leaves fresh mint, torn
- 8 leaves fresh basil, torn
- 1 tablespoon finely chopped lemon peel
- 2 cloves garlic, finely chopped
- 1 cucumber, thinly sliced
- salt and freshly ground black pepper to taste
- 4 tablespoons fresh lemon juice
- 6 tablespoons extra-virgin olive oil

Rinse the arugula thoroughly under cold running water and dry well. • Place in a large salad bowl and add the Feta, tomatoes, onion, olives, mint, basil, lemon peel, garlic, and cucumber. Season with salt and pepper and drizzle with lemon juice and oil. • Toss well and serve.

## Spinach and Feta salad

*Serves: 6*
*Preparation: 10 minutes*
*Recipe grading: easy*

- 2 lb/1 kg fresh spinach leaves
- 6 tablespoons extra-virgin olive oil
- 2 tablespoons white wine vinegar
- 2 tablespoons fresh lemon juice
- 1/2 teaspoon ground cinnamon
- 1/2 teaspoon dry mustard powder
- salt and freshly ground black pepper to taste
- 1 cucumber, thinly sliced
- 1 lb/500 g cherry tomatoes
- 8 oz/250 g Feta cheese, crumbled
- 6 scallions/spring onions, finely chopped

Trim the spinach and rinse thoroughly under cold running water. Dry well and place in a salad bowl. • Place the oil, vinegar, lemon juice, cinnamon, mustard, salt, and pepper in a container with a screw top. Shake well. • Pour half the dressing over the spinach and toss well. • Add the cucumber, tomatoes, Feta, and scallions. • Pour the remaining dressing over the top, toss gently, and serve.

## Fresh spinach and Parmesan salad

*Serves: 4*
*Preparation: 10 minutes*
*Recipe grading: easy*

- 7 oz/250 g fresh spinach leaves
- 2 carrots, peeled and finely grated
- 8 oz/250 g canned corn/sweetcorn or 8 baby corn/sweetcorn cobs
- 8 oz/250 g Parmesan cheese, flaked
- salt and freshly ground black pepper to taste
- juice of 1 lemon
- 4 tablespoons extra-virgin olive oil

Trim the spinach and rinse thoroughly under cold running water. Dry well and place in a salad bowl. • Sprinkle with the carrots and corn. • Top with the Parmesan. • Season with the salt and pepper and drizzle with the lemon juice and oil. • Toss well and serve.

Arugula, corn, and kiwifruit salad

## Pineapple and cantaloupe salad

*Serves: 4*
*Preparation: 20 minutes*
*Recipe grading: easy*

- 1 small cantaloupe/rock melon, cut in half
- 1 small pineapple, skin removed
- 7 oz/200 g green beans, cooked and cut in half
- 12 cherry tomatoes, cut in half
- 1 green bell pepper/capsicum, seeded, cored, and cut in 4

Dressing
- juice of 1 lemon
- 6 tablespoons extra-virgin olive oil
- small bunch parsley
- 3 drops Tabasco sauce
- salt to taste

Peel the cantaloupe and cut in half. Cut the flesh of one half into small cubes and thinly slice the other half. • Cut the pineapple into thin slices. • Place the pineapple slices on serving plates and place the cantaloupe slices on top. Arrange the green beans, cantaloupe cubes, tomatoes, and bell pepper on top. • Process the lemon juice, oil, parsley, and Tabasco sauce in a food processor or blender until well blended. Season with salt. • Pour the dressing over the salad and serve.

## Pear and bell pepper salad

*Serves: 4–6*
*Preparation: 15 minutes*
*Recipe grading: easy*

- 2 large firm-ripe pears, peeled, cored, and cut into thin strips
- juice of 1 lemon
- 3 bell peppers/capsicums, mixed colors, seeded, cored, and cut into thin strips
- 1 clove garlic, finely chopped (optional)
- 1 tablespoon finely chopped parsley
- 4 tablespoons extra-virgin olive oil
- salt and freshly ground black pepper to taste

Place the pears in a salad bowl and drizzle with the lemon juice . • Mix in the bell peppers, garlic, if using, parsley, and oil. Season with salt and pepper. • Toss well and serve.

## Watercress and cantaloupe salad

*Serves: 4*
*Preparation: 15 minutes*
*Recipe grading: easy*

Dressing
- 3 tablespoons fresh lime juice
- 1 teaspoon sugar
- 1 teaspoon finely chopped fresh ginger
- 4 tablespoons extra-virgin olive oil
- salt and freshly ground black pepper to taste

- 10 oz/300 g watercress, shredded
- 1/2 small watermelon, cut in small cubes
- 1/2 small cantaloupe/rock melon, cut in small cubes
- 2 tablespoons slivered almonds, toasted

Dressing: Mix the lime juice, sugar, and ginger in a small bowl. Beat in the oil. Season with the salt and pepper. • Place the watercress, watermelon, and cantaloupe in a large bowl. • Pour the dressing over the top and toss well. • Arrange the salad on individual plates and sprinkle with the almonds.

## Oriental melon salad

*Serves: 4*
*Preparation: 15 minutes*
*Recipe grading: easy*

Dressing
- 2 tablespoons rice vinegar
- 1 tablespoon finely chopped fresh ginger
- 2 teaspoons soy sauce
- 1 teaspoon sugar
- 1 teaspoon sesame oil
- 1/4 teaspoon red pepper flakes
- 4 tablespoons extra-virgin olive oil

- 1 cucumber, thinly sliced
- 1/2 small cantaloupe/rock melon, cut in small cubes
- 2 scallions/spring onions, finely chopped
- 1 tablespoon sesame seeds, toasted

Dressing: Mix the vinegar, ginger, soy sauce, sugar, sesame oil, red pepper flakes, and olive oil in a small bowl. • Place the cucumber, cantaloupe, and scallions in a salad bowl. • Pour the dressing over the salad and toss well. • Sprinkle with the sesame seed and serve.

Pineapple and cantaloupe salad

## Red cabbage and fennel salad with cheese croutons

*Serves: 4*
*Preparation: 20 minutes*
*Cooking: 10 minutes*
*Recipe grading: easy*

Cheese croutons
- 3 thick slices whole-wheat/wholemeal bread, crusts removed and cut into $^1/_2$-inch/1-cm cubes
- 2 tablespoons extra-virgin olive oil
- 3 teaspoons fennel seed, crushed
- salt and freshly ground black pepper to taste

Salad
- 1 jar (1 lb/500 g) pickled red cabbage, drained
- 4 scallions/spring onions, finely chopped
- 1 green bell pepper/capsicum, seeded, cored, and cut into thin strips
- $^1/_2$ yellow bell pepper/capsicum, seeded, cored, and cut into thin strips
- $^1/_2$ fennel bulb, cut into thin slices
- 1 tablespoon pumpkin seeds
- salt and freshly ground black pepper to taste
- $3^1/_2$ oz/100 g Emmental cheese, cut into small cubes
- $3^1/_2$ oz/100 g smoked Provolone cheese, cut into small cubes
- 6 tablespoons extra-virgin olive oil
- juice of $^1/_2$ lemon

Cheese croutons: Preheat the oven to 400°F/200°C/gas 6. • Toss the bread cubes and fennel seeds in the oil. Season with salt and pepper. • Spread the croutons in a baking pan. • Bake for 5 minutes then shake the pan. Bake for 5 minutes more, or until golden brown and crispy. • Let cool completely. • Salad: Place the cabbage, scallions, bell peppers, and fennel in a large bowl. Add the pumpkin seeds and season with salt and pepper. Add the Emmental and Provolone. • Drizzle with the oil and lemon juice and toss well. • Sprinkle with the croutons and serve.

*This eyecatching salad uses vegetables and fruit that are readily available during the cold winter months. Serve it after pizza or pasta for a light lunch or supper.*

## Mandarin, apple, and tomato salad

*Serves: 4*
*Preparation: 20 minutes*
*Recipe grading: easy*

- 3 endive hearts, well-washed
- 1 cup/250 ml sour cream
- juice of 1 lemon
- juice of $^1/_2$ orange
- 7 oz/200 g tomatoes, cut into small cubes
- 5 oz/150 g tart apples, peeled, cored, and cut into small cubes
- 2 mandarins, peeled and cut into small cubes
- 1 scallion/spring onion, finely chopped
- 1 tablespoon finely chopped parsley

Discard any damaged or discolored outer leaves of the endives. Reserve 12–15 attractive outer leaves, and coarsely chop the remainder. • Arrange the outer leaves like the spokes in a wheel on a large serving plate. • Place the sour cream, lemon juice, orange juice, chopped endives, tomatoes, apples, mandarins, scallion, and parsley in a medium bowl and toss well. • Spoon the mixture into the center of the plate and serve.

## Austrian sauerkraut salad

*Serves: 4*
*Preparation: 15 minutes + 30 minutes to marinate*
*Recipe grading: easy*

- 1 kg/500 g sauerkraut, drained
- 2–3 apples, peeled, cored, and finely grated
- 1 tablespoon fresh lemon juice
- 1 onion, finely sliced
- 2 carrots, peeled and finely chopped
- 1 green bell pepper/capsicum, seeded, cored, and cut into thin strips

Dressing
- 2 tablespoons white wine vinegar
- 1 tablespoon extra-virgin olive oil
- 4 tablespoons light/single cream
- salt and freshly ground white pepper to taste
- $^1/_2$ teaspoon sugar
- 1 tablespoon dry white wine (optional)

Place the sauerkraut in a large bowl and break it up with a fork. • Drizzle the apples with the lemon juice to prevent them from turning brown. • Mix the apples and onion into the sauerkraut. Add the carrots and bell pepper. • Dressing: Place the white wine vinegar, oil, and cream in a container with a screw top. Shake well. • Season with the salt, pepper, and sugar. • Pour the dressing over the salad and toss well. Let stand for 30 minutes. • Add the wine, if using, and toss again before serving.

Mandarin, apple, and tomato salad

# Warm potato salad

*Serves: 4*
*Preparation: 15 minutes*
*Cooking: 15 minutes*
*Recipe grading: easy*

- 14 oz/400 g small salad potatoes, such as Charlottes, cut in half
- 1¼ cups/310 ml boiling vegetable stock
- 1 tablespoon red wine vinegar or sherry
- 8 oz/250 g green beans, topped and tailed

Dressing
- 2 tablespoons sherry vinegar
- 2 tablespoons extra-virgin olive oil
- 2 tablespoons sesame oil
- 1 tablespoon vegetable stock
- 1 tablespoon mustard seed
- 1 tablespoon finely chopped chives
- 2 scallions/spring onions, finely chopped

Place the potatoes in a large pot filled with the boiling vegetable stock and red wine vinegar. Cover and cook for 10–15 minutes, or until almost tender. • Add the green beans and cook for 5 minutes, or until tender. • Dressing: Place the vinegar, olive oil, sesame oil, stock, and mustard seed in a small container with a screw top. Shake well. • Drain the potatoes and green beans and arrange on 4 individual serving plates. Drizzle with the dressing. Sprinkle with the chives and scallions and serve.

# Swedish potato salad

*Serves: 4*
*Preparation: 30 minutes + 2 hours to chill*
*Cooking: 12–15 minutes*
*Recipe grading: fairly easy*

Mayonnaise
- 1 egg yolk, at room temperature
- 1 cup/250 ml extra-virgin olive oil
- ⅔ cup/150 ml warm water
- 1–2 tablespoons white wine vinegar
- salt and freshly ground white pepper to taste

- 2 lb/1 kg salad potatoes, such as Charlottes, cut in bite-sized cubes
- 1 onion, finely chopped
- 1 teaspoon freshly grated nutmeg
- 8 hard-boiled eggs, shelled and coarsely chopped
- 4 oz/125 g baby pickled gherkins, finely chopped
- ¼ teaspoon curry powder

Mayonnaise: Place the yolk in a large bowl and beat with an electric mixer at high speed until pale. Gradually add the oil, a little at a time, beating until creamy. Add 1 teaspoon of water, beating constantly and gradually adding the remaining water and vinegar. Add more water if the mayonnaise is too thick and more oil if it is too thin. Season with salt and pepper. Refrigerate until ready to use. • Cook the potatoes in a large pot of salted, boiling water for 15 minutes, or until tender. • Drain well and let cool completely. • Mix the potatoes, eggs, gherkins, onion, and nutmeg in a large bowl. • Pour the mayonnaise over the top. • Toss well and season with salt, pepper, and curry powder. • Refrigerate for at least 2 hours before serving.

## Sweet potato salad

*Serves: 6–8*
*Preparation: 20 minutes + time to cool and chill*
*Cooking: 15–20 minutes*
*Recipe grading: easy*

- 1$^1/_2$ lb/750 g sweet potatoes, peeled and cut into bite-sized cubes
- 1$^1/_2$ lb/750 g salad potatoes, such as Charlottes, cut into bite-sized cubes
- 1 cup/250 ml mayonnaise
- 1 tablespoon fresh lemon juice
- 1 teaspoon freshly ground cumin seeds
- salt to taste
- 2 scallions/spring onions, finely chopped

Cook the potatoes in separate large pots of salted, boiling water for 15–20 minutes, or until tender. • Drain well and let cool completely. • Transfer to a large bowl and add the mayonnaise, lemon juice, and cumin. • Season with salt and sprinkle with the scallions. • Refrigerate for at least 1 hour before serving.

## Russian beet salad

*Serves: 6*
*Preparation: 20 minutes*
*Cooking: 45–60 minutes*
*Recipe grading: fairly easy*

- 1$^1/_2$ lb/750 g beets/red beet
- 1 egg yolk, at room temperature
- 1 tablespoon fresh lemon juice

- salt and freshly ground black pepper to taste
- $^1/_2$ cup/125 ml extra-virgin olive oil
- 1 teaspoon dry mustard powder
- 4 tablespoons light/single cream
- 3 onions, finely chopped
- 2 tablespoons finely chopped dill

Preheat the oven to 400°F/200°C/gas 6. • Place the beets on a baking sheet. • Bake for 45–60 minutes, or until tender. • Remove from the oven and let cool completely. • Peel and cut into thin strips. Arrange on 6 individual serving plates. • Beat the egg yolk and lemon juice until frothy. Season with salt and pepper. • Transfer to a food processor or blender and gradually add the oil, pulsing until smooth and well blended. • Stir in the mustard, cream, onions, and dill and season with the salt and pepper. • Pour over the beets, toss well, and serve.

Russian beet salad

## Orange and olive salad

*Serves: 4*
*Preparation: 15 minutes + 10 minutes to stand*
*Recipe grading: easy*

- 4 ripe, juicy oranges
- 10 green or black olives, pitted and cut into quarters
- white of 1 leek, thinly sliced into rings
- 1 tablespoon finely chopped parsley
- 4 tablespoons extra-virgin olive oil
- salt and freshly ground black or white pepper to taste

Peel the oranges, removing all the white pith and skin. Slice thinly. • Place the oranges in a salad bowl and add the olives, leek, parsley, and oil. Season with salt and pepper. • Toss gently and let stand for 10 minutes before serving.

## Orange and onion salad

*Serves: 4*
*Preparation: 15 minutes + 20 minutes to stand*
*Recipe grading: easy*

- 3 ripe, juicy oranges
- 8 oz/250 g mixed salad greens, well-washed
- 2 red onions, thinly sliced
- 1 cup/100 g black olives, pitted and finely chopped
- 6 tablespoons extra-virgin olive oil
- 2 tablespoons red wine vinegar
- salt and freshly ground black pepper to taste

Peel the oranges, discard any seeds and removing all the white pith and skin. Slice thickly then cut each slice in half. • Place the oranges, salad greens, onions, and olives in a salad bowl. • Mix the oil and vinegar in a small bowl. Season with salt and pepper.

• Pour the dressing over the salad and toss well. • Let stand for 20 minutes before serving.

## Salad with strawberries and apples

*Serves: 4*
*Preparation: 20 minutes + 20 minutes to stand*
*Recipe grading: easy*

Dressing
- 4 tablespoons extra-virgin olive oil
- 2 tablespoons finely chopped chives
- salt and freshly ground black pepper to taste

Salad
- 12 oz/350 g mixed green salad
- 6 oz/180 g endive hearts
- 2 red apples, cored and thinly sliced

- 10 radishes, thinly sliced
- 14 oz/400 g strawberries, cut in half
- 1¹/₂ cups/375 g fresh Ricotta cheese

Dressing: Beat the oil and chives in a small bowl. Season with the salt and pepper. Let stand for 20 minutes. • Salad: Rinse the salad greens and endives thoroughly under cold running water and dry well. Arrange the salad in a large salad bowl. • Place a circle of apple slices on top. Sprinkle with the radishes. • Garnish with the strawberries and Ricotta. • Drizzle with the dressing and serve.

## Carrot and leek salad

*Serves: 4*
*Preparation: 20 minutes + 1 hour to chill*
*Recipe grading: easy*

- 1³/₄ lb/800 g carrots, finely grated
- juice of 1 lemon
- 7 oz/200 g leeks (whites only), very finely sliced

Dressing
- 4 tablespoons extra-virgin olive oil
- 1 tablespoon white wine vinegar
- 1 teaspoon brown sugar
- 1 clove garlic, finely chopped
- 1 tablespoon sesame oil
- 2 teaspoons candied ginger, cut into small cubes
- salt and freshly ground black pepper to taste

Drizzle the carrots with the lemon juice in a medium bowl. • Add the leeks. • Dressing: Mix the olive oil, vinegar, brown sugar, garlic, sesame oil, and ginger in a small bowl. Season with the salt and pepper. • Pour the dressing over the salad and toss well. • Refrigerate for at least 1 hour before serving. • Serve with breadsticks or freshly baked bread.

## Mixed salad greens with balsamic vinegar

*Serves: 6*
*Preparation: 10 minutes*
*Recipe grading: easy*

- 2 lb/1 kg mixed wild salad greens
- salt and freshly ground black pepper to taste
- 4 tablespoons balsamic vinegar
- 4 tablespoons extra-virgin olive oil

Rinse the salad green thoroughly under cold running water and dry well. • Place the leaves in a large salad bowl. Season with salt and pepper and drizzle with the vinegar and oil. • Toss well and serve with freshly baked bread.

*This delicious, easy salad is packed with vitamin C. It is just as good made with oranges or lemons, although in that case, use flakes of Parmesan cheese cut fresh from the round instead of Pecorino.*

## Spinach, grapefruit, and Pecorino cheese salad

*Serves: 4*
*Preparation: 15 minutes*
*Recipe grading: easy*

• 7 oz/200 g fresh baby spinach leaves
• 4 oz/125 g Pecorino romano cheese, flaked
• 1 grapefruit, cut into segments

Dressing
• juice of $^1/_2$ lemon
• 4 tablespoons extra-virgin olive oil
• 1 tablespoon finely chopped chives
• salt and freshly ground black pepper to taste

Rinse the spinach leaves thoroughly under cold running water and dry well. • Arrange the spinach on 4 individual serving plates. Sprinkle with the Pecorino and grapefruit. • Dressing: Mix the lemon juice, oil, and chives in a small bowl. Season with salt and pepper. • Drizzle the dressing over the salads and toss well.

## Mozzarella, tomato, and mixed raw vegetables

*Serves: 4–6*
*Preparation: 15 minutes*
*Recipe grading: easy*

• 14 oz/450 g Mozzarella cheese, thinly sliced
• 4–6 large tomatoes
• 1 cup/250 g mixed raw vegetables, such as zucchini/courgettes, carrots, celery, bell peppers/ capsicums, onion, cut into small cubes
• 1 tablespoon pickled capers, drained
• salt and freshly ground black pepper to taste
• 4 tablespoons extra-virgin olive oil
• 8 leaves fresh basil, torn

Arrange the Mozzarella in a large serving plate. • Cut the tomatoes to the size of the Mozzarella slices and place on top of the Mozzarella. • Place the raw vegetables and capers in a large bowl. Season with salt and pepper and drizzle with the oil. • Toss well. • Spoon the vegetables on top of the tomatoes and Mozzarella. • Sprinkle with the basil and serve.

## Winter salad with Gorgonzola dressing

*Serves: 6*
*Preparation: 20 minutes*
*Recipe grading: easy*

• 2 fennel bulbs
• 2 carrots, peeled and cut into very thin strips
• 1 bunch celery, finely chopped

Spinach, grapefruit, and Pecorino cheese salad

• 1 tart apple, cored and cut into thin slices
• 1 clove garlic, finely chopped
• salt and freshly ground black pepper to taste
• 1 tablespoon lemon juice
• 4 tablespoons extra-virgin olive oil
• 6 oz/180 g Gorgonzola cheese, cut into small cubes
• 1 tablespoon finely chopped parsley

Clean the fennel by discarding the tough outer leaves, then cut the bulbs in half. Rinse under cold running water and dry well. Cut into $^1/_8$-inch (3-mm) thick slices. • Place the fennel, carrots, celery, apple, and garlic in a salad bowl. Season with salt and pepper and drizzle with the lemon juice, and 2 tablespoons of oil. • Heat the Gorgonzola and remaining oil in a small saucepan, stirring constantly until melted. • Drizzle the Gorgonzola dressing over the vegetables. • Sprinkle with the parsley and serve.

## Fontina cheese with pears and walnuts

*Serves: 4–6*
*Preparation: 15 minutes*
*Recipe grading: easy*

• 7 oz/250 g fresh baby spinach leaves
• 1 bunch watercress
• 2 large firm-ripe pears, peeled, cored, and cut into small cubes
• 8 oz/250 g Fontina cheese, cut into small cubes
• 1$^3/_4$ cups/175 g coarsely chopped walnuts
• 3 tablespoons extra-virgin olive oil
• juice of 1 lemon
• salt and freshly ground black pepper to taste

Rinse the spinach leaves and watercress thoroughly under cold running water and dry well. • Arrange the spinach and watercress in a large salad bowl. • Add the pears, Fontina, and walnuts. • Drizzle with the oil and lemon juice and season with the salt and pepper.. • Toss carefully and serve.

• 6 red onions, cut into thin rings
• salt and freshly ground black pepper to taste
• 1 tablespoon white wine vinegar
• 4 tablespoons extra-virgin olive oil
• 2 cucumbers, peeled and thinly sliced
• 1 tablespoon pickled capers, drained
• 6 leaves fresh basil, torn

Place the onions in a large salad bowl. Season with the salt and pepper and drizzle with the vinegar and oil. Toss well and let stand for 30 minutes. • Add the cucumbers and capers and toss well. • Sprinkle with the basil and serve.

## Lentil and herb salad

*Serves: 4*
*Preparation: 20 minutes + 5 minutes to stand*
*Cooking: 35–45 minutes*
*Recipe grading: easy*

• 1 lb/500 g lentils
• 1 large onion studded with 2 cloves
• 1 sprig fresh thyme
• 5 bay leaves
• 3 large carrots
• 1/2 cup/125 ml extra-virgin olive oil
• 2 tablespoons red wine vinegar
• salt and freshly ground black pepper to taste
• 4 cloves garlic, finely chopped
• 2 tablespoons finely chopped parsley

Cook the lentils with the onion, thyme, bay leaves, and carrots in a large pot of salted boiling water for 35–45 minutes, or until tender. • Drain well, shaking to remove excess moisture, and transfer to a salad bowl. Discard the bay leaves, thyme, and cloves. • Cut the onion into thin slices and cut the carrots into small cubes. Add to the lentils. • Drizzle with the oil and vinegar. Season with salt and pepper. • Add the garlic and parsley and toss well. Let stand for 5 minutes before serving.

## Orange and artichoke salad

*Serves: 4*
*Preparation: 15 minutes*
*Recipe grading: easy*

• 6 tender artichoke hearts, cut into small pieces
• 2 oranges, peeled and cut into segments
• 3 oz/90 g Pecorino romano cheese, flaked
• 1 tablespoon finely chopped parsley
• 4 tablespoons extra-virgin olive oil
• juice of 1 lemon
• salt and freshly ground black pepper to taste

Orange and artichoke salad

Place the artichoke in a large salad bowl. • Sprinkle with the orange, Pecorino, and parsley. • Drizzle with the oil and lemon juice and season with the salt and pepper. • Toss well and serve.

## Cucumber and onion salad

*Serves: 6–8*
*Preparation: 15 minutes + 30 minutes to stand*
*Recipe grading: easy*

SALADS

# Lemon and mint salad

*Serves: 4*
*Preparation: 20 minutes + 2 hours to chill*
*Recipe grading: easy*

- 2 lb/1 kg lemons
- 6 tablespoons extra-virgin olive oil
- salt and freshly ground black pepper to taste
- 1 bunch mint, separated into leaves
- 1 green chile pepper, thinly sliced
- 1 red chile pepper, thinly sliced

Peel from the lemon, making sure you remove all the white pithy zest. Cut into small cubes. • Place the lemon cubes in a salad bowl and drizzle with the oil. • Season with the salt and pepper. Sprinkle with the mint leaves and chilies. • Refrigerate for at least 2 hours before serving.

# Asparagus salad

*Serves: 4*
*Preparation: 20 minutes*
*Cooking: 7–10 minutes*
*Recipe grading: easy*

- 2 lb/1 kg asparagus, trimmed
- 6 heads red radicchio
- 12 oz/350 g mushrooms, thinly sliced
- 1/2 cup/125 ml extra-virgin olive oil
- 3 tablespoons fresh lemon juice
- salt and freshly ground black pepper to taste
- zest of 2 lemons, finely chopped
- 10 leaves fresh basil, finely chopped

Cook the asparagus in a large pot of salted, boiling water for 7–10 minutes, or until tender. • Drain well and let cool completely. • Rinse the radicchio thoroughly under cold running water and dry well. • Arrange the leaves on a serving plate and sprinkle with the mushrooms. Place the asparagus on top. • Drizzle with the oil and lemon juice. Season with the salt and pepper and sprinkle with the lemon zest and basil.

Lemon and mint salad

# Dandelion and red onion salad

*Serves: 4*
*Preparation: 20 minutes*
*Recipe grading: easy*

- 2 lb/1 kg dandelion greens
- 2 red onions, cut into thin rings

Dressing
- 3 garlic cloves, finely chopped
- 2 tablespoons coarsely chopped hazelnuts
- 2 tablespoons extra-virgin olive oil
- 1 tablespoon balsamic vinegar
- salt and freshly ground black pepper to taste

Rinse the dandelion greens thoroughly under cold running water and dry well. • Place the dandelion greens in a large salad bowl and sprinkle with the red onion. • Sauté the garlic and hazelnuts in the oil in a skillet (frying pan) over medium heat until the garlic is pale gold. • Pour in the vinegar and season with the salt and pepper. • Drizzle the hot dressing over the salad and toss well.

*This is a hearty salad.
Use your own pickled
vegetables if you have some
on hand.*

## Pasta salad with pickled vegetables and arugula

*Serves: 6*
*Preparation: 25 minutes + time to cool the pasta*
*Cooking: 10–15 minutes*
*Recipe grading: easy*

• 1 lb/500 g whole-wheat pasta shells
• $\frac{1}{8}$ teaspoon saffron strands
• 4 tablespoons extra-virgin olive oil
• 1 bunch arugula/rocket
• 1 tablespoon finely chopped marjoram
• 1 tablespoon capers
• 7 oz/200 g pickled vegetables, finely chopped
• 2 oz/60 g mushrooms in oil

Cook the pasta in a large pot of salted, boiling water for 5 minutes. Add the saffron and cook for 5–10 minutes more, or until the pasta is *al dente*. • Drain well and let cool completely. • Transfer to a large bowl and drizzle with 1 tablespoon of oil. • Rinse the arugula thoroughly under cold running water and dry well. • Finely chop the arugula and add with the marjoram, capers, pickled vegetables, and mushrooms to the salad. • Drizzle with the remaining oil, toss well, and serve.

## Broiled bell pepper pasta salad

*Serves: 4*
*Preparation: 30 minutes*
*Cooking: 10–15 minutes*
*Recipe grading: easy*

- 1 lb/500 g penne pasta
- 4 tablespoons extra-virgin olive oil
- 6 bell peppers/capsicums, mixed colors
- 2 tablespoons capers
- 1 tablespoon raisins
- 1 tablespoon pine nuts
- salt and freshly ground black pepper to taste

Cook the penne in a large pot of salted, boiling water for 10–12 minutes, or until *al dente*. • Drain well and transfer to a serving dish with 1 tablespoon of oil. Let cool completely. • Turn on the broiler (grill). • Broil the bell peppers 4–6 inches (10 to 15 cm) from the heat source, turning them often until blackened all over. Wrap in foil and set aside for 10 minutes. When unwrapped, the skins will peel away easily. Rinse carefully to remove any remaining pieces of burnt skin. • Cut the bell peppers in half and remove the stems and seeds. Cut the flesh into bite-sized pieces. • Mix the oil, capers, raisins, and pine nuts in a small bowl. Season with the salt and pepper. • Spoon over the bell peppers and let stand

*Pasta salad with pickled vegetables and arugula*

for 30 minutes. • Add the bell pepper mixture to the bowl with the pasta, toss well, and serve.

## Summer pasta salad

*Serves: 4*
*Preparation: 20 minutes + time to cool and chill*
*Cooking: 10–12 minutes*
*Recipe grading: easy*

- 1 lb/500 g rigatoni pasta
- 6 tablespoons extra-virgin olive oil
- 8 oz/250 g Mozzarella cheese, cut into small cubes
- 1 cup/100 g black olives, pitted
- 2 tablespoons capers
- 2 cloves garlic, finely chopped
- 4 salad tomatoes, cut into small cubes
- 8 leaves fresh basil, torn

Cook the rigatoni in a large pot of salted, boiling water for 10–12 minutes, or until *al dente*. • Drain well and transfer to a large salad bowl. • Drizzle with 3 tablespoons of oil and let cool completely. • Add the Mozzarella, olives, capers, garlic, tomatoes, basil, and the remaining oil. • Toss well and refrigerate for 30 minutes before serving.

## Cheese and pea pasta salad

*Serves: 4*
*Preparation: 20 minutes*
*Cooking: 10–12 minutes*
*Recipe grading: easy*

- 1 lb/500 g small tubular pasta
- 1¹/₂ cups/180 g peas
- 4 oz/125 g Fontina cheese, cut into very small cubes
- 1 tablespoon finely chopped basil
- 2 firm-ripe tomatoes, coarsely chopped
- 2 tablespoons extra-virgin olive oil
- salt and freshly ground black pepper to taste

Cook the pasta in a large pot of salted, boiling water for 5 minutes. Add the peas and cook for 5–7 minutes more, or until *al dente*. • Drain well and let cool completely. • Transfer to a large bowl and add the Fontina and basil. • Process the tomatoes and oil in a food processor or blender until smooth. • Pour the tomato sauce over the pasta salad and toss well. Season with the salt and pepper and serve.

## Fusilli salad with broiled vegetables

*Serves: 4*
*Preparation: 25 minutes + 1 hour to drain the eggplants*
*Cooking: 10–12 minutes*
*Recipe grading: easy*

- 1 large eggplant/aubergine, cut into ¹/₄-inch/6-mm thick slices
- 2 bell peppers/capsicums, mixed colors, seeded, cored, and cut in strips
- 2 zucchini/courgettes, thinly sliced
- 4 firm-ripe tomatoes, finely chopped
- 14 oz/400 g Mozzarella cheese, cut into small cubes
- 2 tablespoons finely chopped parsley
- salt and freshly ground white pepper to taste
- ¹/₂ cup/125 ml extra-virgin olive oil
- 1 lb/500 g fusilli pasta

Place the eggplants in a colander. Sprinkle with salt and let drain for 1 hour. • Cook the fusilli in a large pot of salted boiling water for 10–12 minutes, or until *al dente*. • Drain well and let cool completely. • Turn on the broiler (grill). • Broil the eggplant, bell peppers, zucchini, and tomatoes 4–6 inches (10–15 cm) from the heat source until slightly browned and tender. • Chop coarsely and transfer the vegetables to a large salad bowl. • Add the Mozzarella and sprinkle with the parsley. Season with salt and pepper and drizzle with the oil. • Add the pasta to the bowl with the vegetables, toss well, and serve.

## Summer salad

*Serves: 4*
*Preparation: 30 minutes*
*Cooking: 5 minutes*
*Recipe grading: easy*

- 5 oz/150 g green beans, topped and tailed
- 1 bunch arugula/rocket
- 2 peaches, stoned and cut in 8
- 2 small fennel bulbs, cut into small pieces
- 5 oz/150 g bell peppers/capsicums, mixed colors, seeded, cored, and cut into thick strips

- juice of 1 lemon
- 6 tablespoons extra-virgin olive oil
- salt and freshly ground black pepper to taste

Cook the green beans in a large pot of salted boiling water for 5 minutes, or until just tender. • Drain well and let cool completely. • Rinse the arugula thoroughly under cold running water and dry well. • Arrange the arugula leaves in a fan shape around the outer edge of the plate. Place the peach slices on top so that you can still see the arugula. Place the green beans in a circle overlapping the peaches, followed by the fennel. • Arrange the bell peppers in the center. • Drizzle with the lemon juice and oil. Season with the salt and pepper and serve.

## Spelt salad

*Serves: 4*
*Preparation: 15 minutes + 10 minutes to stand*
*Cooking: 30–40 minutes*
*Recipe grading: easy*

- 1 lb/500 g spelt
- 16 cherry tomatoes, cut in half
- 1 lb/500 g Mozzarella cheese, cut into small cubes
- 6 scallions/spring onions, finely chopped
- 15 leaves fresh basil, torn
- 2 tablespoons capers
- 1/2 cup/125 ml extra-virgin olive oil
- salt and freshly ground black pepper to taste

Cook the spelt in a large pot of salted boiling water for 30–40 minutes, or until chewy but firm. • Drain well, squeezing out excess moisture. • Transfer to a salad bowl. Add the tomatoes, Mozzarella, scallions, basil, capers, and oil. Season with the salt and pepper. Let stand for 10 minutes before serving.

## Rice salad with cucumber

*Serves: 4*
*Preparation: 15 minutes*
*Cooking: 15–20 minutes*
*Recipe grading: easy*

- 1 1/2 cups/300 g short-grain rice
- 4 tablespoons extra-virgin olive oil
- 20 cherry tomatoes, coarsely chopped
- 1 cucumber, peeled and cut into small cubes
- 1 tablespoon capers
- 10 green or black olives, pitted and finely chopped
- 4 oz/125 g Emmental or Cheddar cheese, cut into small cubes
- 8 leaves fresh basil, torn

Cook the rice in a large pot of salted, boiling water for 15–20 minutes, or until tender. • Drain well. • Transfer to a large salad bowl and drizzle with the oil. Let cool. • Add the tomatoes, cucumber, capers, olives, Emmental, and basil. Toss well and serve.

## Rice salad with vegetables

*Serves: 4*
*Preparation: 15 minutes*
*Cooking: 16–21 minutes*
*Recipe grading: easy*

- 4 oz/125 g baby carrots, cut in half
- 8 oz/250 g baby corn/sweetcorn on the cob
- 1 1/2 cups/300 g short-grain rice
- 1/2 cup/125 ml plain yogurt
- 3 tablespoons finely chopped dill
- 1 tablespoon white wine vinegar
- 1 tablespoon extra-virgin olive oil
- salt and freshly ground black pepper to taste

Blanch the carrots and corn in a large pot of salted, boiling water for 2 minutes. Drain well and transfer to a large salad bowl. • Cook the rice in the same pot for 15–20 minutes, or until tender. • Drain well and let cool completely. • Stir the rice into the bowl with the vegetables. Add the yogurt and dill. • Drizzle with the vinegar and oil. Season with the salt and pepper and serve.

*Summer salad*

remaining lemon juice and oil. • Toss well and serve.

## Green apple salad

*Serves: 4*
*Preparation: 15 minutes*
*Recipe grading: easy*

- 2 large green apples, cored and thinly sliced
- 1 small curly-leaved lettuce
- 4 oz/125 g Parmesan cheese, flaked
- $^1/_2$ cup/125 g raspberries
- $^1/_2$ cup/50 g walnuts, shelled
- juice of 1 lemon
- 4 tablespoons extra-virgin olive oil
- salt and freshly ground white pepper to taste

Arrange the apple slices around the outer edge of a large serving plate. • Rinse the lettuce thoroughly under cold running water and dry well. Coarsely chop the lettuce and place in the center of the plate. Sprinkle with the Parmesan, raspberries, and walnuts. • Drizzle with the lemon juice and oil. Season with the salt and pepper and serve.

## Cheese and grape salad

*Serves: 4*
*Preparation: 15 minutes*
*Recipe grading: easy*

- 10 oz/300 g grapes
- 6 oz/180 g firm goat's cheese, cut into small cubes
- 5 oz/150 g arugula/rocket
- salt and freshly ground black pepper to taste
- 4 tablespoons extra-virgin olive oil

Rinse the grapes thoroughly under cold running water and dry well. Place the grapes on a large serving plate. • Sprinkle with the cheese and arugula. • Season with the salt and pepper and drizzle with the oil. • Toss well and serve.

Green apple salad

## Apple and celery salad

*Serves: 4*
*Preparation: 20 minutes*
*Recipe grading: easy*

- 2 large tart apples, cored and cut in small cubes
- 4 tablespoons fresh lemon juice
- 1 large bunch celery
- 2 cloves garlic, peeled and finely chopped
- $^1/_2$ cup/90 g raisins
- 2 teaspoons cumin seeds
- 4 tablespoons finely chopped parsley
- 1 cup/150 g toasted, lightly salted nuts, such as

peanuts, almonds, or cashews
- salt and freshly ground black pepper to taste
- 6 tablespoons extra-virgin olive oil

Place the apple cubes in a salad bowl. Drizzle with 2 tablespoons of lemon juice to prevent them from turning brown. • Rinse the celery, dry well, and remove all the tough outer filaments. Cut into small pieces. • Add the garlic, raisins, cumin, parsley, and nuts. Season with the salt and pepper and drizzle with the

## Simple bean salad

*Serves: 4*
*Preparation: 15 minutes*
*Recipe grading: easy*

- 10 oz/300 g canned red kidney beans, drained
- 6 oz/180 g canned cannellini beans, drained
- 5 oz/150 g canned borlotti beans, drained
- salt and freshly ground black pepper to taste
- 4 tablespoons extra-virgin olive oil
- 1 tablespoon finely chopped basil

Mix the beans in a salad bowl. • Season with the salt and pepper and drizzle with the oil. • Sprinkle with the basil, toss well, and serve.

## Exotic salad with yogurt

*Serves: 4*
*Preparation: 20 minutes*
*Recipe grading: easy*

- 1 crisp lettuce
- flesh of $^1/_2$ fresh coconut, cut into small pieces
- $^1/_2$ cantaloupe/rock melon, cut into small pieces
- $^1/_2$ red bell pepper/capsicum, seeded, cored, and cut into small pieces

Dressing
- scant 1 cup/200 ml plain yogurt
- 6 tablespoons extra-virgin olive oil
- 1 small red chile pepper, thinly sliced
- $^1/_4$ teaspoon ground coriander seeds

Rinse the lettuce thoroughly under cold running water and dry well. Coarsely chop the lettuce and place in a salad bowl with the coconut, cantaloupe, and bell pepper. • Dressing: Beat the yogurt, oil, chile, and coriander in a small bowl until smooth and well blended. • Drizzle the dressing over the salad and serve.

## Fennel and apple salad

*Serves: 4*
*Preparation: 20 minutes*
*Recipe grading: easy*

Exotic salad with yogurt

Dressing
- $^1/_2$ cup/125 ml apple juice
- 3 tablespoons extra-virgin olive oil
- 2 tablespoons cider vinegar
- 1 teaspoon honey
- salt and freshly ground black pepper to taste

Salad
- 3 oz/90 g arugula/rocket
- 1 large tart apple, cut in 4, cored, and thinly sliced
- 1 fennel bulb, trimmed and thinly sliced
- $^1/_2$ cup/60 g walnuts, toasted

Dressing: Beat the apple juice, oil, vinegar, and honey in a small bowl until well blended. Season with salt and pepper. • Salad: Rinse the arugula thoroughly under cold running water and dry well. • Place the apple, fennel, and arugula in a salad bowl. • Drizzle with the dressing and toss well. • Transfer to individual serving plates, sprinkle with the walnuts, and serve.

## Seasonal salad with tomatoes

*Serves: 6*
*Preparation: 20 minutes*
*Cooking: 3 minutes*
*Recipe grading: easy*

- 1 crisp lettuce, well-washed and coarsely chopped
- 5 oz/150 g Feta cheese, cut into small cubes
- 10 cherry tomatoes, cut in half
- 10 oz/300 g green beans, cooked
- ¹/₂ cup/50 g black olives, pitted

Dressing
- 2 cloves garlic, finely chopped
- 1 tablespoon vinegar
- 6 tablespoons extra-virgin olive oil
- salt and freshly ground black pepper to taste

Place the lettuce in a salad bowl. Sprinkle with the Feta, tomatoes, green beans, and olives. • Dressing: Place the garlic, vinegar, and oil in a small bowl and beat with a whisk. Season with the salt and pepper. • Drizzle the dressing over the salad and toss well.

## Tabbouleh salad

*Serves 4–6*
*Preparation: 20 minutes + 1 hour to soak the bulgur*
*Recipe grading: easy*

- 4 oz/125 g bulgur wheat
- 4 oz/125 g finely chopped parsley
- 4 scallions/spring onions, finely chopped
- 20 leaves fresh mint, finely chopped
- 3 medium tomatoes, finely chopped
- salt and freshly ground black pepper to taste
- juice of 1 lemons
- 6 tablespoons extra-virgin olive oil

Place the bulgur in a bowl and cover with cold water. Let stand for 1 hour. • Drain well. • Transfer to a large salad bowl. • Add the parsley, scallions, mint, and tomatoes. • Season with the salt and pepper and drizzle with the lemon juice and oil. • Toss well and serve.

## Tomato couscous salad

*Serves: 6*
*Preparation: 20 minutes + 5 minutes to stand*
*Cooking: 15 minutes*
*Recipe grading: fairly easy*

- 3 cups/750 ml vegetable stock
- 10 oz/300 g instant couscous
- 2 scallions/spring onions, finely chopped
- 4 plum tomatoes, cut into small cubes
- 2 tablespoons finely chopped basil
- ¹/₂ cup/125 ml extra-virgin olive oil
- 4 tablespoons balsamic vinegar
- salt and freshly ground black pepper to serve

Bring the stock to a boil in a medium saucepan. Add to the couscous and let stand for 15 minutes, or until the couscous has absorbed the stock. • Transfer to a large bowl and break up the couscous with a fork. Let cool completely. • Stir in the scallions, tomatoes, basil, oil, and vinegar. Season with the salt and pepper and serve.

## Gado gado

*Serves: 6*
*Preparation: 20 minutes*
*Cooking: 25 minutes*
*Recipe grading: easy*

- 1 crisp lettuce
- 2 large cooked potatoes, sliced
- 7 oz/200 g lightly cooked green beans, sliced
- 7 oz/200 g shredded cabbage, blanched
- 5 oz/150 g fresh bean sprouts
- 15 cherry tomatoes, cut in half
- 3 hard-boiled eggs, shelled and sliced
- 1 onion, sliced
- 2 scallions/green onions, chopped
- 1–2 fresh red chile peppers, seeded and shredded
- 2 tablespoons finely chopped parsley
- 1 tablespoons extra-virgin olive oil
- 2 eggs, beaten
- ¹/₄ teaspoon salt
- ¹/₂ cup fresh pineapple chunks
- 1 cup shrimp crisps (optional)

Sauce
- 1 tablespoon soy sauce
- 1 tablespoon lemon juice
- 6 tablespoons crunchy peanut butter
- 1 teaspoon red pepper flakes
- ¹/₂ teaspoon salt
- 2 teaspoon sugar
- ³/₄ cup/180 ml thick coconut milk
- 2 tablespoons extra-virgin olive oil

Wash and dry the lettuce and use it to line a salad bowl. Arrange the potato, beans, cabbage, and bean sprouts on top. • Cover with alternate slices of tomato and hard-boiled egg and arrange the onion rings, scallions, and chile pepper on top. Sprinkle with the parsley. • Heat the oil in an omelet pan and pour in the beaten eggs, spreading thinly across the bottom. Cook until firm, then remove and set aside to cool. Cut into thin shreds and pile in the center of the salad. • Add the pineapple chunks and shrimp crisps, if liked, then toss all the ingredients gently (otherwise leave them separate). • To make the sauce, place all the sauce ingredients in a small, heavy-bottomed saucepan and bring to a boil, stirring constantly. Set aside to cool. • Pour over the salad or serve in a separate bowl.

Seasonal salad with tomatoes

# PASTA & GRAINS

Pasta, rice, and polenta—these foods form the basis of the famously healthy "Mediterranean diet." They are all subtle, almost bland in flavor, and team up perfectly with stronger-tasting sauces and toppings. We have also included a good range of some lesser-known Italian gnocchi (dumplings, usually made of potato, egg, and flour) which are simple to make and scrumptious to eat.

*Whole-wheat (or wholemeal) pasta has a delicious nutty flavor that works well with vegetables. The sauce for this dish is based on sautéed onions and zucchini (courgettes), with added zest coming from the chile peppers and basil. Pasta is now available in a wide variety of colors and flavors, including orange pumpkin pasta, red beet root pasta, brown chocolate pasta, green spinach pasta, and golden lemon pasta. Purists tend to snob many of these innovations, but they can be fun and certainly make an eyecatching change on the dinner table!*

Whole-wheat fusilli with onion and basil (see page 120)
Spaghetti with cherry tomatoes (see page 120)

118

*Olives have been a part of the healthy Mediterranean diet for thousands of years. Not only do they add flavor and verve to dishes, but they are also low in calories and high in important mono-unsaturated (healthy) fat. They also contain vitamins A, B1, B2, and C.*

## Spaghetti with cherry tomatoes

*Serves: 4*
*Preparation: 15 minutes*
*Cooking: 15 minutes*
*Recipe grading: easy*

- 2 lb/1 kg cherry tomatoes
- 2 cloves garlic, peeled but whole
- $^1/_2$ teaspoon red pepper flakes
- pinch of oregano
- 4 fresh basil leaves, torn
- 6 tablespoons extra-virgin olive oil
- salt to taste
- 1 lb/500 g spaghetti

Wash and dry the tomatoes, cut each one in half, and place in a bowl with the garlic, red pepper flakes, oregano, and basil. • Heat the oil in a large skillet (frying pan) over high heat and add the contents of the bowl. Cook for 5–6 minutes, gently stirring with a wooden spoon at frequent intervals. Season with salt and remove from heat. Do not overcook the tomatoes: they should still be firm and retain their skins at this stage. • Cook the spaghetti in a large pot of salted, boiling water for about 8–10 minutes. • Drain the spaghetti and add to the tomato mixture in the skillet. Cook for about 5 minutes more over high heat, stirring well, so that the tomato sauce is absorbed by the pasta as it finishes cooking. • Serve immediately.

## Cold spiral pasta with olive sauce

*Serves: 4*
*Preparation: 15 minutes*
*Cooking: 10–15 minutes*
*Recipe grading: easy*

- 1 lb/500 g spiral (or other short) pasta
- $^1/_2$ cup/125 ml extra-virgin olive oil
- 36 large green olives, pitted
- 1 fresh red chile pepper
- 1 bunch fresh parsley
- salt and freshly ground black pepper to taste
- mixed salad greens
- 6 oz/180 g green beans, boiled
- 4–6 small tomatoes
- $^1/_2$ yellow bell pepper/capsicum

Cook the pasta in a large pan of salted, boiling water until *al dente*. • Drain the pasta thoroughly and place in a large serving bowl. Toss with 2 tablespoons of oil and let cool. • Place the olives, chile pepper, parsley, and remaining oil in a food processor and chop finely. • Rinse and dry the salad greens and arrange in the bottom of a large salad dish. • Pour the olive sauce over the cooled pasta and toss well. • Place the pasta on top of the salad greens and garnish the dish with the beans, tomatoes, and bell pepper. • Serve at room temperature or, in summer, slightly chilled.

## Whole-wheat fusilli with onion and basil

*Serves: 4–6*
*Preparation: 15 minutes*
*Cooking: 20 minutes*
*Recipe grading: easy*

- 4 tablespoons extra-virgin olive oil
- 2 large white onions, thinly sliced in rings
- 1 fresh red chile pepper, finely chopped
- 4 tablespoons cold water
- 3 large zucchini/courgettes, cut in small cubes
- salt and freshly ground black pepper to taste
- 1 lb/500 g whole-wheat/wholemeal fusilli
- 6 tablespoons freshly grated Parmesan cheese
- 2–3 tablespoons fresh basil leaves, torn

Heat the oil in a large skillet (frying pan) and sauté the onions and chile for 2–3 minutes. Add the water and cook over medium-low heat until all the water has evaporated. • Add the zucchini and cook for 10–15 minutes more. Season with salt and pepper. • Meanwhile, cook the pasta in a large pan of salted, boiling water until *al dente*. • Drain the pasta, not too thoroughly, and add to the skillet with the sauce. Toss over high heat for 1–2 minutes, or until the water has evaporated. Add the Parmesan and basil and toss again. • Serve hot.

Cold spiral pasta with olive sauce

*Chile peppers work very well in many pasta dishes. They can add zip and zest to the bland flavor of the pasta while underlining the taste of the tomato or other main ingredient in the sauce. Healthwise, chile peppers are a good source of vitamins A, C, and E.*

## Bucatini in spicy eggplant sauce

*Serves: 4*
*Preparation: 20 minutes*
*Cooking: 30 minutes*
*Recipe grading: easy*

- 2 medium eggplants/aubergines
- 6 tablespoons extra-virgin olive oil
- salt and freshly ground black pepper to taste
- 2 large white onions
- 2 cloves garlic, finely chopped
- 4–6 medium tomatoes, peeled and coarsely chopped
- 1–2 fresh chile peppers, finely chopped
- 2 tablespoons capers, rinsed and dried
- 1 lb/500 g bucatini (or other long) pasta
- 6–8 fresh basil leaves, torn
- 2 oz/60 g Pecorino romano cheese, in shavings or flakes

Chop the eggplants into $^{1}/_{2}$-inch (1-cm) cubes. • Heat 4 tablespoons of oil in a large skillet (frying pan) and sauté the eggplants until tender, about 10 minutes. If the pan dries out too much during cooking add a little water. Season with salt and pepper and set aside. • Heat the remaining oil in a large skillet and sauté the onions and garlic until translucent. Add the tomatoes, chile peppers, and capers and cook over medium heat for 15–20 minutes. Add water from the pasta pot if the sauce dries out too much during cooking. • Meanwhile, cook the pasta in a large pan of salted, boiling water until *al dente*. • Drain the pasta, not too thoroughly, and add to the skillet with the eggplant and basil. Toss well until the moisture has all been absorbed, then sprinkle with the Pecorino. • Serve hot.

## Rigatoni with zucchini

*Serves: 4*
*Preparation: 10 minutes*
*Cooking: 25 minutes*
*Level of difficulty: easy*

- 1 lb/500 g rigatoni pasta
- 3 tablespoons butter
- 3 tablespoons extra-virgin olive oil
- 2 cloves garlic, finely chopped
- 6 zucchini/courgettes, sliced in thin wheels
- 1 teaspoon crushed red pepper flakes
- salt and freshly ground black pepper to taste
- 3 tablespoons finely chopped parsley
- $^{1}/_{2}$ cup/60 g freshly grated Parmesan cheese

Cook the rigatoni in a large pot of salted boiling water until *al dente*. • In a large skillet (frying pan) , sauté the garlic in the butter and oil until it starts to change color. Add the zucchini and red pepper flakes. Sauté over high heat until the zucchini begin to turn golden brown. • Lower heat, cover the pan with a lid, and simmer until the zucchini are just tender. Season with salt and pepper. • Drain the pasta and place in a heated serving dish. • Add the zucchini, parsley, and Parmesan, and toss well. • Serve hot.

## Spaghettini with garlic, oil, and chile pepper

*Serves: 4*
*Preparation: 3 minutes*
*Cooking: 10 minutes*
*Level of difficulty: 1*

- 1 lb spaghettini (thin spaghetti)
- 4 cloves garlic, finely chopped
- 2 tablespoons finely chopped parsley
- 1 dried red chile, crumbled
- $^{1}/_{2}$ cup/125 ml extra-virgin olive oil
- salt to taste

Cook the spaghettini in a large pot of salted, boiling water until *al dente*. • While the pasta is cooking, sauté the garlic, parsley, and chile in the oil in a small skillet (frying pan) over low heat until the garlic begins to change color. • Remove from heat and add 2 tablespoons of the cooking water from the pasta pot. Season with salt. • Drain the pasta and place in a heated serving dish. • Pour the sauce over the top and toss well. Serve hot.

Bucatini in spicy eggplant sauce

## Ruote with radicchio

*Serves: 6*
*Preparation: 10 minutes*
*Cooking: 35 minutes*
*Level of difficulty: easy*

- 6 heads red radicchio
- 4 tablespoons butter
- salt and freshly ground black pepper to taste
- 1¼ cups/310 ml heavy/double cream
- 1 quantity Béchamel sauce (see Mushroom cream with sherry, page 56)
- 1 lb/500 g ruote (wheels) or other short pasta shape
- 1 cup/125 g freshly grated Parmesan cheese

Preheat the oven to 350°/180°C/gas 4. • Rinse the radicchio heads thoroughly under cold running water. Dry, and slice lengthwise in quarters. Place in an ovenproof dish greased with the butter. Season with salt and pepper, and pour the cream over the top. Bake for 15 minutes. • Prepare the Béchamel sauce. • Cook the pasta in a large pot of salted, boiling water for half the time indicated on the package. • Mix the pasta with the Béchamel, and place in the ovenproof dish with the radicchio. Mix well. Sprinkle with the Parmesan. • Increase oven temperature to 400°F/200°C/gas 6. • Bake for 20 minutes, or until a golden crust has formed on top. • Serve hot, straight from the ovenproof dish.

## Ziti with cauliflower, raisins, and pine nuts

*Serves: 4*
*Preparation: 15 minutes*
*Cooking: 40 minutes*
*Level of difficulty: easy*

- 1 small cauliflower, about 1 lb/500 g
- salt and freshly ground black pepper to taste
- 1 lb/500 g ziti pasta
- 1 medium onion, thinly sliced
- 6 tablespoons extra-virgin olive oil

## Cannelloni with Ricotta and spinach filling in Béchamel sauce

*Serves: 4*
*Preparation: 40 minutes*
*Cooking: 20 minutes*
*Level of difficulty: fairly easy*

- 1 lb/500 g fresh or 10 oz/300 g frozen spinach
- 4 tablespoons butter
- 1 cup/250 g fresh Ricotta cheese
- 1 cup/125 g freshly grated Parmesan cheese
- 2 eggs
- salt and freshly ground black pepper to taste
- 1 quantity Béchamel sauce (see Mushroom cream with sherry, page 56)
- 12 store-bought cannelloni, spinach or plain

Preheat the oven to 400°F/200°C/gas 6. • Cook the spinach in a pot of salted water until tender (about 5-6 minutes). Drain, squeeze out excess moisture and chop finely. • Put half the butter in a skillet (frying pan) with the spinach. Season with salt and pepper. Cook briefly over high heat until the spinach has absorbed the flavor of the butter. • Transfer to a bowl and mix well with the Ricotta, half the Parmesan, and the eggs. Season with salt and pepper. • Prepare the Béchamel. • Cook the cannelloni in a large pot of salted, boiling water until half-cooked (about 5 minutes). Drain in a colander and pass under cold running water. Dry with paper towels and stuff with the Ricotta and spinach. • Line the bottom of an ovenproof dish with a layer of Béchamel and place the cannelloni in a single layer on it. Cover with the remaining Béchamel sauce. Sprinkle with the remaining Parmesan and dot with butter. • Bake for about 20 minutes, or until a golden crust has formed on top. Serve hot or warm.

- 3 tablespoons small seedless white raisins
- 3 tablespoons pine nuts
- ¼ teaspoon saffron, dissolved in 3 tablespoons hot water
- ½ cup/60 g freshly grated Pecorino cheese

Cook the cauliflower in a large pot of salted, boiling water until just tender. Remove the cauliflower with a slotted spoon, reserving the water. Divide the cauliflower into small florets. • Bring the water back to a boil and add the pasta. • Meanwhile, sauté the onion for 1–2 minutes in the oil in a large, heavy-bottomed saucepan. Add the raisins, pine nuts, and saffron. Stir for 2–3 minutes, then add the cauliflower and continue cooking over very low heat, stirring occasionally. • When the pasta is cooked *al dente*, drain and add to the cauliflower mixture. • Mix carefully, then place in a heated serving dish and sprinkle generously with pepper. • Sprinkle with the Pecorino and serve hot.

## Whole-wheat rigatoni with Pecorino cheese

- 1 lb/500 g whole-wheat/wholemeal rigatoni pasta
- 3 medium potatoes, peeled and cut in small dice
- 4 oz/125 g Pecorino cheese, chopped
- ½ cup/125 ml milk
- 4 tablespoons butter
- salt and freshly ground black pepper to taste
- ½ cup/60 g freshly grated Parmesan cheese

Cook the rigatoni and potatoes in a large pan of salted, boiling water until the pasta is *al dente*. • Place the Pecorino, milk, and butter in the top of a double boiler and cook until the cheese has melted. Season with salt and pepper. • Drain the pasta and potatoes and place in a heated serving dish. • Pour the cheese sauce over the pasta, sprinkle with the Parmesan and serve.

*Cannelloni with Ricotta and spinach filling in Béchamel sauce*

Watercress tagliolini with basil sauce

## Watercress tagliolini with basil sauce

*Serves: 4*
*Preparation: 50 minutes*
*Cooking: 5 minutes*
*Recipe grading: complicated*

- 8 oz/250 g watercress, cleaned
- 1²/₃ cups/250 g all-purpose/plain flour
- 1²/₃ cups/250 g whole-wheat/wholemeal flour
- ¹/₂ teaspoon salt
- ³/₄ cup/180 ml water
- 2¹/₂ oz/75 g fresh basil
- 4 tablespoons extra-virgin olive oil
- 3 oz/90 g cream cheese
- 3 tablespoons pine nuts
- 3 cloves garlic

Cook the watercress in a pan of salted, boiling water for 2–3 minutes. Drain well and finely chop in a food processor. • Place both flours and the salt in a large bowl. Add the watercress and gradually stir in the water a little at a time. You may not need it all. The dough should be reasonably firm. • Transfer the dough to a lightly floured work surface and knead for 7–8 minutes, or until smooth and elastic. • Roll the pasta using a pasta machine or by hand, then cut into tagliolini (thin ribbon pasta). • Place the basil, oil, cream cheese, pine nuts, and garlic in a food processor or blender and chop until smooth and creamy. Add a little hot water from the pasta pan if the sauce is too thick. • Cook the tagliolini in a large saucepan of salted, boiling water for 2–3 minutes, or until *al dente*. • Drain the pasta and place in a heated serving dish. Spoon the sauce over the top and toss gently.

## Spicy fusilli with eggplants

*Serves: 4*
*Preparation: 15 minutes*
*Cooking: 10–15 minutes*
*Recipe grading: easy*

- 6 tablespoons extra-virgin olive oil
- 2 cloves garlic, finely chopped
- 1 large eggplant/aubergine, cut in small cubes
- 1 fresh chile pepper
- salt and freshly ground black pepper to taste
- 1 lb/500 g fusilli (or other short) pasta
- 2 tablespoons salted capers, rinsed and dried
- 2 tablespoons finely chopped fresh oregano
- red pepper flakes, to taste
- 3 tablespoons pine nuts

Heat the oil in a large skillet (frying pan) and sauté the garlic for 5 minutes. • Add the eggplant and chile pepper and cook for 10 minutes, stirring often. Season with salt and pepper. • Meanwhile, cook the pasta in a large pan of salted, boiling water until *al dente*. • Drain the pasta thoroughly and place in the skillet with the eggplant. Add the capers, oregano, red pepper flakes, and pinoli. Toss well. • Serve hot.

## Penne with fresh Ricotta cheese

*Serves: 4*
*Preparation: 5 minutes*
*Cooking: 12 minutes*
*Level of difficulty: easy*

- 1 lb/500 g penne pasta
- 1 cup/250 ml hot milk
- 14 oz/400 g very fresh Ricotta cheese

- 1 tablespoon sugar
- 1 teaspoon ground cinnamon
- salt and freshly ground white pepper to taste
- 1 tablespoon finely chopped fresh marjoram

Cook the penne in a large pot of salted, boiling water until *al dente*. • Combine the milk with the Ricotta, sugar, cinnamon, salt, pepper, and marjoram. Beat with a fork until smooth and creamy. • Drain the pasta well and place in a heated serving dish. Toss with the sauce and serve hot.

## Spring spinach tagliatelle

*Serves: 4*
*Preparation: 10 minutes*
*Cooking: 15 minutes*
*Level of difficulty: fairly easy*

- 1 lb/500 g spinach tagliatelle pasta
- 1¼ cups/250 g fresh or frozen peas
- 4 oz/125 g Gorgonzola cheese, diced

- 1⅓ cups/325 ml light cream
- salt and freshly ground black pepper to taste
- 2 tablespoons finely chopped parsley
- ½ cup/60 g freshly grated Parmesan cheese

Cook the peas in a pot of salted, boiling water. Drain well and set aside. • Place the Gorgonzola and cream in a large heavy-bottomed pan over low heat. Stir until the cheese has melted. • Add the peas, and season with salt and pepper. • Cook the pasta in a large pot of salted, boiling water until al dente. Drain well and place in the pan with the sauce. • Add the parsley and Parmesan. Toss carefully and serve.

## Linguine with green beans and basil sauce

*Serves: 4*
*Preparation: 15 minutes*
*Cooking: 25 minutes*
*Level of difficulty: easy*

- 1½ lb/750 g green beans, cleaned and cut in lengths
- 3 medium new potatoes, peeled and diced
- 1 quantity Basil sauce (see Watercress tagliolini with basil sauce, page 126)
- 1 lb/500 g linguine pasta
- 4 tablespoons butter
- 4 tablespoons freshly grated Pecorino cheese
- 4 tablespoons freshly grated Parmesan cheese

Cook the beans and potatoes in a large pot of salted, boiling water until tender. Scoop out with a slotted spoon and use the same water to cook the pasta. • While the pasta is cooking, prepare the basil sauce. Add 2 tablespoons of boiling water from the pasta pot to make the basil sauce slightly more liquid. • When the pasta is cooked *al dente*, drain and place in a heated serving dish. Toss with the basil sauce, butter, and vegetables. Sprinkle with the cheeses, and serve hot.

Spicy fusilli with eggplants

## Neapolitan-style fusilli

*Serves: 4*
*Preparation: 10 minutes*
*Cooking: 25 minutes*
*Level of difficulty: easy*

- $^1/_2$ cup/125 ml extra-virgin olive oil
- 14 oz/400 g peeled and chopped ripe tomatoes
- 1 tablespoon finely chopped fresh oregano
- salt and freshly ground black pepper to taste
- 1 lb/500 g fusilli pasta
- 8 oz/250 g Mozzarella cheese, diced
- $^1/_2$ cup/60 g freshly grated Pecorino cheese

Cook the oil, tomatoes, oregano, salt, and pepper in a small, heavy-bottomed pan over medium heat for about 25 minutes, stirring frequently. • Remove from heat when the tomatoes begin to separate from the oil. • Meanwhile, cook the fusilli in a large pot of salted, boiling water until *al dente*. Drain well, toss with the sauce, and place in a heated serving dish. Sprinkle with the Mozzarella and Pecorino and toss well. Serve hot.

## Rigatoni with bell peppers

*Serves: 4*
*Preparation: 10 minutes*
*Cooking: 35 minutes*
*Level of difficulty: easy*

- 3 medium bell peppers/capsicums, mixed colors
- 1 large onion, finely chopped
- 2 cloves garlic, finely chopped
- $^1/_2$ cup/125 ml extra-virgin olive oil
- $1^1/_2$ cups/350 g peeled and chopped fresh tomatoes
- 10 basil leaves, torn
- 3 tablespoons boiling water
- salt and freshly ground black pepper to taste
- 2 tablespoons vinegar
- 6 anchovy fillets
- 1 lb/500 g rigatoni pasta

Cut the bell peppers in half, remove the stalks and seeds, and cut into strips about $^1/_4$ inch (6 mm) wide. • Sauté the bell peppers, onion, and garlic in the oil in a large skillet (frying pan) for 8–10 minutes. Add the tomatoes, basil, and boiling water. Season with salt and pepper. Simmer over medium heat for about 20 minutes, or until the bell peppers are tender. • Stir in the vinegar and anchovies, and cook over high heat for 2–3 minutes until the vinegar evaporates. Remove from heat. • Meanwhile, cook the pasta in a large pot of salted, boiling water until al dente. Drain well and place in a heated serving dish. • Pour the sauce over the top and toss well. Serve hot.

# Conchiglie with yogurt and herbs

*Serves: 4*
*Preparation: 15 minutes*
*Cooking: 10–15 minutes*
*Recipe grading: easy*

- 5–6 small, very fresh zucchini/courgettes, with flowers, if possible
- ¹/₂ cup/125 ml thick, full-cream yogurt
- 4 tablespoons finely chopped mixed fresh herbs (mint, marjoram, thyme, parsley, chives, etc)
- 2 tablespoons extra-virgin olive oil
- 2 cloves garlic, finely chopped
- pinch of freshly ground nutmeg
- salt and freshly ground black pepper to taste
- 4 tablespoons freshly grated Parmesan cheese
- 1 lb/500 g conchiglie (or other short) pasta

Rinse the zucchini and clean carefully by trimming one end and detaching the flower.
Tear the flower into large pieces and cut the zucchini lengthwise into very thin slices. • Place the yogurt, herbs, oil, garlic, nutmeg, salt, and pepper in a bowl and mix well. • Cook the pasta in a large pan of salted, boiling water until *al dente*. • Drain the pasta thoroughly and place in a large serving bowl. Add the zucchini and yogurt mixture and sprinkle with the Parmesan. • Toss well and serve.

# Fusilli with mushrooms

*Serves: 4*
*Preparation: 10 minutes*
*Cooking: 20 minutes*
*Level of difficulty: easy*

- 1 lb/500 g white mushrooms
- 3 cloves garlic, finely chopped
- 4 tablespoons extra-virgin olive oil
- 3 tablespoons finely chopped parsley
- salt and freshly ground black pepper to taste
- 1 lb/500 g fusilli pasta

Rinse the mushrooms under cold running water. Trim the stems and slice the stems and caps coarsely. • In a large skillet (frying pan), sauté two-thirds of the garlic in half the oil over medium heat until it begins to color. • Add the mushrooms and half the parsley, season with salt and pepper, and cook for 10–15 minutes, or until the mushrooms are tender. • Meanwhile, cook the fusilli in a large pot of salted, boiling water until *al dente*. Drain well and add to the skillet with the sauce. • Sprinkle with the remaining garlic and parsley and drizzle with the remaining oil. • Toss for 1–2 minutes, then serve.

## Baked whole-wheat tagliatelle

*Serves: 4*
*Preparation: 30 minutes*
*Cooking: 15 minutes*
*Recipe grading: fairly easy*

- 6 tablespoons butter
- 1 onion, finely chopped
- 1 carrot, cut in small cubes
- 7 oz/200 g fava beans/broad beans, hulled
- 5 oz/150 g peas
- salt and freshly ground black pepper to taste
- 2 cups/500 ml milk
- 2 tablespoons all-purpose/plain flour
- ¹/₂ cup/125 ml heavy/double cream
- freshly ground nutmeg to taste
- 1 lb/500 g whole-wheat/wholemeal tagliatelle
- 7 oz/200 g Emmental or Cheddar cheese
- ²/₃ cup/100 g freshly grated Parmesan cheese

Preheat the oven to 400°F/2900°C/gas 6. • Heat 2 tablespoons of butter in a large skillet (frying pan) and sauté half the onion with the carrot, fava beans, and peas for 5 minutes. Season with salt and pepper. • Melt 2 more tablespoons of butter in a saucepan and sauté the remaining onion until translucent. • Stir in the flour, then gradually begin adding the milk, stirring constantly. Bring to a boil and cook over low heat for 5 minutes. • Remove from heat and stir in the cream and nutmeg. • Cook the tagliatelle in a large pan of salted, boiling water until *al dente*. • Drain well and place in a large bowl. Add the vegetables, the cream sauce, and the Emmental or Cheddar, and mix carefully. • Grease a large baking dish with the remaining butter, pour in the mixture, and sprinkle with the Parmesan. • Bake for 15 minutes, or until the Parmesan is nicely browned. • Serve hot.

Baked whole-wheat tagliatelle

## Fettuccine in aromatic vegetable sauce

*Serves: 4*
*Preparation: 15 minutes*
*Cooking: 25 minutes*
*Level of difficulty: easy*

- 4 tablespoons extra-virgin olive oil
- 2 stalks celery, 2 carrots, 2 large onions, small bunch parsley, 2 cloves garlic, all finely chopped
- 1 cup/250 ml dry white wine
- 2 drained canned tomatoes, coarsely chopped
- salt and freshly ground black pepper to taste
- 1 lb/500 g fettuccine pasta
- 1 cup/125 g freshly grated Parmesan cheese

Heat the oil in a large, heavy-bottomed saucepan. Add the celery, carrots, onions, parsley, and garlic and sauté for 10 minutes, or until light golden brown. • Pour in the wine and cook until it has evaporated. • Add the tomatoes and simmer for 10 minutes, adding a little hot water to moisten if necessary. The mixture should be just thick enough to form a light, coating sauce for the pasta. Season with salt and pepper. • Cook the fettuccine in a large pot of salted, boiling water until *al dente*. Drain well, transfer to the pan with the sauce, and toss carefully with the Parmesan. Serve hot.

## Tagliatelle with walnut sauce

*Serves: 4*
*Preparation: 15 minutes*
*Cooking: 10 minutes*
*Level of difficulty: easy*

- ¹/₃ cup/60 g pine nuts
- 1 lb/500 g walnuts, in their shells
- 2 cloves garlic
- 1 cup/100 g finely chopped parsley
- ¹/₂ cup/125 ml extra-virgin olive oil
- salt to taste
- 1 lb/500 g fresh tagliatelle

Preheat the oven to 350°F/180°C/gas 4. Roast the pine nuts in the oven for 5–10 minutes, or until light gold. • Shell the walnuts and chop finely in a food processor with the pine nuts, garlic, parsley, and oil. Season with salt. • Cook the pasta in a large pot of salted, boiling water until *al dente*. • Drain and place in a heated serving dish. Cover with the sauce, toss carefully, and serve hot.

## Tagliolini with artichokes and eggs

*Serves: 4*
*Preparation: 15 minutes*
*Cooking: 30 minutes*
*Level of difficulty: easy*

- 3 tablespoons finely chopped onion
- 5 tablespoons extra-virgin olive oil
- 16 frozen artichoke hearts, thawed
- salt and freshly ground black pepper to taste
- ¹/₂ cup/125 ml water
- 1 lb/500 g tagliolini pasta
- 3 very fresh large eggs
- ¹/₂ cup/60 g freshly grated Pecorino cheese

In a large skillet (frying pan), sauté the onion in the oil until soft. • Cut the artichokes in thin wedges and add to the skillet. Season with salt and pepper. Sauté for 2–3 minutes. • Pour in the water, cover, and cook for 20 minutes, or until the artichokes are tender. • Cook the pasta in a large pot of salted, boiling water until *al dente*. • Break the eggs into a large, heated serving dish, beat with a fork and add half the cheese. • Drain the pasta and toss with the egg, which will harden as it cooks. Toss with the artichokes, sprinkle with the remaining cheese, and serve.

## Tagliatelle with olives and mushrooms

*Serves: 4*
*Preparation: 10 minutes*
*Cooking: 20 minutes*
*Level of difficulty: easy*

- 2 cloves garlic, finely chopped
- 3 tablespoons finely chopped parsley
- ¹/₂ cup/125 ml extra-virgin olive oil
- 12 oz/350 g coarsely chopped mushrooms
- 1 cup/100 g coarsely chopped black olives
- 8 mint leaves, torn
- salt and freshly ground black pepper to taste
- 6 tablespoons boiling water
- 1 lb/500 g tagliatelle pasta

Combine the garlic and parsley in a skillet (frying pan) with the oil and sauté until the garlic begins to color. Add the mushrooms and cook until the liquid they produce has evaporated. • Add the olives, mint, salt, pepper, and boiling water. Simmer for 5 minutes. • Cook the tagliatelle in a large pot of salted, boiling water until *al dente*. Drain and place in a heated serving dish. Toss carefully with the sauce and serve.

Conchiglie with
saffron and broiled vegetables

## Conchiglie with saffron and grilled vegetables

*Serves: 4*
*Preparation: 20 minutes*
*Cooking: 30 minutes*
*Recipe grading: fairly easy*

- 1 large red bell pepper/capsicum
- $^1/_2$ large yellow bell pepper/capsicum
- 1 medium eggplant/aubergine
- 1 lb/500 g conchiglie pasta
- 1 teaspoon saffron threads
- 2 tablespoons finely chopped marjoram
- 4 tablespoons extra-virgin olive oil
- salt and freshly ground black pepper to taste

Remove the seeds and core from the bell peppers, rinse well, and cut into strips. • Heat a grill pan and cook the bell peppers, turning often, until tender, about 10 minutes. • Cut the eggplant lengthwise in slices about $^1/_2$-inch (1-cm) thick. • Cook the slices in the grill pan, browning on both sides. Remove from heat and cut into squares. • Cook the pasta in a large pan of salted, boiling water until *al dente*. • Drain well and transfer to a large serving bowl. Add the grilled vegetables, saffron, marjoram, oil, salt, and pepper. Toss well and serve.

## Penne with summertime sauce

*Serves: 4*
*Preparation: 5 minutes*
*Cooking: 12 minutes*
*Level of difficulty: easy*

- 1 lb/500 g penne pasta
- 10 large ripe tomatoes
- 2 cloves garlic, finely chopped
- 4 tablespoons extra-virgin olive oil
- salt to taste
- 6 oz/180 g Mozzarella cheese, diced
- 1 tablespoon pickled capers, drained
- 12 fresh basil leaves, torn

Cook the penne in a large pot of salted, boiling water until *al dente*. • Peel the tomatoes and chop into bite-sized chunks. Drain off the extra liquid they produce. Place the tomatoes in a serving bowl. Add the garlic and oil and season with salt. • Drain the pasta well and toss with the tomato sauce. Sprinkle with the Mozzarella, capers, and basil, toss well, and serve hot.

## Vegetarian lasagne

*Serves: 6*
*Preparation: 30 minutes + 2 hours to soak soya*
*Cooking: 2 hours*
*Level of difficulty: fairly easy*

- 1 lb/500 g dehydrated tofu pieces
- 2 tablespoons extra-virgin olive oil
- 1 carrot, finely chopped
- 1 stalk celery, finely chopped
- 1 onion, finely chopped
- 1 clove garlic, finely chopped

- 2 tablespoons finely chopped parsley
- $^1/_2$ cup/125 ml dry red wine
- 2 cups/500 g chopped tomatoes
- 1 lb/500 g lasagne
- 2 tablespoons butter
- 1 cup/125 g freshly grated Parmesan cheese
- 1 quantity Béchamel sauce (see Mushroom cream with sherry, page 56)

Place the dehydrated soya in a bowl and cover with cold water. Let soak for 2 hours. Heat the oil in a large skillet (frying pan) and sauté the carrot, celery, onion, garlic, and parsley for 7–8 minutes. • Add the red wine and cook until evaporated. • Add the tomatoes, season with salt and pepper and simmer over low heat for $1^1/_2$ hours. • Preheat the oven to 400°F/200°C/gas 6. • Cook the lasagne 4–5 sheets at a time in a large pot of salted, boiling water for about 2 minutes. Remove with a slotted spoon, plunge into a bowl of cold water to stop the cooking process. Remove quickly, and rinse gently under cold running water. Lay the

sheets out separately on clean cloths to dry. • Prepare the Béchamel and combine with the soya sauce. • Smear the bottom of a large oval baking dish with butter. Line with a single layer of cooked lasagne sheets. Cover with a thin layer of soya and Béchamel sauce. Sprinkle with grated Parmesan, followed by another layer of lasagne. Repeat until there are at least 6 layers. Leave enough sauce to spread a thin layer on top. Sprinkle with Parmesan and add the butter. • Bake for 15–20 minutes, or until golden brown. • Let stand for 10 minutes before serving.

## Walnut lasagne

*Serves: 6*
*Preparation: 30 minutes*
*Cooking: 25 minutes*
*Level of difficulty: fairly easy*

- $^1/_3$ cup/60 g pine nuts
- 1 lb/500 g walnuts, in their shells
- 2 cloves garlic

- 1 cup/100 g parsley
- $^1/_2$ cup/125 ml extra-virgin olive oil
- salt to taste
- 1 lb/500 g lasagne
- 1 quantity Béchamel sauce (see Mushroom soup with sherry, page 56)
- 1 cup/125 g freshly grated Parmesan cheese

Preheat the oven to 350°F/180°C/gas 4. • Roast the pine nuts in the oven for 5–10 minutes, or until lightly browned. Set aside to cool. • Shell the walnuts and combine in a food processor with the pine nuts, garlic, parsley, and oil. Chop finely. Season with salt. • Cook the lasagne sheets and prepare the Béchamel sauce. • Continue in exactly the same way as for Vegetarian lasagne (see recipe on this page).

transfer to a large serving bowl. Add the pecan sauce and the Parmesan and toss well. • Serve hot.

## Penne with artichokes

*Serves: 4*
*Preparation: 30 minutes*
*Cooking: 30 minutes*
*Level of difficulty: easy*

- 6 artichokes
- juice of 1 lemon
- 4 tablespoons extra-virgin olive oil
- 2 cloves garlic, finely chopped
- salt and freshly ground black pepper to taste
- 2 tablespoons finely chopped parsley
- $^1/_2$ cup/125 g freshly grated Pecorino cheese
- 1 lb/500 g penne pasta

Trim the artichoke stems, discard the tough outer leaves, and trim the tops. Cut in half lengthwise and scrape any fuzzy choke away with a knife. Cut into wedges. Place in a bowl of cold water with the lemon juice. Soak for 15 minutes, then drain and pat dry with paper towels. • Heat the oil in a skillet (frying pan) and sauté the garlic until it begins to change color. Add the artichokes and cook over medium-low heat for about 25 minutes, or until the artichokes are tender. Add water if the oil has all been absorbed. Season with salt and pepper. • Meanwhile, cook the penne in a large pot of salted, boiling water until *al dente*. Drain well and add to the pan with the artichokes. • Toss over high heat for 2–3 minutes. Sprinkle with the parsley and Pecorino, and serve.

## Penne with raw zucchini and mint

*Serves: 4*
*Preparation: 10 minutes*
*Cooking 12 minutes*
*Level of difficulty: easy*

## Penne with pecan sauce

*Serves: 4*
*Preparation: 15 minutes*
*Cooking: 10–15 minutes*
*Recipe grading: easy*

- 6 tablespoons extra-virgin olive oil
- 1 medium white onion, coarsely chopped
- 1 lb/500 g penne (or other short) pasta
- 7 oz/200 g shelled pecans
- 2 tablespoons finely chopped parsley
- 2–4 tablespoons fresh cream
- salt and freshly ground black pepper to taste

Penne with pecan sauce

- 6 tablespoons freshly grated Parmesan cheese

Heat 2 tablespoons oil in a large skillet (frying pan) and sauté the onion for 5 minutes, or until translucent. Remove from heat and let cool a little. • Chop the pecans in a food processor with the remaining oil and parsley. • Stir in enough cream to obtain a thick sauce. Season with salt and pepper. • Meanwhile, cook the pasta in a large pan of salted, boiling water until *al dente*. • Drain the pasta thoroughly and

- 6 very fresh small zucchini
- 1 teaspoon fresh lemon juice
- salt and freshly ground black pepper to taste
- 4 tablespoons extra-virgin olive oil
- 6 fresh mint leaves
- 1 lb/500 g penne pasta
- 3 oz/90 g fresh Pecorino cheese, cut in small cubes

Cut the zucchini in julienne strips and place in a bowl (large enough to hold the pasta as well). Add the lemon juice, salt, pepper, oil, and mint leaves. Stir well and let sit for about 20 minutes. • Cook the pasta in a large pan of salted, boiling water until *al dente*. Drain well and place in the bowl with the zucchini. • Toss well, add the Pecorino cheese, toss again, and serve.

## Whole-wheat maltagliati with asparagus and peas

*Serves: 4*
*Preparation: 20 minutes + 30 minutes to rest*
*Cooking: 15 minutes*
*Recipe grading: fairly easy*

### Pasta
- 1 cup/150 g all-purpose/plain flour
- 2/3 cup/100 g whole-wheat/wholemeal flour
- 1 tablespoon sesame seeds
- 1 tablespoon poppy seeds
- 1 tablespoon extra-virgin olive oil
- 2 large eggs
- 1/2 teaspoon salt

### Sauce
- 4 tablespoons butter
- 1 lb/500 g asparagus tips, cut in 1/2 -inch/1-cm pieces
- 5 oz/150 g fresh or frozen peas
- 1/2 cup/125 ml heavy/double cream
- 2 tablespoons finely chopped parsley
- salt and freshly ground black pepper to taste

Whole-wheat maltagliati with asparagus and peas

Place both flours, the poppy seeds, and sesame seeds in a large bowl. Make a well in the center and add the oil, eggs, and salt. Use a wooden spoon to gradually incorporate the eggs and oil. Add 1–2 tablespoons of cold water if necessary and stir until the pasta is firm and well mixed. • Transfer to a lightly floured work surface and knead for 5 minutes, or until smooth and elastic. • Shape into a ball, wrap in a clean cloth, and set aside to rest for 30 minutes. • Roll the pasta out into thin sheets by hand or using a pasta machine. Cut the sheets into irregular diamond shapes. • Set a large saucepan of salted water over high heat and bring to a boil. • Sauce: Heat the butter in a large skillet (frying pan) and sauté the asparagus for 5 minutes. • Add the peas and 2–3 tablespoons of water from the pasta pot. Cook for 5–10 minutes, or until the peas are tender. • Cook the maltagliati in the boiling water until *al dente*. • Drain well and add to the pan with the asparagus along with the cream and parsley. Season with salt and pepper and toss well. • Serve hot.

Spinach and cheese gnocchi

# Spinach and cheese gnocchi

*Serves: 4–6*
*Preparation: 45 minutes + time to dry gnocchi*
*Cooking: 30 minutes*
*Recipe grading: fairly easy*

Gnocchi
- 4 medium potatoes
- 1$\frac{1}{2}$ lb/750 g fresh spinach
- 1 large egg yolk
- 1 cup/150 g all-purpose/plain flour

Sauce
- 8 oz/250 g Fontina cheese, cut in cubes
- $\frac{1}{2}$ cup/125 ml milk
- 6 tablespoons butter
- 6–8 fresh sage leaves
- salt and freshly ground black pepper to taste

Cook the potatoes with their skins on in a large saucepan of salted, boiling water until tender. • Drain and slip off their skins. • Trim the spinach and rinse well under cold running water. Cook in a saucepan of salted, boiling water until tender. Drain well, squeezing out any excess moisture. • Place the spinach and potatoes in a food processor or blender and chop finely. • Transfer to a bowl and stir in the egg yolk, flour, salt, and pepper, mixing well with a wooden spoon to obtain a firm dough. • Working quickly, scoop out pieces of dough and roll them into long sausage shapes about $\frac{1}{2}$-inch (1.5-cm) in diameter on a lightly floured work surface. Cut the sausage shapes into pieces about 1 inch (2.5 cm) long. Set the gnocchi out on a floured clean cloth. Let dry for at least 1 hour. • Cook the gnocchi in batches in a large pan of salted, boiling water. Let the gnocchi bob up to the surface, and then cook for 3–5 minutes more. Scoop them out with a slotted spoon, drain well, and place in a heated dish. Repeat until all the gnocchi are cooked. • While the gnocchi are cooking, place the cheese and milk in a saucepan over low heat and cook, stirring frequently, until the cheese has melted. • Melt the butter in a saucepan with the sage. • Pour the cheese mixture into the bottom of a serving dish and spoon the gnocchi over the top. Pour the butter and sage sauce over the top. Season with salt and pepper and serve. • Spoon a little of the cheese sauce on to your guests' plates as you serve the gnocchi.

# Carrot and potato gnocchi with arugula sauce

*Serves: 6–8*
*Preparation: 35 minutes + time to dry gnocchi*
*Cooking: 45 minutes*
*Recipe grading: fairly easy*

## Gnocchi
- 2 lb/1 kg carrots
- 1 lb/500 g potatoes
- 1 large egg
- 1$^{1}$/$_3$ cups/200 g all-purpose/plain flour
- salt and freshly ground white pepper to taste
- $^{1}$/$_4$ teaspoon freshly grated nutmeg

## Sauce
- 4 oz/125 g arugula/rocket
- 2 cloves garlic
- 4 tablespoons pine nuts
- $^{2}$/$_3$ cup/100 g freshly grated Pecorino romano cheese
- salt and freshly ground black pepper to taste
- $^{1}$/$_2$ cup/125 ml extra-virgin olive oil

Scrape the carrots and cook in a large pan of salted, boiling water until tender. • Cook the potatoes with their skins on in a large saucepan of salted, boiling water until tender. • Drain and slip off their skins. • Mash the carrots and potatoes together and let cool a little. • Stir in the egg, flour, salt, pepper, and nutmeg, mixing well with a wooden spoon to obtain a firm dough. • Working quickly, scoop out pieces of dough and roll them into long sausage shapes about $^{3}$/$_4$-inch (2-cm) in diameter on a lightly floured work surface. Cut the sausage shapes into pieces about 1 inch (2.5 cm) long. Set the gnocchi out on a floured clean cloth and leave for an hour or two to dry. • If liked (this is optional, and slightly tricky, but gives the gnocchi their characteristic shape), press each piece with your thumb onto the tongs of a fork and twist. The gnocchi will have fork marks on one side. • Sauce: Place the arugula, garlic, pine nuts, cheese, salt, and pepper in a blender or food processor and chop finely. Transfer to a bowl and gradually stir in the oil. • Cook the gnocchi in batches in a large pan of salted, boiling water. Cook the gnocchi until they bob up to the surface, and then for 5 minutes more. Scoop them out with a slotted spoon, drain well, and place in a warmed dish. Repeat until all the gnocchi are cooked. • Spoon the arugula sauce over the gnocchi. Toss gently and serve hot.

Carrot and potato gnocchi with arugula sauce

## Spinach gnocchi in sweet tomato sauce

*Serves: 4*
*Preparation: 45 minutes + time to dry gnocchi*
*Cooking: 45 minutes*
*Recipe grading: fairly easy*

• 1 quantity Spinach gnocchi (see page 136)
• 4 tablespoons butter
• 2 onions, cut in thin rings
• 1¹/₂ lb/750 g peeled and chopped tomatoes
• 1 teaspoon sugar
• salt and freshly ground black pepper to taste
• 1 cup/125 g freshly grated Parmesan cheese

Prepare the gnocchi. • Heat the butter in a large skillet (frying pan). Sauté the onions for 8–10 minutes, or until transparent. • Add the tomatoes and sugar and season with salt and pepper. Simmer the sauce over low heat for 35 minutes. • Cook the gnocchi in batches and transfer to a heated serving dish. • Spoon the tomato sauce over the top and toss very gently. • Serve hot.

## Buckwheat spaghetti

*Serves: 4*
*Preparation: 30 minutes + 30 minutes to rest*
*Cooking: 40 minutes*
*Recipe grading: fairly easy*

• 2¹/₂ cups/375 g buckwheat flour
• 1¹/₂ cups/ 225 g all-purpose/plain flour
• 3 eggs
• ¹/₂ cup/125 ml milk
• 8 oz/250 g potatoes, cut in small cubes
• 6 oz/180 g Savoy cabbage, shredded
• ²/₃ cup/180 g butter, melted
• 2 cloves garlic, finely chopped
• 4 leaves fresh sage
• salt and freshly ground black pepper to taste
• 1 cup/125 g freshly grated Parmesan cheese
• 6 oz/180 g Fontina cheese, thinly sliced

Spinach gnocchi with sweet tomato sauce

Preheat the oven to 350°F/180°C/gas 4. • Combine the flours in a large bowl. Add the eggs, milk, and salt and stir to obtain a firm dough. • Knead on a lightly floured work surface until smooth. Set aside for 30 minutes. • Roll the pasta out until about ¹/₈ inch (3 mm) thick. Roll the sheet of pasta loosely and cut into strips ¹/₂ inch (1 cm) wide and 3 inches (8 cm) long. • Bring a large saucepan of salted water to a boil and cook the potatoes and cabbage. Put the potatoes in 5 minutes before the cabbage. • When the potatoes are almost cooked, add the pasta. • When the vegetables and pasta are cooked, drain carefully. • Melt the butter with the garlic and sage in a small saucepan. Cook for 2 minutes. • Butter an ovenproof dish. Place a layer of potato, cabbage, and pasta in the bottom. Drizzle with a little butter, sprinkle with pepper and Parmesan, and cover with slices of Fontina. Repeat this layering process 2 or 3 times until all the ingredients are in the dish. Finish with a layer of Parmesan. • Bake for 25 minutes, or until golden brown on top.

## Baked tomatoes with pasta

*Serves: 4–6*
*Preparation: 20 minutes*
*Cooking: 40 minutes*
*Recipe grading: easy*

• 12 medium tomatoes, with stalks still attached
• 12 basil leaves
• 8 oz/250 g small, tubular pasta
• 2 tablespoons finely chopped parsley
• 6 tablespoons extra-virgin olive oil
• salt and freshly ground black pepper to taste

Preheat the oven to 350°F/180°C/gas 4. • Rinse the tomatoes and dry well. Cut a "hat" off the top of each and set aside. Use a teaspoon to hollow out the pulp and place it in a bowl. Place a basil leaf in the bottom of each tomato. • Cook the pasta in a medium pot of salted, boiling water for half the time indicated on the package. Drain well. • Combine the pasta, tomato pulp, parsley, and

3 tablespoons of the oil. Season with salt and pepper. • Stuff the hollow tomatoes with the mixture. • Grease an ovenproof dish with the remaining oil and arrange the tomatoes carefully inside. Put a "hat" back on each tomato. • Bake for 40 minutes.

## Baked pasta and eggplant

*Serves: 6*
*Preparation: 30 minutes + 1 hour for the eggplants*
*Cooking: 30 minutes*
*Recipe grading: fairly easy*

• 1 lb/500 g eggplant, thinly sliced
• 2 tablespoons coarse sea salt
• 2 cups/500 ml olive oil, for frying
• 1 lb/500 g rigatoni pasta
• salt and freshly ground white pepper to taste
• 4 cloves garlic, peeled and lightly crushed
• 4 tablespoons extra-virgin olive oil
• 1 lb/500 g firm ripe tomatoes, peeled and chopped
• 2 tablespoons butter
• 12 leaves fresh basil, finely chopped
• 1 cup/150 g fine dry bread crumbs
• 1 cup/125 g freshly grated Pecorino cheese

Preheat the oven to 350°F/180°C/gas 4. • Place the eggplant on a slanted cutting board. Sprinkle with the coarse salt and set aside for 1 hour. • Heat the frying oil in a skillet (frying pan) and fry the eggplant until golden brown. Drain on paper towels. • Cook the pasta in a large pot of salted, boiling water for half the time indicated on the package. Drain well and set aside. • Sauté the garlic in the extra-virgin olive oil until pale gold, then remove. • Add the tomatoes and basil, season with salt and pepper, and cook over medium heat for 10 minutes. • Butter an ovenproof dish. • Combine the pasta with the tomatoes and spoon a layer into the dish. Cover with a layer of eggplant. Repeat until the eggplant and pasta mixture are used up. Finish with a layer of eggplant. Sprinkle with the bread crumbs and cheese. • Bake for 20 minutes, or until golden brown. • Serve hot or warm.

Potato gnocchi with asparagus

## Potato gnocchi with asparagus

*Serves: 4*
*Preparation: 30 minutes + time to dry gnocchi*
*Cooking: 45 minutes*
*Recipe grading: fairly easy*

Gnocchi
• 2 lb/1 kg potatoes
• 1 cup/150 g all-purpose/plain flour
• 1 large egg
• $^1/_2$ teaspoon salt

Sauce
• 14 oz/450 g asparagus (tender green tips only), cut in small pieces
• 5 tablespoons butter
• 2 tablespoons all-purpose/plain flour
• 1 cup/250 ml milk
• $^2/_3$ cup/185 ml heavy/double cream
• salt and freshly ground black pepper to taste

• $^1/_4$ teaspoon freshly ground nutmeg
• $^1/_2$ cup/75 g freshly grated Parmesan cheese

Cook the potatoes with their skins on in a large saucepan of salted, boiling water until tender. • Drain and slip off their skins. Mash the potatoes and let cool. • Stir in the egg, flour, and salt to obtain a firm dough. • Scoop out pieces of dough and roll them into long sausage shapes about $^3/_4$ inch (2-cm) in diameter on a lightly floured surface. Cut the sausages into pieces about 1 inch (2.5 cm) long. Let dry for at least 1 hour. • Sauce: Cook the asparagus pieces in a saucepan of boiling water for 4-5 minutes. Drain well. • Sauté the asparagus for 3–4 minutes in half the butter. • Melt the remaining butter in a small saucepan and stir in the flour. • Gradually add the milk. Cook for 5 minutes. • Remove from heat. Add the cream, salt, pepper, nutmeg, and asparagus and chop in a food processor. •

Cook the gnocchi in batches in a large pan of salted, boiling water until they bob up to the surface, and then for 4–5 minutes more. Scoop them out with a slotted spoon, drain well, and place in a warmed dish. Repeat until all the gnocchi are cooked. • Spoon the sauce over the top and toss gently. Serve hot.

## Potato gnocchi baked in a pastry casing

*Serves: 6*
*Preparation: 40 minutes + time to dry gnocchi*
*Cooking: 1 hour*
*Level of difficulty: complicated*

• 1 quantity Potato gnocchi (see preceding recipe)
• 2 cups/300 g all-purpose/plain flour
• 2 egg yolks
• finely grated zest of 1 lemon
• $^1/_8$ teaspoon salt

- ¹/₂ cup/125 g butter, melted
- 1 quantity Béchamel sauce (see Mushroom cream with sherry, page 56)
- ³/₄ cup/90 g freshly grated Parmesan cheese

Prepare the potato gnocchi. • Preheat the oven to 400°F/200°C/gas 6. • Sift the flour into a bowl with the eggs, lemon zest, and salt. Add the butter and mix until the dough is moist and firm. Roll into a ball, cover with plastic wrap, and refrigerate for 1 hour. • Roll the dough out until it is about ¹/₂ inch (1 cm) thick. Grease the bottom and sides of a deep 10-inch (24-cm) ovenproof dish or springform pan and line with the dough. Prick well with a fork. Fill with pie weights or dried beans. • Bake for 20 minutes, or until the pastry is golden brown. • Cook the gnocchi in batches in a large pan of salted, boiling water until they bob up to the surface, and then for 4–5 minutes more. Scoop them out with a

slotted spoon and drain well. Repeat until all the gnocchi are cooked. • Prepare the Béchamel sauce. • Combine the gnocchi and Béchamel and mix gently. Spoon into the baking dish with the pastry. • Sprinkle with the Parmesan cheese. Bake for 10 minutes more. • Remove from the oven and slip the pastry casing containing the gnocchi out of the baking dish. • Serve hot.

## Potato gnocchi with radicchio sauce

*Serves: 4*
*Preparation: 30 minutes + time to dry gnocchi*
*Cooking: 45 minutes*
*Recipe grading: fairly easy*

- 1 quantity Potato gnocchi (see recipe page 140)
- 1 large head of red radicchio (Treviso is best), cleaned and coarsely chopped

- 2 cloves garlic
- 2 tablespoons pine nuts
- 4 tablespoons hulled walnut pieces
- salt and freshly ground black pepper to taste
- ²/₃ cup/100 g freshly grated Pecorino romano cheese
- ¹/₂ cup/125 ml extra-virgin olive oil

Prepare the potato gnocchi. • Place the radicchio, garlic, walnuts, pine nuts, cheese, salt, and pepper in a blender or food processor and chop finely. Transfer to a bowl and gradually stir in the oil. • Cook the gnocchi in batches in a large pan of salted, boiling water until they bob up to the surface, and then for 4–5 minutes more. Scoop them out with a slotted spoon, drain well, and place in a heated dish. Repeat until all the gnocchi are cooked. • Spoon the radicchio sauce over the gnocchi. Toss gently and serve hot.

Potato gnocchi with radicchio sauce

Rigatoni with peas and basil

## Rigatoni with peas and basil

*Serves: 4*
*Preparation: 15 minutes*
*Cooking: 10–15 minutes*
*Recipe grading: easy*

• bunch of fresh basil
• 6–8 fresh mint leaves
• 2 cloves garlic, finely chopped
• salt and freshly ground white pepper to taste
• 4 tablespoons freshly grated Ricotta salata cheese
• 6–8 tablespoons extra-virgin olive oil
• 1 lb/500 g rigatoni pasta
• 14 oz/400 g fresh or frozen peas

Rinse the basil and mint under cold running water. Remove any large stems and place in a food processor or blender with the garlic, salt, and pepper. Chop for 2–3 minutes, then add the cheese and chop finely. Transfer the sauce to a small bowl and gradually beat in enough of the oil to make a thick pesto sauce. • Meanwhile, cook the pasta and peas in a large pan of salted, boiling water until the pasta is cooked *al dente* and the peas are tender. • Drain the pasta and peas thoroughly and place in a large serving bowl. • Spoon the herb sauce over the top and toss well • Serve hot.

## Potato gnocchi with four-cheese sauce

*Serves: 6*
*Preparation: 20 minutes + time to dry gnocchi*
*Cooking: 30 minutes*
*Level of difficulty: fairly easy*

• 1 quantity Potato gnocchi (see recipe, page 140)
• 1 quantity Béchamel sauce (see Mushroom cream with sherry, page 56)
• 8 oz/250 g Fontina cheese, freshly grated
• 4 oz/125 g Gorgonzola cheese, coarsely chopped
• 4 oz/125 g Mascarpone cheese
• 1 cup/125 g freshly grated Parmesan cheese
• salt and freshly ground black pepper to taste

Prepare the potato gnocchi. • Prepare the Béchamel sauce. • When the Béchamel is ready, add the four cheeses and stir over low heat until they have melted and the sauce is smooth and creamy. Season with salt and pepper. • Cook the gnocchi in batches in a large pan of salted, boiling water until they bob up to the surface, and then for 4–5 minutes more. Scoop them out with a slotted spoon, drain well, and place in a heated dish. Repeat until all the gnocchi are cooked. • Pour the cheese sauce over the top. Toss gently and serve.

## Fried gnocchi

*Serves: 4*
*Preparation: 50 minutes*
*Cooking: 40 minutes*
*Level of difficulty: fairly easy*

• 5 egg yolks, + 1 whole egg, beaten
• 1 tablespoon sugar
• 1 cup/150 g potato flour

- 2 cups/500 ml whole milk
- 1 cup/250 g butter
- pinch each of nutmeg, cinnamon, and salt
- $^1/_4$ cup/30 g all-purpose/plain flour
- 1 cup/125 g fine dry bread crumbs
- $^1/_2$ cup/60 g freshly grated Parmesan cheese

Beat the egg yolks in a bowl with the sugar until smooth. • Place the potato flour in a heavy-bottomed saucepan. Gradually stir in the milk. Add the egg mixture, 2 tablespoons of the butter, the nutmeg, cinnamon, and salt. Mix well with a wooden spoon. • Place the pan over medium heat and, stirring constantly, bring to a boil. Boil over low heat for 10 minutes, stirring all the time. Remove from heat. • Turn the gnocchi batter out onto a flat work surface. Using a spatula dipped in cold water, spread it to about $^1/_2$ inch (1 cm) thick and leave to cool for 30 minutes. • Roll the batter into marble-sized balls. Dust with flour, drop them into the beaten egg, then roll them in the bread crumbs. • Heat the remaining butter in a large skillet

(frying pan) and fry until golden brown. • Place on a heated serving dish, sprinkle with Parmesan, and serve.

## Roman gnocchi with Gorgonzola

*Serves: 6–8*
*Preparation: 15 minutes*
*Cooking: 30 minutes*
*Recipe grading: fairly easy*

### Gnocchi

- 1$^1/_2$ quarts/1.5 liters milk
- 14 oz/400 g semolina
- 4 tablespoons butter
- 5 large egg yolks
- salt to taste

### Sauce

- 3 tablespoons butter
- 3 tablespoons all-purpose/plain flour
- 2 cups/500 ml hot milk
- salt and freshly ground black pepper to taste

- 8 oz/250 g Gorgonzola cheese, cut in small cubes
- 4 tablespoons freshly grated Parmesan cheese

Preheat the oven to 450°F/225°C/gas 7. • Gnocchi: Bring the milk to a boil in a medium saucepan. • Gradually pour the semolina into the milk, stirring all the time. Cook for 10–15 minutes, stirring constantly. • Remove from heat and stir the egg yolks in one at a time, followed by the butter and salt. The mixture should be thick, but still soft. Let cool a little. • Pour the gnocchi out onto a lightly oiled work surface and spread to about $^1/_2$ inch (1 cm) thick. Use a glass or cookie cutter to cut out rounds about 2 inches (5 cm) in diameter. • Arrange the gnocchi in an oiled baking dish, overlapping a little, roof-tile style. • Sauce: Melt the butter in a medium saucepan and stir in the flour. • Gradually add the milk and cook over low heat, stirring constantly, for 5 minutes. Season with salt and pepper. • Sprinkle the Gorgonzola over the gnocchi in the baking dish and pour the sauce over the top. Sprinkle with Parmesan. • Bake for 15 minutes, or until nicely browned.

## Baked polenta with tasty tomato topping

*Serves: 4*
*Preparation: 20 minutes*
*Cooking: 45 minutes*
*Recipe grading: easy*

- 1 lb/500 g package polenta
- 4 tablespoons extra-virgin olive oil
- 2 cloves garlic, finely chopped
- 14 oz/450 g fresh or canned tomatoes, peeled and chopped
- fresh basil leaves, torn
- salt and freshly ground black pepper to taste

Cook the polenta following the instructions on the package. If preferred, buy a fast cooking or precooked polenta so that cooking time is reduced to about 10 minutes. • Drizzle or spray a clean work surface with cold water and turn the hot polenta out onto it. Spread to about $1/2$ inch (1 cm) thick and leave to cool. • Preheat the oven to 400°F/200°C/gas 6. • Lightly oil a large baking dish. • Heat the oil in a large skillet (frying pan) and sauté the garlic for 5 minutes. Add the tomatoes and basil and cook for 20 minutes, or until reduced. Season with salt and pepper. • Use a glass or cookie cutter to cut out disks of polenta about 2 inches (5 cm) in diameter. • Arrange the polenta disks in the baking dish, overlapping them slightly roof-tile fashion. • Spoon the hot sauce over the top and sprinkle with the Parmesan. • Bake for 10–15 minutes, or until the cheese is lightly browned. • Serve piping hot straight from the oven.

## Polenta and beans

*Serves: 6*
*Preparation: 20 minutes + 12 hours to soak the beans*
*Cooking: 1 hour 45 minutes*
*Level of difficulty: easy*

- 1$1/3$ cups/330 g dried cranberry, borlotti, or pinto beans
- $1/2$ onion, finely chopped
- 1 tablespoon finely chopped fresh sage or rosemary
- salt and freshly ground black pepper to taste
- 2$1/4$ cups/330 g coarse-grain yellow cornmeal

Soak the beans overnight in a large bowl of water. • Sauté the onion in a large, heavy-bottomed saucepan. • Add the strained beans, sage or rosemary, and sufficient cold water to cover the beans (about 5 cups.1.25 liters). Bring to a boil, then cover and simmer gently for 1 hour. • When the beans are nearly done, add salt and pepper to taste and gradually stir in the cornmeal. • Cook slowly for 45 minutes, stirring continuously, and adding a little warm water now and then if necessary. The polenta should be fairly soft, not stiff. • Turn out onto a board or platter and serve.

## Polenta with leeks

*Serves: 4*
*Preparation: 15 minutes*
*Cooking: 1 hour*
*Level of difficulty: 1*

- 1 lb/500 g package polenta
- 1 lb/500 g leeks, (white part only)
- 3 tablespoons butter
- salt and freshly ground white pepper to taste
- 1$1/2$ cups/375 ml light cream
- 4 tablespoons milk

Cook the polenta following the instructions on the package. If preferred, buy a fast cooking or precooked polenta so that cooking time is reduced to about 10 minutes. • Cut the leeks into $1/8$-inch (3-mm) thick slices. • Melt the butter in a heavy-bottomed saucepan over medium heat, add the leeks, cover and cook for 5 minutes, or until the leeks have wilted. • Season with salt and pepper. Add the cream and milk and cook for 20–25 minutes. • When the polenta is done (it

should be very thick, almost stiff), turn it out onto a heated serving dish. • Serve hot with the leek sauce passed separately.

## Buckwheat polenta

*Serves: 4*
*Preparation: 25 minutes + 30 minutes to rest*
*Cooking: 1 hour*
*Level of difficulty: fairly easy*

- 1$3/4$ quarts/1.75 liters water
- 1 tablespoon coarse sea salt
- 1$1/3$ cups/200 g coarse-grain yellow cornmeal
- 1$1/3$ cups/200 g buckwheat flour
- $1/2$ cup/125 g butter
- 3 oz/90 g salted anchovy fillets, rinsed and boned
- 10 oz fresh Toma (or Fontina) cheese

Bring the water to a boil with the coarse salt. Sprinkle in the cornmeal and the buckwheat flour, stirring continuously with a whisk to prevent lumps forming. • Cook over medium heat, stirring almost continuously for about 40 minutes. • When the polenta is ready (it should be stiff), turn out onto a platter or cutting board and let cool for at least 30 minutes. • Preheat the oven to 400°F/200°C/gas 6. • Melt three-quarters of the butter in a small saucepan. • Use the remaining butter to grease a fairly deep ovenproof dish. • Cut the polenta into pieces about $3/4$ inch (2 cm) thick. Place a layer of polenta pieces (use about one-third) in the greased dish and sprinkle with one-third of the anchovies, sliced cheese, and melted butter. Repeat the operation, using half the remaining polenta, all the remaining anchovies and cheese, and about half the remaining melted butter. • Cover with a final layer of polenta and drizzle the remaining butter over the top. • Bake for 20 minutes, or until golden brown on top.

*Baked polenta with tasty tomato topping*

## Pistacchio risotto

*Serves: 4*
*Preparation: 15 minutes*
*Cooking: 25 minutes*
*Level of difficulty: fairly easy*

- 4 tablespoons butter
- 1 onion, finely chopped
- 5 oz/150 g pistacchios
- 2 cups/400 g short-grain rice (preferably Italian arborio)
- $^{1}/_{2}$ cup/125 ml dry white wine
- $1^{1}/_{2}$ quarts/1.5 liters vegetable stock (bouillon cube)
- 4 tablespoons freshly grated Parmesan cheese
- salt and freshly ground white pepper to taste

Melt half the butter in a large, heavy-bottomed saucepan. Add the onion and sauté over medium heat until transparent. • Add the pistacchios and rice, increase the heat, and stir for 2 minutes. • Pour in the wine, and stir until absorbed. • Stir in $^{1}/_{2}$ cup (125 ml) of the stock. Cook, stirring often, until the stock is absorbed. Continue adding the stock, $^{1}/_{2}$ cup (125 ml) at a time, stirring often until each addition is absorbed, until the rice is tender, 15–18 minutes. • Add the Parmesan when the rice is almost cooked. • Season with salt and pepper, add the remaining butter, and mix well. • Serve hot.

## Risotto with Gorgonzola cheese

*Serves: 4*
*Preparation: 10 minutes*
*Cooking: 25 minutes*
*Level of difficulty: easy*

- 2 tablespoons butter
- $^{1}/_{2}$ small onion, finely chopped
- 2 cups/450 g short-grain rice (preferably Italian arborio)
- $^{2}/_{3}$ cup/180 ml dry white wine
- $1^{1}/_{2}$ quarts/1.5 liters vegetable stock (bouillon cube)
- 10 oz/300 g Gorgonzola cheese, chopped
- salt and freshly ground white pepper to taste
- $^{1}/_{3}$ cup/70 g freshly grated Parmesan cheese

Melt the butter in a large, heavy-bottomed saucepan. • Add the onion and sauté until soft. • Add the rice and cook, stirring constantly, for 2 minutes. • Pour in the wine and when it has been absorbed, stir in $^{1}/_{2}$ cup (125 ml) of the stock. Cook, stirring often, until the stock is absorbed. Continue adding the stock, $^{1}/_{2}$ cup (125 ml) at a time, stirring often until each addition is absorbed, until the rice is tender, 15–18 minutes. • About 3–4 minutes before the rice is ready, add the Gorgonzola and mix well. Season with salt and pepper. • Add the Parmesan and serve.

## Orange risotto with Fontina cheese

*Serves: 4*
*Preparation: 15 minutes*
*Cooking: 20 minutes*
*Level of difficulty: easy*

- 2 large unwaxed oranges
- 1 small onion, finely chopped
- $^{1}/_{2}$ cup/125 g butter
- 2 cups short-grain rice (preferably Italian arborio)
- $^{1}/_{2}$ cup/125 ml dry white wine
- $1^{1}/_{2}$ quarts/1.5 liters vegetable stock (bouillon cube)
- 4 oz/125 g Fontina cheese, diced
- salt and freshly ground white pepper to taste

Peel the oranges, taking care to use only the outermost, orange layer. Chop the peel in tiny dice. Squeeze the juice and set aside. • In a heavy-bottomed pan, sauté the onion in three-quarters of the butter until soft. • Add the rice and cook for 2 minutes, stirring constantly. • Pour in the wine, and

when it has been absorbed, stir in $^{1}/_{2}$ cup (125 ml) of the stock. Cook, stirring often, until the stock is absorbed. Continue adding the stock, $^{1}/_{2}$ cup (125 ml) at a time, stirring often until each addition is absorbed, until the rice is tender, 15–18 minutes. Stir in the Fontina cheese and orange peel 5 minutes before the rice is cooked. • Just before removing from heat, season with salt and pepper and pour in the orange juice. Stir well and serve.

## Asparagus risotto

*Serves: 4*
*Preparation: 15 minutes*
*Cooking: 25 minutes*
*Level of difficulty: fairly easy*

- $1^{3}/_{4}$ lb/800 g asparagus
- 4 tablespoons butter
- 1 small onion, finely chopped
- 2 cups/450 g short-grain rice (preferably Italian arborio)
- $^{1}/_{2}$ cup/125 ml dry white wine
- 6 cups vegetable stock (bouillon cube)
- $^{1}/_{3}$ cup/70 g freshly grated Parmesan cheese
- salt and freshly ground white pepper to taste

Rinse the asparagus and trim the white part off the stalks. Cut the green tips in 2 or 3 pieces. • Melt three-quarters of the butter in a deep, heavy-bottomed saucepan. Add the onion and sauté for 1 minute. Add the asparagus and sauté for 5 minutes. • Add the rice and pour in the wine. Stir well. • When the wine has been absorbed, stir in $^{1}/_{2}$ cup (125 ml) of the stock. Cook, stirring often, until the stock is absorbed. Continue adding the stock, $^{1}/_{2}$ cup (125 ml) at a time, stirring often until each addition is absorbed, until the rice is tender, 15–18 minutes. • Add the remaining butter and the Parmesan. Mix well. • Season with salt and pepper and serve.

*Pistachio risotto*

## Apple and zucchini risotto

*Serves: 4–6*
*Preparation: 15 minutes*
*Cooking: 20 minutes*
*Recipe grading: easy*

• 2 tablespoons extra-virgin olive oil
• 1 large onion, finely chopped
• 1 small red bell pepper, cut in small squares
• 2 large zucchini/courgettes, cut in small cubes
• 2 cups/400 g short-grain rice
• 3 cups/750 ml vegetable stock (bouillon cube)
• 2 tart-tasting apples (Granny Smiths are ideal), peeled, cored, and thinly sliced, drizzled with 4 tablespoons fresh lemon juice (to stop them from turning brown)
• 4 small potatoes, cut in small cubes
• 2 teaspoons curry powder
• 1 teaspoon saffron threads
• 2 tablespoons chopped fresh dill
• salt and freshly ground black pepper to taste

Heat the oil in a large skillet (frying pan) and sauté the onion, bell pepper, and zucchini over medium heat for 5 minutes. • Increase the heat to high and add the rice. Cook for 2 minutes, stirring constantly. • Begin stirring in the stock, $^1/_2$ cup (125 ml) at a time. After about 8 minutes, add the apples and potatoes. Add more stock and cook and stir until each addition has been absorbed, until the rice and potatoes are tender, about 15–18 minutes. • Just before the rice is cooked, add the curry powder, saffron, and dill. Season with salt and pepper and stir well. • Serve hot.

## Artichoke risotto

*Serves: 4*
*Preparation: 20 minutes*
*Cooking: 30 minutes*
*Level of difficulty: easy*

• 6 artichokes
• juice of 1 lemon

Apple and zucchini risotto

• 3 tablespoons butter
• 1 small onion, finely chopped
• 2 cups/400 g short-grain rice (preferably Italian arborio)
• 1$^1/_2$ quarts/1.5 liters vegetable stock (bouillon cube)
• salt and freshly ground black pepper to taste
• 2 tablespoons finely chopped parsley
• $^1/_2$ cup/70 g freshly grated Pecorino cheese

Trim the artichokes stems, cut off the tops, and discard the tough outer leaves. Cut in half and remove the fuzzy chokes. Soak in a bowl of cold water with the lemon juice for 10 minutes. • Melt the butter in a large, heavy-bottomed saucepan. Add the onion and sauté until soft. • Drain the artichokes, slice thinly, and add to the onion. Sauté for 5 more minutes. • Add the rice and cook for 2 minutes. Increase the heat slightly. Stir in $^1/_2$ cup (125 ml) of the stock. Cook, stirring often, until the stock is absorbed. Continue adding the stock, $^1/_2$ cup (125 ml) at a time, stirring often until each addition is absorbed, until the rice is tender, 15–18 minutes. Season with salt and pepper. • Add the parsley and Pecorino, stir well, and serve.

## Rice with artichokes and peas

*Serves: 4*
*Preparation: 10 minutes*
*Cooking: 25 minutes*
*Level of difficulty: easy*

• 12 frozen artichoke hearts, thawed
• 1 lemon
• 1 medium onion, thinly sliced
• 4 tablespoons extra-virgin olive oil
• 1–2 cloves garlic, finely chopped
• 1 cup/180 g peas, fresh or frozen
• salt and freshly ground black pepper to taste
• about $^1/_2$ cup/125 ml water
• 2 cups/450 g short-grain rice (preferably Italian arborio)
• $^1/_2$ cup/70 g freshly grated Pecorino cheese

Cut the thawed artichoke hearts in halves or quarters. • Sauté the onion in the oil. Add the garlic, cook for 1 minute. • Add the artichokes and peas. Season with salt and pepper and moisten with half the water. Cook until the water has been absorbed. • Add the rice and stir for 1 minute, then add the remaining water. Stir in $^1/_2$ cup (125 ml) of the stock. Cook, stirring often, until the stock is absorbed. Continue adding the stock, $^1/_2$ cup (125 ml) at a time, stirring often until each addition is absorbed, until the rice is tender, 15–18 minutes. • Sprinkle with the cheese and serve.

## Eggplant risotto

*Serves: 4*
*Preparation: 10 minutes + 1 hour for the eggplants*
*Cooking: 25 minutes*
*Level of difficulty: easy*

• 2 large eggplants/aubergines
• 2 tablespoons coarse sea salt
• 3 cloves garlic, finely chopped
• 2 tablespoons finely chopped parsley
• 6 tablespoons extra-virgin olive oil
• 2 cups/400 g short-grain rice (preferably Italian arborio)
• 1$^1/_4$ quarts/125 liters vegetable stock (bouillon cube)
• salt and freshly ground black pepper to taste

Rinse the eggplants and cut in cubes. Sprinkle with the coarse salt and place on a slanted cutting board for 1 hour to degorge. • Sauté the garlic and parsley in the oil in a heavy-bottomed pan. • Add the eggplant and cook over medium heat until the eggplants are soft. • Add the rice and cook for 2 minutes, stirring constantly • Stir in $^1/_2$ cup (125 ml) of the stock. Cook, stirring often, until the stock is absorbed. Continue adding the stock, $^1/_2$ cup (125 ml) at a time, stirring often until each addition is absorbed, until the rice is tender, 15–18 minutes. • Season with salt and pepper and serve hot.

Brown rice pilaf
with leeks

## Brown rice pilaf with leeks

*Serves: 4*
*Preparation: 30 minutes*
*Cooking: 25 minutes*
*Level of difficulty: easy*

- 1 lb/500 g leeks, cut in wheels
- 1 quantity Béchamel sauce (see Mushroom cream with sherry, page 56)
- 1 small onion, finely chopped
- 4 tablespoons butter
- $^1/_2$ teaspoon saffron threads
- $1^1/_2$ cups/350 g brown rice
- 3 cups/750 ml vegetable stock (bouillon cube)
- salt and freshly ground black pepper to taste

Cook the leeks in salted, boiling water for 5–10 minutes, or until tender. Drain well. • Heat the butter in a large heavy-bottomed saucepan over medium heat. Add the onion and sauté until translucent. • Add the rice and stir over high heat for 2 minutes. • Add the stock and saffron and bring to a boil. Season with salt and pepper. Cover the pan with a piece of aluminum foil and simmer over low heat for about 25 minutes, or until the stock has all been absorbed and the rice is tender. • Prepare the Béchamel sauce and stir the leeks into it. • Place the pilaf on a heated serving dish and spoon the leek sauce over the top. • Serve hot.

## Strawberry risotto

*Serves: 4*
*Preparation: 15 minutes*
*Cooking: 25 minutes*
*Level of difficulty: fairly easy*

- 1 small onion, cut in 4 or 6 pieces
- 2 tablespoons extra-virgin olive oil
- 2 cups/400 g short-grain rice (preferably Italian arborio)
- 4 tablespoons dry white wine
- 1 quart/1 liter vegetable stock (bouillon cube)
- 12 oz/350 g fresh strawberries
- 2 tablespoons butter
- 2 tablespoons freshly grated Parmesan cheese
- 2 tablespoons heavy/double cream

Sauté the onion in the oil in a large frying pan over medium heat until soft. Discard the onion. • Add the rice and cook for 2 minutes, stirring constantly. Pour in the wine and cook until it evaporates. Stir in $^1/_2$ cup (125 ml) of the stock. Cook, stirring often, until the stock is absorbed. Continue adding the stock, $^1/_2$ cup (125 ml) at a time, stirring often until each addition is absorbed, until the rice is tender, 15–18 minutes. • Meanwhile, wash, clean and slice the strawberries, reserving 6 whole ones. Add the sliced strawberries to the rice 5 minutes before the end of cooking time. • When the rice is cooked, remove from heat and stir in the butter, Parmesan and cream. Garnish with the whole strawberries and serve.

## Onion and Parmesan risotto

*Serves 4*
*Preparation: 5 minutes*
*Cooking: 25 minutes*
*Recipe grading: easy*

- 4 tablespoons butter
- 2 tablespoons very finely chopped onion
- 2 cups/400 g short-grain rice (preferably Italian arborio)
- $^1/_2$ cup/125 ml dry white wine
- 1 quart/1 liter vegetable stock (bouillon cube)
- $^3/_4$ cup/90 g freshly grated Parmesan cheese
- salt and freshly ground white pepper to taste
- 3 tablespoons extra-virgin olive oil

Melt half the butter in a heavy-bottomed saucepan. Add the onion and sauté until transparent. • Add the rice and cook over high heat, stirring continuously, for 2 minutes. • Add the wine and cook until it has evaporated. Stir in $^1/_2$ cup (125 ml) of the stock. Cook, stirring often, until the stock is absorbed. Continue adding the stock, $^1/_2$ cup (125 ml) at a time, stirring often until each addition is absorbed, until the rice is tender, 15–18 minutes. • Stir in half the Parmesan and season with salt and pepper to taste. • Turn off the heat, cover tightly and let stand for 2 minutes. • Dot the surface of the rice with the remaining butter, in thin slivers. Sprinkle with the remaining cheese and stir quickly but gently. • Add the oil and stir once more. • Serve hot.

## Mushroom risotto

*Serves: 4*
*Preparation: 20 minutes + 20 minutes to soak*
*Cooking: 25 minutes*
*Level of difficulty: easy*

- 1 oz/30 g dried porcini mushrooms
- 1 cup/250 ml warm water
- 4 tablespoons extra-virgin olive oil
- 1 small onion, finely chopped
- $^1/_2$ cup/125 ml dry white wine
- 2 cups/400 g short-grain rice (preferably Italian arborio)
- 1$^1/_2$ quarts/1.5 liters vegetable stock (bouillon cube)
- 2 tablespoons finely chopped parsley
- salt and freshly ground black pepper to taste

Soak the mushrooms in the water for 20 minutes. Drain, reserving the water, and chop coarsely. • Heat the oil in a large, heavy-bottomed saucepan over medium heat. Add the onion and sauté until transparent. • Add the mushrooms and sauté for 2–3 minutes. • Add the rice and cook for 2 minutes, stirring constantly. • Add the wine and cook until it has evaporated. Stir in the mushroom water. • Stir in $^1/_2$ cup (125 ml) of the stock. Cook, stirring often, until the stock is absorbed. Continue adding the stock, $^1/_2$ cup (125 ml) at a time, stirring often until each addition is absorbed, until the rice is tender, 15–18 minutes. • Season with salt and pepper. • Add the parsley, mix well, and serve hot.

Onion and Parmesan risotto

## Golden mushroom polenta

*Serves: 4*
*Preparation: 5 minutes*
*Cooking: 50 minutes*
*Level of difficulty: fairly easy*

- 1 lb/500 g package polenta
- 1 lb/500 g mixed wild mushrooms
- 6 tablespoons extra-virgin olive oil
- 1 onion, finely chopped
- 2 tablespoons finely chopped parsley
- 6 fresh sage leaves, finely chopped
- 2 cups/500 ml oil, for frying

Cook the polenta following the instructions on the package. If preferred, buy a fast cooking or precooked polenta so that cooking time is reduced to about 10 minutes. • While the polenta is cooking, clean the mushrooms, rinse under cold running water and chop coarsely. • Heat the oil in a large skillet (frying pan) and sauté the onion until soft. • Add the mushrooms, parsley and sage, and cook over medium heat for 10 minutes, stirring frequently. • Add the mushroom mixture to the polenta just before the polenta is cooked. • Dampen a clean work surface and spread the mixture out in a layer about $^1/_2$ inch (1 cm) thick. Leave to cool. • Cut the polenta in slices about 2 x 4 inches (5 x 10 cm). • Heat the oil in a large skillet until very hot and fry the polenta in batches until golden brown on both sides. Drain on paper towels. • Serve hot.

## Buckwheat polenta with cheese

*Serves: 4*
*Preparation: 5 minutes*
*Cooking: 50 minutes*
*Level of difficulty: fairly easy*

- $1^3/_4$ quarts/1.75 liters water
- 1 tablespoon coarse sea salt
- 3 cups/450 g buckwheat flour
- 1 cup/250 ml butter
- 8 oz/250 g Fontina, Asiago, or Fontal cheese (or a mixture of the three), cut in slivers

Bring the water and salt to a boil. • Sift in the buckwheat flour, stirring with a whisk, and add half the butter. • Cook, stirring frequently, for 40 minutes. The polenta will be rather soft. • Add the cheese and continue stirring over fairly low heat. • After 3 minutes add the remaining butter. • Cook for 5–8 minutes more and the polenta will be ready. • Serve hot.

## Baked polenta in cheese sauce

*Serves: 4*
*Preparation: 20 minutes + time to cool polenta*
*Cooking: 1 hour 15 minutes*
*Level of difficulty: fairly easy*

- 1 lb/500 g package polenta
- 3 tablespoons butter
- 1 tablespoon all-purpose/plain flour
- 1 cup/250 ml milk
- pinch of nutmeg
- 6 oz/180 g Emmental (or Gruyère, or similar) cheese, thinly sliced

- 6 oz/180 g Gorgonzola cheese, chopped
- 1/2 cup/60 g freshly grated Parmesan cheese

Cook the polenta following the instructions on the package. If preferred, buy a fast cooking or precooked polenta so that cooking time is reduced to about 10 minutes. • Set aside to cool for at least 3 hours. • Preheat the oven to 400°F/200°C/gas 6. • Melt 2 tablespoons of butter in a saucepan. Add the flour and cook over low heat for 1–2 minutes, stirring continuously. • Begin adding the milk, a little at a time, stirring continuously until the sauce is smooth. Season with the nutmeg. • Turn up the heat and gradually add the Emmental, Gorgonzola, and Parmesan, stirring constantly until smooth. • Use the remaining butter to grease an ovenproof baking dish large enough to hold the polenta and sauce in a layer about 2 inches (5 cm) thick. • Cut the polenta into

3/4-inch (2 cm) cubes. • Cover the bottom of the dish with half the polenta and pour half the sauce over the top. Put the remaining polenta on top and cover with the remaining sauce. • Bake in a preheated oven at for 25–30 minutes, or until the top is golden brown.

## Polenta with pizza topping

*Serves: 4*
*Preparation: 5 minutes*
*Cooking: 1 hour 5 minutes*
*Level of difficulty: fairly easy*

- 1 lb/500 g package polenta
- 2 tablespoons extra-virgin olive oil
- 2 cloves garlic, finely chopped
- 14 oz/400 g peeled and chopped tomatoes
- 1–2 tablespoons capers, rinsed
- salt and freshly ground black pepper to taste

- 8 oz/250 g Mozzarella cheese, sliced

Cook the polenta following the instructions on the package. If preferred, buy a fast cooking or precooked polenta so that cooking time is reduced to about 10 minutes. • Heat 4 tablespoons of the oil in a large skillet (frying pan) and sauté the garlic until pale gold. • Add the tomatoes and capers and season with salt and pepper. Cook over low heat for 25 minutes, or until the oil begins to separate from the tomatoes. • Preheat the oven to 400°F/200°C/gas 6. • Oil an ovenproof baking dish large enough to contain a layer of polenta about 1 inch (2.5 cm) cm thick. • When the polenta is ready, transfer it to the dish and level with a spatula. • Spoon the sauce over the top. Arrange the Mozzarella evenly on top and drizzle with the remaining oil. • Cook in a preheated oven for about 15 minutes. • Serve hot.

Baked polenta in a cheese sauce

# STEWED & BAKED DISHES

**M**ost of the hearty and nutritious dishes in this chapter can be served as meals in themselves or as the main course at a lunch or dinner party. The recipes come from all over the world and include Indian curries, Southeast Asian stir-fries, Chinese bean curd stews, Italian vegetable lasagnes, baked French crêpes, North African tajines, and krauti dishes from Germany, the Czech Republic, and much much more.

Traditionally, a clafoutis is a rustic French dessert tart made with cherries baked in an egg custard. We have borrowed the name for this hearty vegetable casserole because it is made in a similar way. In this case the sweet pastry tart base is replaced with slices of toasted bread that are covered with the vegetables. The egg and cream "custard" is then poured over the top and the whole thing is baked in a hot oven for 20–25 minutes, or until the egg and cheese sauce is set. Feel free to vary the vegetables according to the season and what you have in your garden or refrigerator.

Brie and vegetable clafoutis (see page 156)
Savory onions and tomatoes (see page 173)

*Delicious Parmesan cheese is made from raw cow's milk. It is very nutritious — it takes about four gallons (16 liters) of fresh milk to produce just two pounds (one kilogram) of the cheese. Parmesan is rich in calcium, phosphorus, and protein.*

## Zucchini lasagne

*Serves: 4*
*Preparation: 25 minutes*
*Cooking: 45 minutes*
*Recipe grading: fairly easy*

- 6 tablespoons extra-virgin olive oil
- 1¹/₂ lb/750 g zucchini/courgettes, cut into thin strips lengthwise
- 1³/₄ cups/100 g fresh bread crumbs
- 2 tablespoons butter, cut up
- 1 clove garlic, finely chopped
- 5 shallots, coarsely chopped
- 2 carrots, cut into small cubes
- 8 oz/250 g asparagus tips, finely chopped
- ³/₄ cup/180 ml heavy/double cream
- salt to taste
- 1 cup/125 g freshly grated Parmesan cheese

Preheat the oven to 400°F/200°C/gas 6. • Heat 2 tablespoons of oil in a large skillet (frying pan) over medium heat and brown the zucchini. • Remove from the skillet and set aside. • Sauté the bread crumbs in the same skillet with 2 tablespoons of oil, 1 tablespoon of butter, and the garlic for 5 minutes. • Remove from the skillet and set aside. • Sauté the shallots and carrots in the remaining oil over medium heat until lightly browned. • Add the asparagus and cream and cook for 10 minutes. Season with the salt. • Line a baking dish with a layer of the zucchini strips. Cover with a layer of the asparagus mixture and sprinkle with the bread crumbs and Parmesan. Repeat until all the ingredients are in the dish, finishing with a layer of bread crumbs and Parmesan. • Dot with the remaining butter. • Bake for 15–20 minutes, or until browned. • Serve hot.

## Brie and vegetable clafoutis

*Serves: 4*
*Preparation: 20 minutes*
*Cooking: 45 minutes*
*Recipe grading: fairly easy*

- 1 shallot, finely chopped
- 4 tablespoons extra-virgin olive oil
- 3 oz/90 g zucchini/courgettes, cut into small cubes
- 3 oz/90 g carrots, cut into small cubes
- 3 oz/90 g asparagus tips, chopped
- 3 oz/90 g fresh fava/broad beans
- salt to taste
- 8–10 slices firm-textured bread
- 1 teaspoon paprika
- 1 tablespoon all-purpose/plain flour
- 6 tablespoons milk
- 6 tablespoons heavy/double cream
- 2 eggs
- 5 oz/150 g Brie cheese, thinly sliced
- 1 cup/125 g freshly grated Parmesan cheese

Preheat the oven to 350°F/180°C/gas 4. • Sauté the shallot in the oil in a large skillet (frying pan) over medium heat until softened. • Add the zucchini, carrots, asparagus, and fava beans and cook for 5 minutes. Season with the salt. • Grease two baking sheets with oil. • Place the bread on the baking sheets and dust with the paprika. Toast in the oven until lightly browned. • Remove and set aside. • Mix the flour and milk in a small bowl. • Heat the cream and eggs in a medium saucepan over medium heat, stirring constantly. Add the milk mixture and stir until the sauce begins to thicken. • Line the base of a large baking dish with the toast and cover with the Brie. Spoon the vegetables over the top. • Pour the sauce over the top and sprinkle with the Parmesan. • Bake for 20–25 minutes, or until the vegetables are tender and the topping is nicely browned. • Serve hot.

## Baked zucchini omelet

*Serves: 2–4*
*Preparation: 15 minutes*
*Cooking: 30 minutes*
*Recipe grading: easy*

- 3 eggs, lightly beaten
- ²/₃ cup/150 ml milk
- 1 tablespoon finely chopped parsley
- salt and freshly ground black pepper to taste
- 1¹/₄ cups/150 g fresh or frozen peas, thawed if frozen
- 12 zucchini/courgettes with flowers attached, cut into rounds
- 2 tablespoons butter

Preheat the oven to 400°F/200°C/gas 6. • Butter a large round baking dish. • Beat the eggs, milk, and parsley in a small bowl until frothy. Season with the salt and pepper. • Sauté the peas and zucchini in the butter in a large skillet (frying pan) over medium heat until the zucchini are lightly browned. Season with the salt and pepper. • Arrange the vegetables in the prepared baking dish and pour the egg mixture over the top. • Bake for 15–20 minutes, or until the omelet is cooked and the vegetables are tender. • Serve hot or at room temperature.

*Zucchini lasagne*

## Fresh Ricotta and zucchini crêpes

*Serves: 6*
*Preparation: 45 minutes*
*Cooking: 20 minutes*
*Recipe grading: fairly easy*

Crêpes
• 1²/₃ cups/250 g all-purpose/plain flour
• 2 cups/500 ml milk
• 4 eggs
• 1 tablespoon finely chopped thyme
• 1 tablespoon finely chopped marjoram
• 1 tablespoon finely chopped parsley
• ¹/₈ teaspoon salt
• 1 tablespoon butter

Ricotta filling
• 12 oz/350 g zucchini/courgettes, cut into rounds
• 2 tablespoons butter
• 24 zucchini flowers, carefully washed
• 1²/₃ cups/400 g Ricotta cheese
• ¹/₂ cup/60 g pine nuts, toasted
• ¹/₂ teaspoon freshly ground nutmeg
• 1¹/₄ cups/310 ml cream
• 1 tablespoon freshly grated Parmesan cheese

Crêpes: Mix the flour and milk in a large bowl. • Add the eggs and beat until well blended. • Beat in the thyme, marjoram, and parsley. Season with salt. • Melt the butter in a small skillet (frying pan) over medium heat. • Pour in just enough batter to cover the bottom of the skillet, tilting it so that it thinly covers the surface. • Cook until the crêpe is light gold on the underside. Use a large spatula to flip the crêpe and cook the other side. Repeat until all the batter has been used. Stack the cooked crêpes one on top of the other in a warm oven. • Preheat the oven to 400°F/200°C /gas 6. • Butter a large baking dish. • Ricotta filling: Sauté the zucchini in the butter in a large skillet over medium heat for 5–10 minutes. • Add the zucchini flowers, Ricotta, pine nuts, and nutmeg. Cook for 2–3 minutes, then remove from heat. • Place 2–3 tablespoons of filling in the center of each crêpe. Fold the crêpes in half and then in half again to form triangles. • Arrange the filled crêpes in the prepared baking dish. • Pour the cream over the top and sprinkle with the Parmesan. • Cover with aluminum foil and bake for 10 minutes. • Remove the foil and bake for 8–10 minutes more, or until the crêpes are crispy and and the cheese is golden brown.

## Crêpes stuffed with spinach and goat's cheese

*Serves: 6*
*Preparation: 30 minutes*
*Cooking: 45 minutes*
*Recipe grading: fairly easy*

• 1 quantity Crêpes (see Fresh Ricotta and zucchini crêpes, this page)
• 1³/₄ lb/800 g Swiss chard
• 2 cloves garlic, cut in half
• 2 tablespoons butter
• salt and freshly ground black pepper to taste
• 7 oz/200 g fresh creamy goat's cheese
• ¹/₂ teaspoon ground nutmeg
• 1 quantity Béchamel sauce (see Mushroom soup with sherry, page 56)
• ¹/₂ cup/60 g freshly grated Gruyère cheese

Prepare the crêpes and set aside. • Preheat the oven to 350°F/180°C/gas 4. • Butter a large baking dish. • Cook the spinach in a large pot of salted, boiling water for 5 minutes. Drain well, squeeze out excess moisture, and chop finely. • Sauté the garlic in the butter in a large skillet (frying pan) until pale gold. Discard the garlic. • Sauté the spinach in the same skillet for 5 minutes. Season with the salt and pepper. • Spread the goat's cheese over the crêpes and dust with the nutmeg. • Place 2 tablespoons of spinach on one half of each crêpe. • Fold the crêpes in half and then in half again to form triangles. • Arrange the crêpes, overlapping, in the prepared baking dish. • Pour the Béchamel sauce over the top and sprinkle with the Gruyère. • Bake for 20–25 minutes, or until the cheese is golden brown. • Serve hot.

Fresh Ricotta and zucchini crêpes

## Chinese vegetables with omelet

*Serves: 4*
*Preparation: 40 minutes*
*Cooking: 20 minutes*
*Recipe grading: fairly easy*

- 2 tablespoons water
- 2 tablespoons soy sauce
- 2 teaspoons cornstarch/cornflour
- 1 teaspoon white wine
- 4 oz/125 g bean curd or tofu, coarsely chopped
- 6 tablespoons extra-virgin olive oil
- 2 oz/60 g dried bean thread, soaked in warm water for 10 minutes and drained
- 2 oz/60 g yellow chive
- 4 oz/125 g fresh spinach leaves, stalks removed
- 1 cup/250 ml vegetable stock
- $^3/_4$ teaspoon salt
- 6 scallions/spring onions, finely chopped
- 4 oz/125 g bean sprouts
- 3 eggs, lightly beaten

Mix 1 tablespoon of water, 1 tablespoon of soy sauce, 1 teaspoon of cornstarch, and the white wine in a large bowl. Add the bean curd and let marinate for 10 minutes. • Stir in 1 tablespoon of oil. • Chop the soaked bean thread into short lengths. • Rinse the chive and spinach thoroughly under cold running water and dry well. Chop into short lengths. • Heat a large wok over medium heat and add 3 tablespoons of oil. • Sauté the bean curd for 3 minutes. Remove from the wok and set aside. • Sauté the chive and spinach for 3 minutes, or until slightly wilted. • Remove from the wok and set aside. • Add 1 tablespoon of oil and sauté the scallions until lightly browned. Add the bean thread, vegetable stock, remaining soy sauce, and $^1/_2$ teaspoon salt. • Cook until the sauce has reduced, then stir in the bean sprouts. Cook for 3 more minutes then add the bean curd mixture.

Transfer to a serving dish. • Beat the eggs with the remaining water, cornstarch, and salt in a medium bowl until frothy. • Heat the remaining oil in a large skillet (frying pan) over medium heat. • Pour in the beaten egg mixture, tilting the pan so that the batter thinly covers the bottom. • Cook until light golden brown on the underside. Use a large spatula to flip the omelet and cook until golden. • Drape the omelet over the top of the serving dish. • Serve hot.

## Ginger stir-fried vegetables

*Serves: 4*
*Preparation: 20 minutes*
*Cooking: 10–15 minutes*
*Recipe grading: easy*

- 3 tablespoons vegetable stock (bouillon cube)
- 2 tablespoons dry sherry
- 1 teaspoon granulated sugar
- 1 teaspoon cornstarch/cornflour
- 1 teaspoon salt
- 4 oz/125 g fresh shiitake mushrooms, stems removed
- 2 tablespoons extra-virgin olive oil
- 8 oz/250 g carrots, cut into thin strips
- 8 oz/250 g leeks, thinly sliced
- 8 oz/250 g cabbage, shredded
- 2 cloves garlic, finely chopped
- 2 teaspoons finely chopped fresh ginger root

Mix the stock, sherry, sugar, cornstarch, and salt in a small bowl until well blended. • Cut the mushroom caps into $^1/_8$-inch (3-mm) thick slices. • Heat a large wok over medium heat and add the oil. • Sauté the carrots and leeks for 3 minutes. • Add the mushrooms, cabbage, garlic, and ginger. Sauté for 2 minutes, or until the carrots are tender but still have a slight bite. • Pour in the stock mixture and cook for 2 minutes more. • Serve hot.

## Bean curd with coconut and mixed vegetables

*Serves: 4–6*
*Preparation: 15 minutes*
*Cooking: 10 minutes*
*Recipe grading: easy*

- 6 shiitake mushrooms, stems removed
- 1 small broccoli, broken into 8 florets
- 1 small cauliflower, broken into 8 florets
- 2 cloves garlic, finely chopped
- 1 tablespoon sesame oil
- 12 baby corn/sweetcorn cobs
- 8 sugar peas/mangetout
- 1 small eggplant, cut into small chunks
- $^3/_4$ cup/180 ml coconut milk
- 2 tablespoons soy sauce
- 1 tablespoon vegetarian oyster sauce (optional)
- 1 lb/500 g bean curd or tofu
- 1 baby bok choy, cut in 4
- 1 scallion/spring onion, finely chopped

Cut the mushroom caps into $^1/_8$-inch (3-mm) thick slices. • Blanch the broccoli and cauliflower in a large pot of salted, boiling water for 1 minute. • Drain well and set aside. • Sauté the garlic in the oil in a large wok or skillet (frying pan) over high heat until pale gold. • Add the broccoli, cauliflower, corn, sugar peas, mushrooms, and eggplant. Cover and cook for 5–7 minutes, or until vegetables are almost tender. • Stir in the coconut milk, soy sauce, and oyster sauce. • Add the bean curd, bok choy, and scallion. Cover and cook for 2 minutes, or until the vegetables are tender. Season with the pepper. • Transfer to a heated serving dish and serve hot.

Chinese vegetables with omelet

Pineapple and coconut curry

## Pineapple and coconut curry

*Serves: 4*
*Preparation: 25 minutes*
*Cooking: 20 minutes*
*Recipe grading: fairly easy*

Spice paste
• 4–6 dried red chile peppers, crumbled
• 1 teaspoon coriander seeds
• 2 cloves garlic, finely chopped
• 6 shallots, finely chopped
• 1 teaspoon ground turmeric
• 1 tablespoon finely chopped fresh ginger root

Stew
• 2 tablespoons extra-virgin olive oil
• 3 cups/750 ml coconut milk
• 1 ripe pineapple, peeled and cut into small cubes
• 2 star anise, chopped

• one 3-inch/8-cm stick cinnamon
• $^1/_4$ teaspoon ground cloves
• $^1/_8$ teaspoon ground nutmeg
• 1 stalk lemongrass, finely chopped
• 1 tablespoon fresh lime juice
• salt and freshly ground black pepper to taste
• $^1/_2$ cup/125 ml coconut cream
• 2 shallots, finely chopped and lightly fried, to garnish

Spice paste: Grind the chilies, coriander seeds, garlic, shallots, turmeric, and ginger root in a pestle and mortar until crushed. • Stew: Heat the oil in a large wok or skillet (frying pan) and sauté the spice paste until aromatic. • Pour in the coconut milk and bring to a boil, stirring constantly. • Add the pineapple, star anise, cinnamon, cloves, nutmeg, lemongrass, and lime juice. Season with

salt and pepper. Cook over medium heat until the pineapple is heated through, 5–7 minutes. • Stir in the coconut cream and cook for 2–3 minutes more. • Transfer to a heated serving dish. • Garnish with the fried shallots and serve hot.

## Sweet potato curry

*Serves: 4*
*Preparation: 25 minutes*
*Cooking: 30 minutes*
*Recipe grading: fairly easy*

• 2 red bell peppers/capsicums, cut into thin strips
• 1 onion, thinly sliced
• 1 tablespoon extra-virgin olive oil
• 1 clove garlic, finely chopped
• 1 tablespoon Thai green curry paste

- 1 lb/500 g sweet potatoes, peeled and cut into small cubes
- 1 (14-oz/400-ml) can coconut milk
- ¹/₂ cup/125 ml water
- 8 oz/250 g sugar peas
- 1 tablespoon finely chopped cilantro/coriander

Sauté the bell peppers and onion in the oil in a large work or skillet (frying pan) over medium heat for 5 minutes. • Add the garlic and curry paste and cook, stirring constantly, for 5 more minutes. • Add the sweet potatoes, coconut milk, and water. Cover and simmer, stirring occasionally, for 15 minutes, or until the potatoes are almost tender. • Add the sugar peas and simmer, uncovered, until the sauce has thickened slightly and the vegetables are well cooked. • Sprinkle with the cilantro and serve hot on a bed of boiled basmati rice.

# Yellow lentil and vegetable curry

*Serves: 6*
*Preparation: 20 minutes*
*Cooking: 45 minutes*
*Recipe grading: fairly easy*

- 2 cups/200 g small yellow lentils
- 2 onions, finely sliced
- 2 tomatoes, chopped
- 2 sprigs curry leaves
- ¹/₂ teaspoon ground turmeric
- 1 quart/1 liter water
- 1 teaspoon salt
- 1³/₄ lb/800 g mixed vegetables, such as carrots, potatoes, eggplants/aubergines, cauliflower, and green beans, cut into small cubes
- ¹/₂ cup/90 g tamarind pulp soaked in 1 cup/250 ml water, strained
- 1 cup/100 g freshly grated coconut blended with 6 tablespoons water

- ¹/₂ teaspoon sugar
- 1 tablespoon finely chopped cilantro/coriander
- 2 tablespoons extra-virgin olive oil
- 1 teaspoon mustard seeds
- 3–4 dried red chile peppers, crumbled

Cook the lentils, onions, tomatoes, curry leaves, turmeric, water, and salt in a large saucepan over medium heat for 15–20 minutes. • Add the vegetables that take longer to cook, such as carrots and potatoes, along with the tamarind liquid, coconut, and sugar. Cook for 15 minutes, or until the vegetables are softening and the lentils have broken down. • Add the remaining vegetables and cilantro and cook for 10 minutes more. • Heat the oil in a small saucepan. Sauté the mustard seed and chilies until aromatic. • Add to the vegetable curry, stir well, and cook for 2 minutes more. • Serve hot.

Yellow lentil and vegetable curry

Curry with dhal balls

## Potato curry

*Serves: 4*
*Preparation: 20 minutes*
*Cooking: 30 minutes*
*Recipe grading: fairly easy*

• 4 medium potatoes, peeled and cut into small cubes
• 2 scallions/spring onions, finely chopped
• 2 cloves garlic, lightly crushed
• 1 green chile pepper, finely chopped
• 1 teaspoon coarse salt
• seeds of 2 cardamom pods, lightly crushed
• 2 tablespoons extra-virgin olive oil
• 1 teaspoon butter
• 1 small cinnamon stick
• ²/₃-inch/1.5 cm piece ginger, finely sliced
• 2 tomatoes, finely chopped
• 1 teaspoon mustard seeds
• 1 tablespoon garam masala
• ¹/₂ cup/125 ml plain yogurt
• salt and freshly ground black pepper to taste
• 1 tablespoon finely chopped fresh cilantro/ coriander

Boil the potatoes in a large pot of salted, boiling water for 10 minutes, or until tender. • Drain and set aside. • Grind the scallions, garlic, chile, salt, and cardamom seeds to a paste in a pestle and mortar. • Heat the oil and butter in a small saucepan over low heat. Cook the paste for 3 minutes. • Add the cinnamon, ginger, tomatoes, mustard seeds, and garam masala. • Cook for 10 minutes, stirring constantly. • Stir in the yogurt and cook until thickened. • Add the potatoes and simmer for 5 minutes. • Season with the salt and pepper. Sprinkle with the cilantro and serve.

## Curry with dhal balls

*Serves: 4*
*Preparation: 40 minutes*
*Cooking: 45 minutes*
*Recipe grading: fairly easy*

• 10 oz/300 g Urad or blackgrain dhal, without the black skin, soaked in cold water for 3 hours and drained
• 2 small red chile peppers, finely chopped
• ¹/₂ teaspoon ground turmeric
• salt and freshly ground black pepper to taste
• 2 carrots, finely grated
• 6 dried red chile peppers, crumbled
• ³/₄ teaspoon ground fenugreek
• ¹/₂ cup/90 g tamarind pulp blended with 1 quart/1 liter water, strained
• 2 tablespoons extra-virgin olive oil
• 1 teaspoon cumin seeds

Vegetarian tajine

- ¹/₂ teaspoon mustard seeds
- 6 curry leaves

Process the dhal, fresh chilies, and turmeric in a food processor until a paste has formed. • Season with salt and pepper and add the carrots. • Shape into balls or oblongs 1-inch (2.5-cm) in diameter and arrange in a steamer lightly greased with oil. • Steam for 10 minutes then set aside. • Grind the dried chilies and fenugreek to a paste with a pestle and mortar. • Stir the ground spices into the tamarind water in a medium bowl. • Heat the oil in a small saucepan over medium heat. Add the cumin seeds, mustard seeds, and curry leaves and cook until aromatic. • Pour in the tamarind mixture and bring to a boil. Simmer for 20 minutes. • Add the dhal balls and simmer for 10 minutes more. • Serve hot.

## Vegetarian tajine

*Serves: 4–6*
*Preparation: 20 minutes*
*Cooking: 35–45 minutes*
*Recipe grading: fairly easy*

- 3 tomatoes
- 2 onions, coarsely chopped
- 4 scallions/spring onions, bulbs only
- 6 tablespoons extra-virgin olive oil
- 3 carrots, cut into rounds
- 3 zucchini/courgettes, finely chopped
- ¹/₈ teaspoon ground cinnamon
- 1 teaspoon cumin seeds
- ¹/₈ teaspoon ground cloves
- 1 tablespoon finely chopped mint
- 1 bunch mixed fresh herbs, finely chopped
- 2 cups/500 ml vegetable stock (bouillon cube)

- salt and freshly ground black pepper to taste

Preheat the oven to 350°F/180°C/gas 4. • Blanch the tomatoes in a large pot of salted, boiling water for 1 minute. Peel, gently squeeze out as many seeds as possible, then chop the flesh into small cubes. • Sauté the onions and whole scallion bulbs in half the oil over medium heat in a tajine or a flameproof dish until lightly browned. • Add the tomatoes, carrots, and zucchini. Cook for 10 minutes, stirring often. • Add the remaining oil, cinnamon, cumin seeds, cloves, half the mint, and the herbs. Pour in the vegetable stock and season with salt and pepper. • Cover with the dish with aluminum foil and bake for 35–45 minutes, or until the vegetables are tender. • Remove the foil, garnish with the remaining mint, and serve hot.

## Bean curd with mushrooms

*Serves: 6*
*Preparation: 20 minutes*
*Cooking: 25 minutes*
*Recipe grading: fairly easy*

- 2 cups/500 ml olive oil, for frying
- 2 lb/1 kg bean curd or tofu, cut into small chunks
- 3 tablespoons extra-virgin olive oil
- 2 scallions/spring onions, thinly sliced
- 1 tablespoon finely chopped fresh ginger root
- 1 lb/500 g button mushrooms
- $^1/_2$ cup/125 g finely sliced bamboo shoots
- 1 cup/250 ml vegetable stock (bouillon cube)
- $2^1/_2$ tablespoons soy sauce
- 1 teaspoon sesame oil
- freshly ground black pepper to taste
- 4 bok choy, cooked and cut in half
- 2 teaspoons cornstarch/cornflour
- 1 tablespoon water

Heat the frying oil in a wok to very hot. • Fry the bean curd in two batches for 5–7 minutes, or until golden brown all over. • Drain well and drain on paper towels. • Discard the frying oil. • Sauté the scallions and ginger in the 3 tablespoons of extra-virgin oil in the wok over medium heat for 5 minutes. • Add the mushrooms and cook for 5 more minutes. • Stir in the bamboo shoots, vegetable stock, soy sauce, sesame oil, and the fried bean curd. Season with the pepper. • Bring to a boil and simmer for 3 minutes. • Add the bok choy and cook for 2 minutes more. • Mix the cornstarch and water in a small bowl. Stir into the bean curd mixture to thicken. • Transfer to a heated serving dish and serve hot.

Bean curd with mushrooms

## Porcini mushroom stew

*Serves: 4*
*Preparation: 20 minutes*
*Cooking: 25–30 minutes*
*Recipe grading: easy*

- 2 lb/1 kg fresh porcini mushrooms
- 3 cloves garlic, finely chopped
- 1 tablespoon finely chopped parsley
- 4 tablespoons extra-virgin olive oil
- salt and freshly ground black pepper to taste
- 1–2 tablespoons hot water
- 4–6 medium tomatoes, peeled and chopped

Cut the ends off the mushroom stalks. Rinse thoroughly under cold running water and dry well. • Slice the caps into thin strips and dice the stalks. • Sauté the garlic and parsley in the oil over low heat for 3 minutes. • Add the mushroom stalks. Season with the salt and pepper and cook for 5 minutes. • Stir in the caps and cook for 5 minutes more. Add enough hot water to make sure the mushrooms are moist. • Stir in the tomatoes and simmer for 15–20 minutes, or until the moisture the tomatoes produce has been absorbed. • Serve hot.

## Stuffed mushrooms

*Serves: 4*
*Preparation: 20 minutes*
*Cooking: 25–30 minutes*
*Recipe grading: easy*

- 12 fresh medium Caesar's mushrooms
- 1 clove garlic, finely chopped
- 2 large slices firm-textured bread, crusts removed, soaked in warm milk and squeezed dry
- salt and freshly ground black pepper to taste
- 1 egg + 1 egg yolk
- $1^1/_2$ cups/180 g freshly grated Parmesan cheese
- $^1/_2$ teaspoon dried oregano
- 1 tablespoon finely chopped parsley
- 1 tablespoon finely chopped marjoram
- 4 tablespoons extra-virgin olive oil

Preheat the oven to 350°F/180°C/gas 4. • Grease a large baking dish with oil. • Detach the stems from the mushrooms. Rinse the caps and stems thoroughly under cold running water and dry well. Peel the caps and leave them whole. Chop the stems finely. • Mix the mushroom stems, garlic, and bread in a large bowl. Season with the salt and pepper. • Add the egg and egg yolk, Parmesan, oregano, parsley, marjoram, and 1 tablespoon of oil. • Use the mixture to stuff the mushroom caps, pressing it in carefully with your fingertips. • Arrange the stuffed mushroom caps in the prepared baking dish and drizzle with the remaining oil. • Bake for 25–30 minutes, or until the mushrooms are tender and well cooked. • Serve hot or at room temperature.

## Mushrooms with pine nuts and almonds

*Serves: 4*
*Preparation: 10 minutes*
*Cooking: 20 minutes*
*Recipe grading: easy*

- 2 large potatoes, cut into small cubes
- 4 tablespoons extra-virgin olive oil
- 2 cloves garlic, finely chopped
- $1^1/_2$ lb/650 g white mushrooms, cleaned and coarsely chopped
- salt and freshly ground black pepper to taste
- $^2/_3$ cup/120 g pine nuts
- $^1/_2$ cup/50 g flaked almonds
- 1 tablespoon finely chopped mint

Sauté the potatoes and garlic in the oil in a large skillet (frying pan) over medium heat for 2 minutes. • Add the mushrooms and season with the salt and pepper. Cover and cook for 5 minutes. • Uncover and stir in the pine nuts and almonds. Cook for 10 minutes more, or until the mushrooms are tender and the moisture released during cooking has evaporated. • Sprinkle with the mint and cook for 1 minute. • Serve hot.

# Spicy bean curd

*Serves: 6*
*Preparation: 20 minutes + 30 minutes to soak*
*Cooking: 10 minutes*
*Recipe grading: easy*

- 2 teaspoons dried black mushrooms
- 2 teaspoons dried bean curd strips
- 2 tablespoons vegetable oil
- 2 stalks celery, finely chopped
- 2 cloves garlic, peeled and finely chopped
- 2 red chile peppers, finely chopped
- 2 lb/1 kg bean curd or tofu, cut into $^1/_2$-inch/ 1-cm cubes
- 1$^1/_2$ cups/375 ml vegetable stock (bouillon cube)
- 1 tablespoon soy sauce
- 1 tablespoon sesame oil
- $^1/_2$ teaspoon sugar
- 1 tablespoon water
- 1 teaspoon cornstarch/cornflour
- freshly ground black pepper to taste
- 1 tablespoon finely chopped parsley

Soak the dried mushrooms in warm water for 15 minutes. • Soak the bean curd strips in warm water for 15 minutes. • Chop the soaked bean curd finely and set aside. • Heat the oil in a large wok or skillet (frying pan) over medium heat. Sauté the celery and garlic for 5 minutes. • Add the mushrooms, soaked bean curd, and chilies and sauté for 3 minutes. • Stir in the bean curd, vegetable stock, soy sauce, sesame oil, and sugar. Cook for 5 minutes, or until the liquid has reduced slightly. • Mix the water and cornstarch in a small bowl. Stir into the wok to thicken the mixture. • Season with pepper, garnish with the parsley, and serve.

# Sweet spicy bean curd

*Serves: 6*
*Preparation: 20 minutes*
*Cooking: 10 minutes*
*Recipe grading: easy*

- 2 tablespoons extra-virgin olive oil
- 2 lb/1 kg bean curd or tofu, cut into $^1/_2$-inch/1-cm cubes
- 2 scallions/spring onions, finely chopped
- 2 cloves garlic, finely chopped
- 1 teaspoon finely chopped fresh ginger root
- 2 small red chile peppers, finely chopped
- 1 tablespoon dry sherry
- 1$^1/_2$ tablespoons soy sauce
- 1 cup/250 ml + 1 tablespoon water
- $^1/_2$ teaspoon salt
- 1$^1/_2$ teaspoons cornstarch/cornflour

Heat the oil a large wok or skillet (frying pan) over medium-high heat. • Sauté the bean curd, half the scallions, half the garlic, and ginger for 5 minutes. • Add the chilies and cook for 1 minute. • Stir in the sherry, soy sauce, 1 cup (250 ml) of water, and salt. Bring to a boil and cook for 3 minutes. • Mix the remaining water and cornstarch in a small bowl. Stir into the bean curd

mixture to thicken. • Sprinkle with the remaining scallion and garlic. • Transfer to a heated plate and serve hot.

## Potatoes with mixed spices

*Serves: 4*
*Preparation: 15 minutes*
*Cooking: 30 minutes*
*Recipe grading: easy*

- 1 teaspoon cumin seeds
- 1 teaspoon onion seeds
- 1 teaspoon fennel seeds
- 6 curry leaves
- 4 tablespoons extra-virgin olive oil
- 2 onions, finely chopped
- 2 cloves garlic, finely chopped
- 1 teaspoon finely chopped fresh ginger root
- 2 small red chile peppers, thinly sliced
- salt to taste
- 6 medium potatoes, sliced

Grind the cumin, onion, and fennel seeds with the curry leaves to a smooth paste in a pestle and mortar. • Heat the oil in a large wok or skillet (frying pan). • Cook the spice mixture, onions, garlic, ginger, and chilies until the onions are transparent. • Season with salt. • Add the potatoes. Cover and cook for 15–20 minutes, or until the potatoes are tender. • Serve hot.

## Sweet and sour bean curd

*Serves: 6*
*Preparation: 20 minutes*
*Cooking: 17–20 minutes*
*Recipe grading: easy*

- 2 tablespoons extra-virgin olive oil
- 2 lb/1 kg bean curd or tofu, cut into small cubes
- 2 onions, cut into small pieces
- 2 large bell peppers/capsicums, mixed colors, seeded, cored, and cut into small chunks
- 2 teaspoons finely chopped fresh ginger root

- 3 cups/750 ml vegetable stock (bouillon cube)
- 1 can (1 lb/500 g) pineapple chunks
- 2 tablespoons brown sugar
- 2 teaspoons curry powder
- 2 teaspoons white wine vinegar
- 2 tablespoons cornstarch/cornflour
- 4 tablespoons water
- 1 tablespoon finely chopped cilantro/coriander

Heat the oil a large wok or skillet (frying pan) over medium heat. • Sauté the bean curd for 7–10 minutes, or until browned all over. • Remove and set aside. • Sauté the onions, bell peppers, and ginger in the same pan until the onions have softened. • Pour in the vegetable stock and add the pineapple, sugar, curry powder, vinegar, and the bean curd. Bring to a boil and simmer for 5 minutes. • Mix the water and cornstarch in a small bowl. Stir into the bean curd mixture to thicken. • Sprinkle with the cilantro and serve.

- ¹/₄ teaspoon ground nutmeg
- ¹/₄ teaspoon paprika

Place the bread in a medium bowl and pour the milk over the top. Let stand for 15 minutes, or until the milk has been absorbed. • Rinse the spinach under cold running water. Do not drain but place in a saucepan and cook, with just the water clinging to its leaves, for 3 minutes. Drain, press out excess moisture, chop coarsely, and set aside. • Melt 3 tablespoons of butter in a large skillet (frying pan) and sauté the spinach. • Transfer a third of the spinach to a food processor. Add the soaked bread, Parmesan, eggs, almonds, remaining butter, and nutmeg. Season with salt and pepper. Process until very finely chopped. • Preheat the oven to 375°F/190°C/gas 5. • Butter six small pudding molds or ramekins. • Spoon the chopped spinach mixture into the bottom and up the sides of the molds, pressing it firmly with the back of a spoon. • Fill the center of the molds with the whole spinach leaves. Sprinkle with the carrots and cover with the remaining spinach leaves. • Half fill a large roasting pan with hot water and place the molds in the waterbath. • Bake for 50 minutes. • Remove the molds from the waterbath and set aside for 10 minutes. • Carefully invert the molds and turn the spinach dumplings onto serving plates. • White wine sauce: Bring the wine to a boil with the shallot. Simmer until the wine has reduced by half. • Stir in the cream and bring to a boil once more. Cook until a thick sauce has formed. • Season with salt and pepper and spoon over the mounds. • Dust with the paprika and nutmeg and serve.

Spinach dumplings with white wine sauce

## Spinach dumplings with white wine sauce

*Serves: 6*
*Preparation: 45 minutes*
*Cooking: 50 minutes*
*Recipe grading: fairly easy*

- 10 oz/300 g firm-textured bread, crusts removed and cut into small cubes
- ³/₄ cup/180 ml milk
- 2¹/₂ lb/1.25 kg fresh spinach leaves, destalked
- 6 tablespoons butter
- ¹/₂ cup/60 g freshly grated Parmesan cheese
- 2 eggs
- 2 oz/60 g finely chopped almonds
- ¹/₈ teaspoon ground nutmeg
- salt and freshly ground black pepper to taste
- 7 oz/200 g carrots, peeled and cut in small cubes

White wine sauce
- 1 cup/250 ml dry white wine
- 1 shallot, finely chopped
- 1¹/₄ cups/310 ml light/single cream
- salt and freshly ground black pepper to taste

## Fried mixed mushroom parcels

*Serves: 6*
*Preparation: 30 minutes*
*Cooking: 1 hour*
*Recipe grading: fairly easy*

- 1 1/2 lb/750 g potatoes
- 10 oz/300 g mixed mushrooms
- 1 clove garlic, finely chopped
- 2 cups/500 ml olive oil, for frying
- 2 tablespoons extra-virgin olive oil
- 1 tablespoon finely chopped parsley
- salt to taste
- 2 eggs
- 4 tablespoons all-purpose/plain flour
- 1 cup/125 g fine dry bread crumbs

Preheat the oven to 350°F/180°C/gas 4. • Bake the potatoes in their skins for 30–40 minutes, or until well cooked. • Rinse the mushrooms carefully under cold running water and dry well. Slice thinly. • Sauté the garlic in 2 tablespoons of extra-virgin olive oil in a skillet (frying pan) over medium heat for 2–3 minutes. • Add the mushrooms and sauté for 10 minutes, or until tender. • Add the parsley and season with salt. Remove from the heat and set aside. • Remove the potatoes from the oven and let cool for 15 minutes. • Peel and mash the insides until smooth. • Transfer to a large bowl and stir in the eggs and flour. Use your hands to work the mixture until smooth and well combined. • Shape into balls to resemble medium-sized potatoes. Press a hollow into the center of each "potato" with your index finger and spoon in a little mushroom mixture. Close up the ball, sealing the mushrooms inside. • Roll in the bread crumbs until well coated. • Heat the frying oil in a deep fryer or skillet to very hot. • Fry the parcels in small batches for 5–7 minutes, or until golden brown all over. • Drain well on paper towels. • Serve hot.

## Spinach and lentil stew

*Serves: 4*
*Preparation: 20 minutes*
*Cooking: 25 minutes*
*Recipe grading: easy*

- 2 cloves garlic, finely chopped
- 2 tablespoons extra-virgin olive oil
- 3 cups/750 ml vegetable stock (bouillon cube)
- 1 cup/100 g lentils
- 8 oz/250 g potatoes, cut into small cubes
- 2 tablespoons fresh lemon juice
- 6 oz/180 g fresh spinach leaves, stalks removed
- 1/4 teaspoon paprika
- salt to taste
- freshly ground black pepper to taste
- 2 tablespoons finely chopped parsley
- 2 tablespoons finely chopped mint

Fried mixed mushroom parcels

Sauté the garlic in the oil in a large saucepan over medium heat for 2–3 minutes. • Pour in the vegetable stock and lentils and bring to a boil. Lower the heat, cover and simmer for 10 minutes. • Add the potatoes and cook for 12–15 minutes, or until the potatoes and lentils are tender. • Add the lemon juice, spinach, and paprika. Cook for 2–3 more minutes, or until the spinach has wilted. Season with the salt and pepper. Sprinkle with the parsley and mint and serve hot.

## Garbanzo bean pancakes with two cheeses

*Serves: 6*
*Preparation: 40 minutes*
*Cooking: 8–10 minutes*
*Recipe grading: fairly easy*

Pancakes
- $^2/_3$ cup/150 ml water
- $^2/_3$ cup/100 g garbanzo bean/chickpea flour
- 2 eggs
- 6 tablespoons milk
- 1 tablespoon butter, melted
- $^1/_3$ cup/50 g all-purpose/plain flour
- salt to taste

Cheese filling
- 1 cup/250 g Ricotta cheese
- $^2/_3$ cup/150 g fresh, creamy goat's cheese
- $^3/_4$ cup/90 g freshly grated Parmesan cheese
- 1 tablespoon finely chopped marjoram
- 1 tablespoon finely chopped parsley
- 1 clove garlic, finely chopped
- salt and freshly ground black pepper to taste
- 1 tablespoon butter, cut up
- arugula/rocket, to serve

Pancakes: Mix the water and garbanzo bean flour in a small bowl until well blended. • Beat the eggs and milk in a large bowl until frothy. • Stir in the butter, flour, and garbanzo flour mixture until smooth. Season with the salt. • Grease a small skillet (frying pan) with oil. • Pour 2 tablespoons of the batter into the skillet, tilting the pan so that the batter covers the surface. • Cook until the pancake is light golden underneath. Use a large spatula to flip the pancake and cook until gold on the other side. Repeat until all the batter has been used. • Preheat the oven to 400°F/

Garbanzo bean pancakes
with two cheeses

200°C/gas 6. • Butter a large baking dish. • Cheese filling: Mix the Ricotta, goat's cheese, $^1/_2$ cup (60 g) of Parmesan, the marjoram, parsley, and garlic in a large bowl until well blended. Season with salt and pepper. • Spread the pancakes with the filling and roll them up tightly. • Place the pancakes seam-side down in the baking dish. • Dot with the remaining Parmesan and dot with the butter. • Bake for 8–10 minutes, or until lightly browned. • Serve warm on a bed of arugula.

# Red cabbage and glazed chestnuts

*Serves: 4*
*Preparation: 20 minutes*
*Cooking: 35–45 minutes*
*Recipe grading: fairly easy*

- 1 medium red cabbage, weighing about 2 lb/1 kg
- 2 tablespoons extra-virgin olive oil
- 1 tablespoon sugar
- 1 onion, finely chopped
- 2–3 apples, peeled, cored, and coarsely chopped
- 3–4 cloves
- 2 bay leaves
- salt and freshly ground black pepper to taste
- 3–4 tablespoons white wine vinegar
- 1 cup/250 ml vegetable stock (bouillon cube)

Remove the tough outer leaves from the cabbage and cut it in half. Remove the hard core and chop the leaves finely. • Heat the oil in a large saucepan over medium heat. Add the sugar and cook until it begins to caramelize. • Stir in the onion and apples and cook, stirring constantly, until the apples and onion begin to soften and caramelize. • Add the cabbage, cloves, bay leaves, and salt, then gradually pour in the vinegar and stock. The cooking liquid should just fill the bottom of the pan, so don't use too much at once. • Simmer, covered, over low heat for 30–40 minutes,

or until the cabbage is tender. • Season with the salt and pepper. Serve hot.

# Rhubarbkraut

*Serves: 4*
*Preparation: 20 minutes*
*Cooking: 35 minutes*
*Recipe grading: easy*

- 1 jar (1 lb/500 g) sauerkraut
- 1 tablespoon sugar
- 4–5 sticks pink rhubarb, washed and cut into small chunks
- 1 onion, finely sliced
- 2 stalks celery, finely chopped
- 2 tablespoons extra-virgin olive oil
- 2 tablespoons all-purpose/plain flour
- $^3/_4$ cup/180 ml vegetable stock
- 3 tablespoons sour cream
- salt and freshly ground black pepper to taste
- 1 tablespoon finely chopped parsley

Drain the sauerkraut and rinse under cold running water. • Heat a small saucepan over medium heat. Add the sugar and cook until it begins to caramelize. • Add the rhubarb and cook, stirring constantly, until softened. • Sauté the onion and celery in the oil in a large deep skillet (frying pan) over low heat until softened. • Sprinkle with the flour and pour in the vegetable stock, stirring constantly. Bring to a boil and add the sauerkraut. Cook for 20 minutes. • Add the rhubarb and simmer for 10 minutes more. Stir in the sour cream, season with the salt and pepper, and garnish with the parsley. • Serve hot.

# Czech sauerkraut

*Serves: 4*
*Preparation: 20 minutes*
*Cooking: 35 minutes*
*Recipe grading: easy*

- 1 large onion, finely chopped
- 1 clove garlic, finely chopped
- 1 tablespoon extra-virgin olive oil
- 2–3 apples, peeled, cored, and finely chopped
- 1 jar (1$^1/_2$ lb/650 g) sauerkraut
- 1 teaspoon caraway seeds
- 6 juniper berries, crushed
- 1 cup/250 ml hot water
- salt and freshly ground black pepper to taste
- $^1/_2$ cup/125 ml dry white wine (optional)

Sauté the onion and garlic in the oil in a large deep skillet (frying pan) until lightly browned. • Add the apples, sauerkraut, caraway seeds, and juniper berries. Stir well and pour in $^1/_2$ cup (125 ml) of water. Cover and cook for 30 minutes, adding the remaining water if the mixture begins to dry. • Season with salt and pepper and pour in the wine, if using. Cook for 2 minutes more. • Serve hot with boiled potatoes or bread dumplings.

# Savory onions and tomatoes

*Serves: 6*
*Preparation: 15 minutes*
*Cooking: 45 minutes*
*Recipe grading: easy*

- 2 lb/1 kg onions, peeled and sliced
- $^1/_2$ cup/125 ml extra-virgin olive oil
- 1 red bell pepper/capsicum and 1 yellow bell pepper/capsicum, cleaned and cut in small pieces
- 1$^1/_4$ lb/625 g ripe tomatoes, peeled
- salt to taste
- freshly ground black pepper to taste

Sauté the onions in the oil in a large, heavy-bottomed saucepan until golden brown. • Add the bell peppers and cook for 10 minutes more. • Roughly chop the tomatoes and add to the pan. Season with salt and pepper. Simmer over a low heat for 30 minutes, stirring frequently. • Serve hot or at room temperature.

Green-jaded bean curd

## Green-jaded bean curd

*Serves: 6*
*Preparation: 15 minutes + 15 minutes to soak*
*Cooking: 30 minutes*
*Recipe grading: fairly easy*

- 3 dried black mushrooms
- 10 oz/300 g fresh spinach leaves
- 4 lb/2 kg bean curd or tofu
- 2 egg whites
- 2 teaspoons sugar
- 1 tablespoon + 1 teaspoon sesame oil
- $^3/_4$ teaspoon salt
- $^1/_2$ teaspoon freshly ground black pepper
- 1 cup/250 ml vegetable stock (bouillon cube)
- 1 tablespoon water
- 1 tablespoon cornstarch/cornflour

Soak the mushrooms in the warm water for 15 minutes, or until softened. • Drain well and finely chop. • Rinse the spinach thoroughly under cold running water and dry well. • Remove the stems and finely chop the leaves. • Cut the hard edges off the bean curd and use a fork to mash the curd in a large bowl. • Add the spinach, egg whites, sugar, 1 teaspoon sesame oil, $^1/_2$ teaspoon salt, and pepper. • Continue to mash until puréed. • Sprinkle a 2-quart/2-liter bowl with the remaining sesame oil. • Pour in the bean curd purée. • Steam for 20 minutes over medium heat, or until the bean curd does not stick to a chopstick when pierced. • Carefully invert the mold and turn the bean curd onto a serving plate. • Bring the stock and remaining salt to a boil in a medium saucepan. Add the mushrooms. • Mix the water and cornstarch in a small bowl and add to the stock to thicken. • Pour this mixture over the bean curd. Spoon the mushrooms on top and around the sides, and serve hot.

## Quick veggie stew

*Serves: 4*
*Preparation: 15 minutes*
*Cooking: 15–20 minutes*
*Recipe grading: easy*

- 2 onions, coarsely chopped
- 8 oz/250 g mushrooms, thinly sliced
- 2 cloves garlic, finely chopped
- 1 tablespoon finely chopped parsley
- 1 tablespoon finely chopped marjoram
- 2 bay leaves
- 2 tablespoons extra-virgin olive oil
- 2 cups/500 ml vegetable stock (bouillon cube)
- 1 zucchini/courgette, cut into small cubes
- 1 carrot, cut into small cubes
- 4 potatoes, peeled and cut into small cubes
- 8 oz/250 g cauliflower, broken into florets

- 1 tomato, finely chopped
- salt to taste
- freshly ground black pepper to taste

Sauté the onions, mushrooms, garlic, parsley, marjoram, and bay leaves in the oil in a large saucepan until the onions have are transparent. • Pour in the vegetable stock and add the zucchini, carrot, potatoes, and cauliflower. Bring to a boil, cover, and simmer over medium heat for 10–15 minutes, or until the vegetables are tender. • Add the tomato, discard the bay leaves, and season with the salt and pepper. • Serve hot.

## Mixed cheese pie

*Serves: 4–6*
*Preparation: 1 hour*
  *+ 1 hour to rest the dough*
*Cooking: 25–30 minutes*
*Recipe grading: fairly easy*

Dough
- $^1/_2$ oz/15 g fresh yeast or 1 package ($^1/_4$ oz/7 g) active dry yeast
- 2 cups/500 ml warm milk
- 1 teaspoon sugar
- $1^1/_3$ cups/200 g all-purpose/plain flour
- $^1/_4$ teaspoon salt

Filling
- 8 oz/250 g mixed cheeses, such as Mozzarella, Provolone, Fontina, and Valdostana, cut into small cubes
- 2 tablespoons all-purpose/plain flour
- 1 cup/250 ml milk
- freshly ground black pepper to taste
- 3 eggs, separated

Dough: Mix the yeast, milk, and sugar in a small bowl. Set aside for 5 minutes, or until foamy. • Sift the flour and salt into a bowl and make a well in the center. • Pour in the yeast mixture and stir to obtain a firm dough.

• Transfer to a lightly floured work surface and knead for 5–7 minutes, or until smooth and elastic. • Shape into a ball, place in an oiled bowl, and cover with a clean cloth. • Let rise for 1 hour, or until doubled in bulk. • Preheat the oven to 400°F/ 200°C/gas 6. • Butter a large oval baking dish. • Roll the dough out on a lightly floured surface until it is large enough to cover the bottom of sides of the baking dish. • Place the dough in the prepared baking dish. • Filling: Mix the cheeses, flour, and milk in a medium saucepan. Season with pepper and cook over low heat until the cheeses have melted. • Add the egg yolks, beating until just blended. Remove from heat and set aside. • Beat the egg whites in a large bowl with an electric mixer at high speed until stiff peaks form. • Fold the whites into the cheese filling. • Pour into the dough base. • Bake for 25–30 minutes, or until the filling is golden brown on top. • Serve hot.

Mixed cheese pie

*Globe artichokes are a delicious winter vegetable originally from the Mediterranean region. They are a good source of potassium, magnesium, and folate. When choosing artichokes, go for plump, heavy buds with tightly packed leaves and good purple-green coloring.*

## Sweet and sour artichokes

*Serves: 4*
*Preparation: 25 minutes*
*Cooking: 40 minutes*
*Recipe grading: easy*

- 8 very young fresh artichokes
- $^1/_2$ lemon
- $2^1/_2$ tablespoons all-purpose/plain flour
- 6 tablespoons extra-virgin olive oil
- $2^1/_2$ tablespoons finely chopped onion
- 1 tablespoon capers
- 12 green olives, pitted and finely chopped
- 1 small carrot, cut into small cubes
- 2 stalks celery, finely chopped
- scant $^1/_2$ cup/100 ml hot water
- salt and freshly ground black pepper to taste
- 4 tomatoes
- 4 anchovy filets
- 4 tablespoons red wine vinegar
- $2^1/_2$ teaspoons sugar

Remove the outer leaves of the artichokes and the top third of the leaves. Remove the choke and peel the remaining stalk. Rub all over with the lemon to prevent discoloring. • Cut each artichoke lengthwise into six pieces. • Roll the artichokes in the flour. • Sauté the artichokes in the oil in a flameproof casserole over high heat for 3 minutes. • Remove the artichokes, letting the excess oil drain back into the casserole, and set aside. • Add the onion, capers, olives, carrot, celery, and hot water. Season with the salt and pepper and simmer over medium heat for 10 minutes. • Add the tomatoes, artichokes, and anchovies. Simmer, covered, over low heat for 25 minutes. • Mix the vinegar and sugar and stir into the vegetables. Cook for 5 minutes more. • Serve warm or at room temperature.

## Kouliabaka

*Serves: 10–12*
*Preparation: 1 hour + 1 hour 15 minutes to rest the dough*
*Cooking: 20–25 minutes*
*Recipe grading: complicated*

### Dough
- $^1/_2$ oz/15 g fresh yeast or 1 package ($^1/_4$ oz/7 g) active dry yeast
- 4 tablespoons warm milk
- 1 teaspoon sugar
- $1^2/_3$ cups/250 g all-purpose/plain flour
- $^1/_2$ teaspoon salt
- 6 tablespoons butter, melted
- 2 eggs

### Filling
- 4 oz/125 g buckwheat
- $1^2/_3$ cups/400 ml vegetable stock
- 1 bay leaf
- 6 tablespoons butter
- salt and freshly ground black pepper to taste
- 1 onion, finely chopped
- 1 tablespoon extra-virgin olive oil
- 8 oz/250 g Savoy cabbage, outer leaves removed, finely shredded
- 8 oz/250 g mushrooms, finely sliced
- 6 tablespoons sour cream
- 1 bunch fresh dill
- 1 egg yolk

Dough: Mix the yeast, milk, and sugar in a small bowl. Set aside for 5 minutes, or until foamy. • Sift the flour and salt into a large bowl and make a well in the center. Stir in the yeast mixture and add the butter and eggs. Stir until a smooth dough has formed. Turn the dough onto a lightly floured work surface and knead for 5–7 minutes, or until smooth and elastic. • Shape into a ball, place in an oiled bowl, and cover with a clean cloth. Let rise in a warm place for 45 minutes, or until doubled in bulk. • Turn out of the bowl and knead briefly. Return to the bowl, cover with the cloth, and let rest for 30 minutes more. • Roll the dough out to fit a medium baking sheet. • Line the sheet with parchment paper, lift the dough onto it, and cover with the cloth. • Preheat the oven to 425°F/220°C/gas 7. • Filling: Toast the buckwheat in a hot skillet (frying pan), shaking the pan until the buckwheat is brown and starts to pop. • Pour in 1 cup (250 ml) of vegetable stock and crumble in the bay leaf. Cover and simmer for 10 minutes. • Stir in 4 tablespoons of butter and season with salt and pepper. Set aside to cool. • Sauté the onion in the oil and 1 tablespoon of butter in a large skillet until transparent. Add the cabbage and sauté until tender. • Gradually pour in the remaining stock. Season with salt and pepper. Remove from heat and let cool. • Sauté the mushrooms for 3 minutes in the remaining butter. • Stir in the sour cream and cook for 2–3 minutes. • Sprinkle with the dill. • Spoon a layer of buckwheat over one half of the dough, followed by a layer of cabbage and the mushroom sauce. Fold the other half over the filling. Seal the edges by dampening with water and crimping the dough edges upwards with your finger and thumb. Brush the top with the yolk. • Bake for 20–25 minutes, or until it sounds hollow when tapped. Let cool for 15 minutes before slicing. Serve warm with sour cream or butter.

Sweet and sour artichokes

# Cheese and vegetable pancakes

*Serves: 4*
*Preparation: 50 minutes*
*Cooking: 8–10 minutes*
*Recipe grading: fairly easy*

Pancakes
- 2 tablespoons butter
- 2 eggs
- $^3/_4$ cup/125 g all-purpose/plain flour
- $^1/_8$ teaspoon salt
- 1 cup/250 ml milk

- 1 carrot, cut into matchsticks
- 2 zucchini/courgettes, cut into matchsticks
- white of 1 leek, very finely sliced
- 4 tablespoons extra-virgin olive oil
- 1$^2/_3$ cups/300 g Ricotta cheese

- 1 egg
- 1$^3/_4$ cups/215 g freshly grated Pecorino cheese
- $^3/_4$ cup/90 g freshly grated Parmesan cheese
- 1 clove garlic, finely chopped
- 14 oz/400 g spinach leaves, blanched
- 3 tablespoons heavy/double cream
- freshly ground black pepper to taste

Pancakes: Melt the butter in a small skillet (frying pan). • Beat the eggs, flour, and salt in a large bowl until well blended. • Gradually stir in the milk and melted butter until smooth. • Pour 2 tablespoons of the batter into the skillet (frying pan), tilting the pan so that the batter thinly covers the surface. • Cook until light gold on the bottom. Use a large spatula to flip the pancake and cook the other side. • Repeat until all the batter has been used. • Preheat the oven to 400°F/200°C/gas 6. •

Sauté the carrot, zucchini, and leek in 2 tablespoons of the oil in a skillet over medium heat for 5 minutes. • Remove from heat and transfer to a baking dish. • Beat the Ricotta, egg, Pecorino, and $^1/_2$ cup (60 g) of Parmesan in a large bowl until well blended. • Spread the mixture over the pancakes and roll them up loosely. • Use a sharp knife to trim edges of the pancakes. • Place half the pancakes on top of the vegetables in the baking dish. • Sauté the garlic in the remaining oil in a large skillet over medium heat. Add the spinach and sauté for 7–8 minutes. • Transfer to the baking dish and arrange the remaining pancakes on top. • Drizzle with the cream, season with pepper, and sprinkle with the remaining Parmesan. • Bake for 8–10 minutes, or until the cheese is golden brown. • Serve hot.

# Asparagus spirals

*Serves: 4*
*Preparation: 45 minutes*
*Cooking: 1 hour*
*Recipe grading: complicated*

### Pancakes
- 2 eggs
- $^3/_4$ cup/125 g all-purpose/plain flour
- $^1/_8$ teaspoon salt
- 1 cup/250 ml milk
- 2 tablespoons butter, melted

### Filling
- 14 oz/400 g fresh spinach leaves, stalks removed
- $^3/_4$ cup/180 g fresh creamy goat's cheese
- 1 cup/250 g Ricotta cheese
- salt to taste
- $^1/_8$ teaspoon ground nutmeg
- 1 lb/500 g tender asparagus spears
- $^2/_3$ cup/150 ml light/single cream
- 1 tablespoon butter, cut up
- $^3/_4$ cup/90 g freshly grated Parmesan cheese

Preheat the oven to 400°F/200°C/gas 6. • Beat the eggs, flour, and salt in a large bowl until well blended. • Gradually stir in the milk and half the melted butter. • Place a baking sheet in the oven for 5 minutes. • Remove from the oven and drizzle with a little of the remaining butter. Spoon one sixth of the batter onto the baking sheet. • Bake for 5 minutes, or until the batter is cooked. • Slip the pancake onto a plate and repeat until all the batter is cooked. • Filling: Cook the spinach in a little salted, boiling water for 6–7 minutes, or until tender. Drain and chop finely. Place in a large bowl. • Cook the asparagus in a little salted, boiling water for 10 minutes, or until tender. Drain and chop finely. Place in the bowl with the spinach. • Stir in the goat's cheese and Ricotta and season with salt and nutmeg. • Spread the filling over the pancakes and carefully roll them up. Use a sharp knife to slice each pancake into rounds about 1 inch (2.5 cm) thick. • Butter a baking dish. • Place the pancake rounds in the baking dish, placing them on one end so that they look like spirals. • Drizzle with the cream, dot with the butter, and sprinkle with the Parmesan. • Bake for 15 minutes, or until the cheese has is golden brown. • Serve hot.

Asparagus spirals

## Stuffed zucchini

*Serves: 4*
*Preparation: 20 minutes*
*Cooking: 20 minutes*
*Recipe grading: easy*

- 4 zucchini/courgettes
- 1 tablespoon finely chopped parsley
- 1 clove garlic, finely chopped
- $^1/_2$ cup/60 g fine dry bread crumbs
- $^1/_2$ cup/60 g freshly grated Parmesan cheese
- 1 egg
- 2 tablespoons milk
- 1 scallion/spring onion, finely chopped
- 4 tablespoons butter
- 2 tablespoons chopped tomatoes
- salt and freshly ground black pepper to taste
- 1 cup/250 ml water

Trim the ends off the zucchini and cut in half lengthwise. Scoop out the centers and finely chop the flesh. • Mix the zucchini flesh, parsley, garlic, bread crumbs, Parmesan, egg, and milk in a medium bowl. • Spoon the mixture into the hollowed-out zucchini. • Sauté the scallion in the butter in a large deep skillet (frying pan) over medium heat until softened. • Add the tomatoes and season with salt and pepper. • Arrange the zucchini in the skillet with the tomato mixture. Pour in the water. • Cook over medium heat for 20 minutes. • Serve hot.

## Stuffed green bell peppers

*Serves: 4–6*
*Preparation: 1 hour*
*Cooking: 1 hour*
*Recipe grading: complicated*

- 6 fat green bell peppers/capsicums

Stuffing
- 2 onions, finely chopped
- 4 tablespoons butter
- 1 cup/200 g long-grain rice
- 1 tablespoon pine nuts
- 2 tablespoons sunflower seeds
- 1 tablespoon pumpkin seeds
- 2 tablespoons golden raisins/sultanas
- 1 cup/250 ml water
- salt and freshly ground black pepper to taste
- 3 tablespoons finely chopped parsley
- 1 tablespoon finely chopped mint
- 1 tablespoon finely chopped savory
- 2 tablespoons finely chopped dill

- 3 cups/750 ml vegetable stock, flavored with 1 teaspoon tomato concentrate and 1 teaspoon paprika
- 2 egg yolks
- 2 tablespoons all-purpose/plain flour
- 2 tablespoons fresh lemon juice
- salt and freshly ground black pepper to taste
- 1 tablespoon finely chopped dill

Wash and dry the bell peppers. Cut the top, or a "hat" off each and set aside. Remove the cores, seeds, and ribs from inside the bell peppers. • Stuffing: Sauté the onions in the butter in a medium saucepan over low heat until pale gold. • Stir in the rice, pine nuts, sunflower seeds, pumpkin seeds, and raisins. • Pour in the water and bring to a boil. Cover and cook for 10 minutes. Season with salt and pepper and sprinkle with the parsley, mint, savory, and dill. • Place the peppers in a saucepan just big enough to hold them all snugly standing upright. • Divide the stuffing equally among the bell peppers. Cover each bell pepper with its hat "hat." • Pour the stock into the saucepan. • Simmer over medium-low heat for 25–30 minutes, or until the peppers are tender and the stuffing is well cooked. • Carefully transfer the bell peppers to an ovenproof dish, reserving the cooking liquid. Place the bell peppers in a warm oven. • Beat the egg yolks, flour, and lemon juice in a small bowl. • Stir this mixture into 2 cups (500 ml) of the cooking liquid from the bell peppers. • Cook for 5 minutes over medium heat, stirring constantly. • Season with salt and pepper then pour the sauce over the peppers. • Sprinkle with the dill and serve.

## Tomatoes baked with Parmesan, parsley, and garlic

*Serves: 4–6*
*Preparation: 35 minutes*
*Cooking: 30–35 minutes*
*Recipe grading: easy*

- 10 firm-ripe tomatoes
- 5 cloves garlic, finely chopped
- 6 tablespoons finely chopped parsley
- $^1/_2$ cup/60 g fine dry bread crumbs
- $^1/_2$ cup/60 g freshly grated Parmesan cheese
- $^1/_2$ cup/125 ml extra-virgin olive oil
- salt and freshly ground black pepper to taste

Preheat the oven to 350°F/180°C/gas 4. • Butter a baking dish. • Cut the tomatoes in half and gently squeeze out as many seeds as possible. Sprinkle with salt and let drain upside-down in a colander for 20 minutes. • Stir together the garlic and parsley in a medium bowl. Add the bread crumbs and Parmesan. Use a fork to gradually work in the oil. Season with the salt and pepper. • Use a teaspoon to spoon the filling into the tomato halves, pressing it down with your fingertips so that it sticks to the inside of the tomatoes. • Place the filled tomatoes in the prepared dish. • Bake for 30–35 minutes, or until lightly browned. • Serve hot.

*Stuffed zucchini*

Cheese and potato pie

## Cheese and potato pie

*Serves: 4*
*Preparation: 40 minutes*
*Cooking: 20–25 minutes*
*Recipe grading: easy*

• 1³/₄ lb/800 g potatoes
• ¹/₂ cup/125 g butter, cut up
• 8 oz/250 g Parmesan cheese, thinly sliced
• salt to taste
• freshly ground black pepper to taste
• 1 cup/250 ml milk

Boil the potatoes in their skins for 15–20 minutes, or until tender but still firm. • Drain well and let cool for 15 minutes. • Peel and let cool completely. • Preheat the oven to 400°F/200°C/gas 6. • Butter a baking dish. • Cut the potatoes into ¹/₂-inch (1-cm) slices and arrange in layers in the prepared baking dish. • Dot each layer with the butter and sprinkle with Parmesan. Season with salt and pepper. Pour in the milk. • Bake for 20–25 minutes, or until golden brown. • Serve hot.

## Three-bean chilli

*Serves: 4–6*
*Preparation: 20 minutes*
*Cooking: 35–45 minutes*
*Recipe grading: easy*

• 3 tablespoons extra-virgin olive oil
• 4 tablespoons butter
• one 2-inch/4–5-cm piece root ginger, peeled and grated
• seeds of 4 cardamom pods
• 1 tablespoon ground coriander seeds
• 5 cloves garlic, finely chopped
• 2 onions, finely chopped
• 2 small red chile peppers, seeded and finely sliced
• 2 small green chile peppers, seeded and finely sliced
• 1 tablespoon tomato concentrate/purée
• 1 cup/200 g canned garbanzo beans/ chickpeas
• 1 cup/200 g canned kidney beans
• 1 cup/200 g canned pinto or flageolet beans
• 2 cups/500 ml chopped tomatoes
• 2 bay leaves

• salt and freshly ground black pepper to taste
• 1 tablespoon finely chopped parsley
• 1 teaspoon finely chopped cilantro/coriander

Heat the oil and butter in a large skillet (frying pan) over high heat. Add the ginger, cardamom, coriander seeds, and garlic and sauté for 3 minutes. • Add the onions, chilies, and tomato concentrate. Sauté for 5 minutes over medium heat. • Stir in the beans, tomatoes, and bay leaves. Cover and simmer over very low heat for 30–40 minutes, stirring often. The chilli should be thick and moist, but not mushy. • Season with salt and pepper and sprinkle with the parsley and cilantro just before serving. • Serve hot.

## Split-pea purée

*Serves: 6*
*Preparation: 25 minutes*
*Cooking: 2 hours 10–20 minutes*
*Recipe grading: fairly easy*

• 12 oz/350 g split yellow peas
• 1 quart/1 liter water + more as needed

- 1 large onion, finely chopped
- 2 tablespoons extra-virgin olive oil
- ¹/₂ teaspoon ground turmeric

Flavored butter
- 2 cloves garlic, lightly crushed
- 2 scallions/spring onions, finely chopped
- 2 shallots, finely chopped
- 1 teaspoon finely chopped mint
- ¹/₂ small green chile pepper, seeded and finely chopped
- 2 tablespoons butter
- ¹/₂ teaspoon dried red chile pepper
- 1 teaspoon ground coriander seeds
- ¹/₂ teaspoon ground cumin seeds
- 2 teaspoons fresh lemon juice
- 1 teaspoon fresh lime juice
- salt to taste
- freshly ground black pepper to taste
- 1 tablespoon finely chopped cilantro/ coriander
- 2 lemons, cut in 4
- 1 red onion, finely sliced

Wash the split peas thoroughly under cold running water. Place in a large saucepan and cover with the water. Bring to a boil, then skim the froth off. • Add the onion, oil, and turmeric. Simmer for 2 hours, or until the peas have broken down almost completely. Add more water if needed. Let cool completely and use a potato masher to purée. • Flavored butter: Sauté the garlic, scallions, shallots, mint, and green chile in the butter in a skillet (frying pan) over low heat for 3 minutes. • Grind the red chile, coriander, and cumin to a paste in a pestle and mortar. Mix with the lemon and lime juices in a small bowl. • Add the paste to the skillet and cook for 2 minutes more. • Stir the butter into the split pea purée. Simmer, covered, for 5–10 minutes, or until the purée is the consistency of porridge. • Season with salt and pepper. Sprinkle with the cilantro. • Serve with the lemon quarters and red onion.

## Stuffed eggplants

*Serves: 4*
*Preparation: 20 minutes*
*Cooking: 30–35 minutes*
*Recipe grading: easy*

- 4 small eggplants/aubergines
- 8 oz/250 g Mozzarella cheese, cut into small cubes
- 1 clove garlic, finely chopped
- 3 tablespoons extra-virgin olive oil
- salt to taste
- freshly ground black pepper to taste
- 3 firm-ripe tomatoes, cut into small cubes

Preheat the oven to 350°F/180°C/gas 4. • Rinse the eggplants thoroughly under cold running water and cut in half lengthwise. Scoop out the centers and chop the flesh into small cubes. • Mix the eggplant flesh, Mozzarella, and garlic in a medium bowl. Drizzle with 2 tablespoons of oil and season with salt and pepper. • Arrange the hollowed-out eggplant halves in a baking dish. Spoon the filling mixture into the eggplants. Sprinkle with the chopped tomatoes. • Bake for 30–35 minutes, or until the topping is bubbling and the eggplants are well cooked. • Serve hot or at room temperature.

## Baked fennel with Parmesan cheese

*Serves: 4*
*Preparation: 30 minutes*
*Cooking: 15–20 minutes*
*Recipe grading: fairly easy*

- 6 large fennel bulbs
- 1 onion, thinly sliced
- 4 tablespoons all-purpose/plain flour
- $^1/_2$ cup/125 g butter
- 4 tablespoons heavy/double cream
- salt and freshly ground black pepper to taste
- $1^1/_4$ cups/150 g freshly grated Parmesan cheese

Preheat the oven to 375°F/190°C/gas 5.
• Butter a baking dish. • Clean the fennel by removing the tough outer leaves. Trim the stalks and cut each bulb in half. • Cook the fennel in salted, boiling water for 8–10 minutes, or until tender. • Drain well and pat dry with a clean cloth. Cut each half in 2 or 3 pieces. • Dip the fennel and onion in the flour. Sauté the fennel and onion in 4 tablespoons of butter in a skillet (frying pan) over medium heat until golden brown. • Add the cream and season with the salt and pepper. • Cook, covered over low heat for 12–15 minutes, or until the sauce has reduced. • Arrange the fennel and onion in layers with the sauce in the prepared baking dish. Sprinkle with the Parmesan and dot with the remaining butter. • Bake for 15–20 minutes, or until the top is light gold. • Serve hot.

Baked fennel with Parmesan cheese

# Baked eggplants with Parmesan cheese

*Serves: 6*

*Preparation: 30 minutes + 1 hour to drain the eggplants*

*Cooking: 1 hour*

*Recipe grading: fairly easy*

- 3 large eggplants/aubergines, peeled and cut into ¼-inch/5-mm slices
- 1 cup/150 g all-purpose/plain flour
- 4 eggs, lightly beaten
- 3 cups/750 ml olive oil, for frying
- 2 cups/500 ml tomato sauce (store-bought or homemade)
- 12 oz/350 g Mozzarella cheese
- 2½ cups/310 g freshly grated Parmesan cheese
- 2 tablespoons butter

Place the eggplant slices in a colander, sprinkle with salt, and let drain for 1 hour. • Preheat the oven to 350°F/180°C/gas 4. • Dip the eggplant slices in the flour, coating well, followed by the beaten eggs. • Heat the oil in a deep fryer or skillet (frying pan) to very hot. • Fry the eggplants in batches for 5–7 minutes, or until tender and well cooked. • Drain well on paper towels. • Place a layer of tomato sauce in a baking dish and cover with a layer of fried eggplants and Mozzarella. Sprinkle with some Parmesan. Repeat this layering process until all the ingredients are in the dish, finishing with a layer of tomato sauce and Parmesan. Dot the top with the butter. • Bake for 30–35 minutes, or until lightly browned. • Serve hot.

Baked eggplants with Parmesan cheese

# Cabbage parcels

*Serves: 4–6*
*Preparation: 45 minutes*
*Cooking: 50 minutes*
*Recipe grading: fairly easy*

Stuffing
- 1 large onion, finely chopped
- 6 tablespoons butter
- 1 clove garlic, finely chopped
- $^1/_2$ teaspoon ground caraway seeds
- 14 oz/400 g mixed mushrooms, washed, dried, and finely chopped
- 1 teaspoon paprika
- 1 tablespoon finely chopped thyme
- 5 tablespoons heavy/double cream
- 2 oz/60 g strong-flavored firm-textured cheese, such as Cheddar or Pecorino
- salt and freshly ground black pepper to taste
- 1 Savoy cabbage, weighing about 2 lb/1 kg, outer leaves and hard core removed
- 1 teaspoon tomato concentrate/purée (optional)
- 1 cup/250 ml vegetable stock (bouillon cube)
- 2 tomatoes, peeled and chopped
- 1 tablespoon finely chopped parsley

Stuffing: Sauté the onion in the butter in a skillet (frying pan) over medium heat until lightly browned. • Add the garlic and caraway seeds and cook for 2 minutes. • Stir in the mushrooms, paprika, and thyme. Cook over high heat for 5 minutes, or until the cooking liquid the mushrooms release has evaporated. • Stir in 3 tablespoons of cream and the cheese. Season with salt and pepper and set aside to cool. • Blanch the cabbage leaves in a large pot of salted, boiling water for 3 minutes. Drain well and

Zucchini and carrot mold

spread out each leaf with your fingers. • Spoon a little of the stuffing onto each of the flattened leaves. Fold over the edges of each leaf all the way round and carefully roll up. Tie with kitchen string. • Cook the cabbage parcels in the remaining butter in a flameproof casserole for 2–3 minutes. • Stir the tomato concentrate into the stock until well blended. Pour over the cabbage parcels and sprinkle with the tomatoes. • Cover and cook for 25 minutes over low heat. • Stir in the remaining cream and sprinkle with the parsley. Season with salt and pepper and simmer for 10 minutes more. • Serve hot.

# Zucchini and carrot mold

*Serves: 4–6*
*Preparation: 40 minutes*
*Cooking: 1 hour 30 minutes*
*Recipe grading: fairly easy*

- 2–3 tablespoons butter
- $^1/_2$ cup/75 g fine dry bread crumbs
- $1^1/_4$ lb/625 g zucchini/courgettes, thinly sliced
- 4 tablespoons extra-virgin olive oil
- 2 onions, finely chopped
- 4 medium carrots, finely chopped
- 1 quantity Béchamel sauce (see Mushroom soup with sherry, page 56)
- $^1/_2$ cup/60 g freshly grated Parmesan cheese
- 2 eggs, lightly beaten
- 2 tablespoons finely chopped mint
- salt and freshly ground black pepper to taste

Preheat the oven to 400°F/200°C/gas 6. • Butter a 10-inch (25-cm) ring mold and sprinkle with the bread crumbs. • Sauté one-fifth of the zucchini in 1 tablespoon of oil in a large skillet (frying pan) over medium heat for 5 minutes. Set aside. • Line the prepared mold with the zucchini by sticking them one by one to the butter and bread crumbs until the mold is covered. • Sauté the carrots and onions in the remaining oil for 5 minutes. • Add the

remaining zucchini and cook, covered, for 10–15 minutes, or until the vegetables are tender. • Prepare the Béchamel sauce. Let cool for 10 minutes. • Mix the Parmesan, eggs, vegetables, and mint into the Béchamel. Season with salt and pepper. • Pour the mixture into the mold, taking care not to knock the zucchini off the sides. • Half fill a large roasting pan with hot water and place the mold in the waterbath. • Bake for 50 minutes. • Cool for 10 minutes. Carefully invert and turn onto a serving plate. • Serve hot or at room temperature.

# Baked vegetables

*Serves: 4–6*
*Preparation: 35 minutes*
*Cooking: 50–60 minutes*
*Recipe grading: fairly easy*

- 1 pumpkin, weighing about $1^1/_4$ lb/575 g
- 4 bell peppers/capsicums, mixed colors
- 2 red onions, cut in 4
- 16 cherry tomatoes
- 4 cloves garlic
- 2 fresh red chile peppers
- 5 tablespoons extra-virgin olive oil
- 1 tablespoon honey
- 2 tablespoons finely chopped thyme
- 1 teaspoon coarsely ground sea salt

Preheat the oven to 400°F/200°C/gas 6. • Halve the pumpkin, remove the seeds, and peel. Cut the flesh into small chunks and spread out in a large roasting pan. • Cut the tops and stalks off the peppers, halve lengthways, and remove the seeds and ribs. • Place bell peppers, onions, cherry tomatoes, garlic, and chilies in the roasting pan with the pumpkin. Drizzle with the oil and honey. Sprinkle with the thyme and salt. • Bake for 50–60 minutes, or until lightly browned. • Cool for 5 minutes. Spoon the juices from the pan over the top. • Serve hot or at room temperature.

## Cauliflower mold with black olives

*Serves: 4*
*Preparation: 25 minutes*
*Cooking: 45 minutes*
*Recipe grading: easy*

- 2 lb/1 kg cauliflower head, cut into large florets
- ¹/₂ quantity Béchamel sauce (see Mushroom soup with sherry, page 56)
- ¹/₂ cup/60 g freshly grated Parmesan cheese
- 20 black olives, pitted and finely chopped
- 3 eggs, lightly beaten
- salt and freshly ground black pepper to taste
- ¹/₄ teaspoon ground nutmeg

Preheat the oven to 350°F/180°C/gas 4. • Butter a 10-inch (25-cm) ring mold and sprinkle with fine dry bread crumbs. • Cook the cauliflower in a large pot of salted boiling water for 5–7 minutes. Drain well and set aside. • Chop the cauliflower coarsely. • Stir in the Béchamel, Parmesan, olives, and eggs. Season with the salt, pepper, and nutmeg. • Pour the mixture into the prepared mold. • Fill a large roasting pan with hot water and place the mold in the waterbath. • Cook for 45 minutes. • Carefully invert and turn out onto a serving plate. • Serve hot or at room temperature

## Baked onions with potatoes and cheese

*Serves: 4*
*Preparation: 30 minutes*
*Cooking: 20–25 minutes*
*Recipe grading: easy*

- 3 lb/1.5 kg potatoes
- 8 onions, cut into thick slices
- 1 tablespoon extra-virgin olive oil
- ¹/₂ cup/125 g butter
- 1 cup/250 ml dry white wine
- ¹/₂ cup/125 ml vegetable stock (bouillon cube)

- salt and freshly ground black pepper to taste
- 1¹/₄ cups/310 ml milk
- 3 eggs, lightly beaten
- 1 cup/125 g freshly grated Parmesan cheese
- 1 cup/125 g freshly grated Gruyère cheese
- 2 tablespoons fine dry bread crumbs

Cook the potatoes in their skins in a large pot of salted, boiling water for 20–25 minutes, or until tender. Drain and cover to keep warm. • Place the onions, oil, 6 tablespoons of butter, wine, and stock in a large saucepan. Season with salt and pepper. Cover and simmer for 25–30 minutes, or until the onions are tender. • Preheat the oven to 350°F/ 180°C/gas 4. • Butter a baking dish. • Peel the potatoes and mash until smooth. • Heat the milk in a large saucepan. Stir in the potatoes and 5 tablespoons of butter. Remove from heat and cool for 10 minutes. • Mix the potato mixture with the eggs and season with the salt and pepper. Add ²/₃ cup (80 g) Parmesan. • Spread half the potato mixture in the prepared baking dish in an even layer. • Drain the cooked onions and spread over the potatoes. Sprinkle with the Gruyère and cover with the remaining potatoes. • Sprinkle with bread crumbs and remaining Parmesan. • Bake for 20–25 minutes, or until light golden brown on top. • Serve hot.

## Onions stuffed with brown rice and oregano

*Serves: 4*
*Preparation: 45 minutes*
*Cooking: 40 minutes*
*Recipe grading: fairly easy*

- 1¹/₄ cups/250 g brown rice
- 8 large onions
- 2 cups/200 g black olives, pitted
- 3 eggs, lightly beaten
- 2 teaspoons dried oregano
- ¹/₂ cup/60 g freshly grated Parmesan cheese

- 1 cup/125 g freshly grated Pecorino cheese
- salt and freshly ground black pepper to taste
- 4 tablespoons extra-virgin olive oil
- 1 cup/250 ml dry white wine
- 1 cup/250 ml vegetable stock (bouillon cube)
- 2 tablespoons butter

Cook the rice in a large pot of salted, boiling water for 15–20 minutes, or until tender. Drain well. • Preheat the oven to 350°F/180°C/gas 4. • Cut the bottoms off the onions and slice off the tops. • Cook the onions in a large pot of salted, boiling water for 8–10 minutes, or until slightly softened. Drain and let cool completely. • Scoop the flesh out of the onions, leaving a ¹/₂-inch (1-cm) thick shell. Reserve the flesh. • Chop half the olives finely. • Beat the eggs, rice, half the oregano, Parmesan, Pecorino, and olives in a large bowl. Season with salt and pepper. • Spoon the mixture into the onions and sprinkle with the remaining oregano. • Cut the remaining olives in half. • Mix 4 table-spoons of the reserved onion flesh, the halved olives, and 1 tablespoon of oil in a small bowl. Season with salt and pepper. • Pour into a baking dish. • Arrange the stuffed onions in the dish and pour in the remaining oil, wine, and vegetable stock. Dot the onions with the butter. • Bake for 40 minutes, or until tender and well cooked. • Serve hot.

Onions stuffed with brown rice and oregano

# SIDE DISHES

**S**ide dishes should always be chosen carefully to complement the dishes they accompany. They should draw out the flavors of the main dishes, or contrast with them in interesting ways. In this sense, vegetarian meals can require a little more forethought and planning than a traditional "meat and vegetables" combination. The nutritional value of the dishes should also be taken into consideration—for example, many grains and legumes served together provide complete proteins, often lacking in vegetarian diets.

*Bell peppers (also known as capsicums, or just plain peppers) are a summer vegetable that work beautifully with a range of ingredients and flavors. The simple baked dish shown here has distinctly Mediterranean overtones, with olives, capers, oregano, and olive oil. Generally speaking, bell peppers go well with tomatoes, onions, Parmesan, and fresh cheeses such as Mozzarella and Caprino (goat's cheese). They also combine well with balsamic vinegar, garlic, basil, chile peppers, and olive oil.*

Baked bell peppers (see page 192)
Spinach and Ricotta croquettes
(see page 192)

190

## Spinach and Ricotta croquettes

*Serves: 4*
*Preparation: 20 minutes*
*Cooking: 25–30minutes*
*Recipe grading: fairly easy*

- 1¼ lb/600 g fresh spinach leaves, stalks removed
- ¾ cup/180 g Ricotta cheese
- ½ cup/75 g all-purpose/plain flour
- 2 eggs, lightly beaten
- salt and freshly ground black pepper to taste
- 2 cups/500 ml olive oil, for frying

Rinse the spinach leaves thoroughly under cold running water. Do not drain but place in a saucepan and cook, with just the water clinging to their leaves, for 3 minutes. Drain, press out excess water, and chop finely. • Mix the spinach, Ricotta, 2 tablespoons of flour, and the eggs in a large bowl. Season with salt and pepper. • Heat the oil in a deep fryer or skillet (frying pan) until very hot. • Shape the spinach mixture into balls the size of walnuts. • Roll in the remaining flour until well coated. • Fry the croquettes in batches in the oil for 5–7 minutes, or until golden brown and crisp. • Drain well on paper towels. • Sprinkle with salt and serve hot.

## Baked bell peppers

*Serves: 4–6*
*Preparation: 15 minutes*
*Cooking: 25–30 minutes*
*Recipe grading: : easy*

- 3 lb/1.5 kg red bell peppers/capsicums, seeded, cored, and cut into large chunks
- 1½ lb/750 g onions, thickly sliced
- 20 green olives, pitted
- 2 tablespoons capers in salt, rinsed
- 6 tablespoons extra-virgin olive oil
- salt to taste
- 1 tablespoon finely chopped oregano

Preheat the oven to 400°F/200°C gas 6. • Place the bell peppers in a large baking dish. Sprinkle with the onions, olives, and capers. Drizzle with the oil and season with the salt. • Bake for 25–30 minutes, or until the bell peppers are tender. • Sprinkle with the oregano and serve hot.

## Sautéed vegetables with egg white omelet

*Serves: 6*
*Preparation: 20 minutes*
*Cooking: 20 minutes*
*Recipe grading: easy*

- 8 egg whites
- salt to taste
- 1 scallion/spring onion, finely chopped
- 3 tablespoons butter
- 8 oz/250 g carrots, peeled and cut into thin sticks
- 1 cup/250 ml water
- 1 tablespoon finely chopped thyme
- 1 tablespoon finely chopped marjoram
- 2 tablespoons extra-virgin olive oil
- 15 oz/450 g asparagus tips, cut in half
- 4 oz/125 g fresh fava/broad beans
- 1 tablespoon finely chopped parsley
- 1 tablespoon freshly grated Parmesan cheese

Beat the egg whites and ⅛ teaspoon salt in a large bowl with an electric mixer at high speed until stiff peaks form. • Sauté the scallion in 1 tablespoon of butter in a skillet (frying pan) over medium heat until lightly browned. • Melt 1 tablespoon of butter in a skillet over medium heat. Pour in the beaten whites and cook until set. Turn out onto a board and cut into thin strips. • Sauté the carrots in the remaining butter over medium heat. Season with salt. • Pour in the water and cook for 8–10 minutes, or until tender. • Sauté the thyme and marjoram in the oil in a large skillet until aromatic. • Add the asparagus and cook until tender. • Stir in the carrots, fava beans, and parsley. Cook for 1 minute. • Add the omelet strips and sprinkle with the Parmesan. • Serve hot.

*Sautéed vegetables with egg white omelet*

*In tropical areas where the coconut palm grows wild, this plant is a staple food item, consumed as oil, milk, and food. Fresh coconut is a great ingredient for vegans as it can replace eggs, cheese, and milk as a source of protein.*

## Vegetables with spicy coconut sauce

*Serves: 4*
*Preparation: 25 minutes*
*Cooking: 25 minutes*
*Recipe grading: easy*

Sauce
• 1 tablespoon chopped fresh ginger root
• 8 small red chilies, seeded
• 4 cloves garlic
• 4 shallots
• 1 tablespoon palm sugar
• 3 cups/750 g freshly grated coconut
• 1 quart/1 liter water
• 3 salam leaves
• salt to taste

Vegetables
• 3 oz/90 g green beans, topped and tailed
• 3 oz/90 g carrots, peeled and cut into rounds
• 3 oz/90 g bean sprouts
• fried onion, to garnish

Sauce: Process the ginger, chilies, garlic, shallots, and palm sugar in a food processor until very finely chopped. • Transfer to a large saucepan and stir in the coconut, water, and salam leaves. Season with salt. Bring to a boil and simmer over medium heat until the sauce begins to thicken. • Remove from heat and let cool completely. • Vegetables: Steam the green beans and carrots until tender. • Arrange the vegetables on a large serving plate. • Blanch the bean sprouts in a large pot of salted, boiling water for 1 minute. • Drain well and add to the serving plate. • Drizzle the sauce over the top and garnish with the fried onions. • Serve hot, with boiled rice.

## Noodles with vegetables

*Serves: 4*
*Preparation: 15 minutes*
*Cooking: 15 minutes*
*Recipe grading: fairly easy*

• 1 tablespoon finely chopped fresh ginger root
• 1 clove garlic, finely chopped
• 1 tablespoon extra-virgin olive oil
• 2 carrots, cut into thin sticks
• 1 zucchini/courgette, cut into thin sticks
• 3 scallions/spring onions, cut into thin sticks
• 1 teaspoon sesame oil
• 1 cup/250 ml water
• 1 cup/250 ml coconut milk
• 1 tablespoon soy sauce
• 1 1/2 teaspoons red curry paste
• 10 oz/300 g white somen noodles
• 1/2 cup/50 g finely chopped peanuts
• 2 tablespoons finely chopped cilantro/coriander

Sauté the ginger and garlic in the olive oil in a large skillet (frying pan) for 2–3 minutes. • Add the carrots, zucchini, scallions, and sesame oil and sauté until the vegetables are tender but crunchy. • Transfer the vegetables to a medium bowl and set aside. • Pour the water, coconut milk, soy sauce, and red curry paste into the skillet. Cook for 6–8 minutes, or until the sauce has reduced by half. • Add the vegetables and stir until well coated. • Cook the noodles in a large pot of salted, boiling water for 2 minutes, or until tender. • Drain well and transfer to the skillet. Toss well. • Transfer to a heated serving dish. • Sprinkle with the peanuts and cilantro and serve hot.

## Spiced cucumber yogurt

*Serves: 2–4*
*Preparation: 10–15 minutes*
*Recipe grading: easy*

• 1 small cucumber, peeled and cut in half
• 1 1/2 teaspoons salt
• 1 cup/250 ml plain yogurt
• 1 tablespoon finely chopped mint

Use a teaspoon to scrape the seeds from the cucumbers. Grate finely and place in a large bowl. • Sprinkle with the salt and let stand for 5–10 minutes. • Drain and stir in the yogurt and mint until well blended.

## Spiced banana yogurt

*Serves: 4*
*Preparation: 10 minutes*
*Recipe grading: easy*

• 1 cup/250 g plain yogurt
• 1/2 cup/125 ml heavy/double cream
• 1/2 teaspoon finely chopped red chile pepper
• 2 ripe bananas, mashed
• 1/8 teaspoon salt
• 1 green chile pepper, seeded and thinly sliced

Beat the cream in a small bowl with an electric mixer at high speed until thick. • Fold the cream into the yogurt. Add the red chile and bananas and mix well. • Season with salt and garnish with the green chile.

Vegetables with spicy coconut sauce

## Boston baked beans

*Serves: 6*
*Preparation: 45 minutes + 1 hour to soak the beans*
*Cooking: 5 hours*
*Recipe grading: fairly easy*

- 1 lb/500 g haricot beans
- 3 onions
- 4 cloves
- 6 tablespoons dark molasses/black treacle
- $^3/_4$ cup/150 g firmly packed light brown sugar
- 2 teaspoons dry mustard powder
- 1 cup/250 ml water
- salt and freshly ground black pepper to taste

Cook the beans in a large pot of salted, boiling water for 2 minutes. • Remove from heat and let soak for 1 hour. • Preheat the oven to 300°F/150°C/gas 2. • Add 1 onion to the beans and bring to a boil. Simmer for 30 minutes more, or until the beans are tender. • Drain well and discard the onion. • Pierce the remaining onions with the cloves and arrange in a large baking dish. • Mix the molasses, sugar, mustard, and water in a small bowl until well blended. Season with salt and pepper. • Spoon the beans into the baking dish and drizzle with the molasses mixture. • Bake for 4 hours, or until the beans are cooked and the liquid has been absorbed. • Serve hot with crusty bread.

## Baby onions with carrots

*Serves: 4–6*
*Preparation: 20 minutes*
*Cooking: 30 minutes*
*Recipe grading: fairly easy*

- 7 oz/200 g baby onions
- 7 oz/200 g carrots, cut into small sticks
- 2 cups/500 ml + 4 tablespoons water
- 7 oz/200 g zucchini/courgettes, cut into small sticks
- 1 tablespoon butter

*Serve this dish with a lightly aromatic dry white wine on a summer's evening together with rice or potatoes and a mix of vegetables cooked over a herbal scented wood fire.*

## Onions sautéed with tomatoes and bell peppers

*Serves: 4*
*Preparation: 20 minutes*
*Cooking: 35–40 minutes*
*Recipe grading: easy*

- 2 firm-ripe tomatoes
- $^1/_2$ red bell pepper/capsicum, seeded, cored, and finely chopped
- 1 small green chile pepper, seeded and finely chopped
- 4 tablespoons extra-virgin olive oil
- 2 lb/1 kg onions, each cut in 4
- salt to taste
- 2 tablespoons finely chopped marjoram

Peel the tomatoes, squeeze gently to remove as many seeds as possible, and chop coarsely. • Sauté the bell pepper and chile in the oil in a medium saucepan over high heat for 7–10 minutes, or until the bell peppers begin to soften. • Add the tomatoes and onions. Season with salt, cover and cook for 35–40 minutes, or until the vegetables are tender. • Remove from heat and let cool completely. • Sprinkle with the marjoram and serve.

- 1 teaspoon sugar
- salt and freshly ground white pepper to taste

Cook the onions and carrots with the water in a pressure cooker with the lid securely closed for 5 minutes. • Drain well and set aside. • Sauté the onions, carrots, and zucchini in the butter in a large skillet (frying pan) over medium heat for 5 minutes. Add the 4 tablespoons of water and sprinkle with the sugar. Season with the salt and pepper. • Cook until the vegetables have a glossy, caramelized finish. • Serve hot.

## Sweet and sour onions

*Serves: 4*
*Preparation: 25 minutes*
*Cooking: 35–45 minutes*
*Recipe grading: easy*

- $1^1/_2$ cups/375 ml dry white wine
- $1^1/_2$ cups/375 ml white wine vinegar
- 1 cup/250 ml balsamic vinegar
- 1 cup/200 g sugar
- 5 tablespoons extra-virgin olive oil
- 1 clove garlic, lightly crushed
- 10 cloves
- 2 bay leaves
- $1^1/_2$ teaspoons black peppercorns
- 2 lb/1 kg baby onions

Bring the wine, white wine vinegar, balsamic vinegar, sugar, oil, garlic, cloves, bay leaves, and peppercorns to a boil in a large saucepan. • Add the onions and simmer for 8–10 minutes, or until tender but crunchy. • Transfer the onions to a large jar. • Bring the liquid to a boil again and cook for 15–20 minutes, or until the liquid has reduced to 2 cups (500 ml). Pour the liquid over the onions and let cool completely. • Fasten the jar tightly and refrigerate for 1 week before serving.

Onions sautéed with tomatoes and bell peppers

# Marinated eggplants

*Serves: 4*

*Preparation: 20 minutes + 1 hour to degorge the
   eggplants + 24 hours to marinate*

*Cooking: 5–7 minutes*

*Recipe grading: easy*

- 4 large eggplants/aubergines, thinly sliced
- 1–2 tablespoons coarse sea salt
- $^1/_2$ cup/125 ml extra-virgin olive oil
- 2 cloves garlic, thinly sliced
- 8–10 fresh sage leaves, torn
- 2 cups/500 ml best-quality wine vinegar

Place the eggplants in a colander. Sprinkle
with the salt and leave 1 hour. • Heat the oil
in a large skillet (frying pan) until very hot.
• Rinse the eggplants and dry well. • Fry in
batches for 5–7 minutes, or until golden
brown on both sides. • Drain well on paper
towels. • Place a layer of eggplant in a deep
serving dish and sprinkle with garlic and
sage leaves. Repeat until all the ingredients
are in the dish. • Pour in sufficient wine
vinegar to cover the top layer completely. •
Marinate for 24 hours before serving.

# Marinated porcini mushrooms

*Serves: 4*

*Preparation: 20 minutes + 24 hours to marinate*

*Cooking: 7 minutes*

*Recipe grading: easy*

- 2 lb/1 kg small porcini mushrooms
- 2 cups/500 ml white wine vinegar
- 2 cups/500 ml dry white wine
- 3 bay leaves
- 10 white peppercorns
- 1 teaspoon salt
- 10–15 leaves fresh mint, torn
- extra-virgin olive oil to cover

Rinse the mushrooms thoroughly under
cold running water, trimming off any
dirty pieces. • Bring the vinegar, wine,
bay leaves, and peppercorns to a boil in a
large saucepan. • Add the mushrooms
and cook for 7 minutes. • Drain well. •
Let marinate for 24 hours. They must
lose all their humidity before going in the
jars. • Pack the mushrooms in sterilized
jars and sprinkle each with a little salt and
mint. • Pour in enough oil to cover. • Use
a knife to make sure no pockets of air
remain. • Seal and store for at least a
month before serving.

# Olive pâté

*Serves: 2*

*Preparation: 20 minutes*

*Recipe grading: easy*

- 14 oz/400 g green or black olives, pitted
- 6 tablespoons extra-virgin olive oil + extra to
  cover
- freshly ground white pepper to taste

Process the olives in a food processor or
blender until finely chopped. Add
enough of the oil to make a creamy paste.
Season with pepper. • Transfer to
sterilized jars, cover with oil, and seal. • If
liked, add herbs or spices, such as garlic
or parsley, to the olives before chopping
them. Serve this pâté on slices of warm
toast or as a pasta sauce.

## Marinated artichokes

*Serves: 8*
*Preparation: 20 minutes*
*Cooking: 4–5 minutes*
*Recipe grading: easy*

- 24 small artichokes
- 2 cups/500 ml white wine vinegar
- 2 cups/500 ml water
- 10 white peppercorns
- 3 bay leaves
- $^1/_8$ teaspoon salt
- extra-virgin olive oil to cover

Clean the artichokes, cutting off the stalks and removing all the tough outer leaves so that only the tender heart remains. Cut in half, removing the fuzzy choke inside. • Heat the vinegar, water, peppercorns, and bay leaves in a large saucepan over medium heat. Simmer the artichokes for 4–5 minutes. • Drain well and sprinkle with salt. • Pack in sterilized jars and pour in enough oil to cover. Use a knife to make sure no pockets of air remain. Seal and store for at least a month before serving.

## Marinated zucchini

*Serves: 2–4*
*Preparation: 20 minutes + 24 hours to marinate*
*Cooking: 25 minutes*
*Recipe grading: easy*

- 8 zucchini/courgettes
- 4 tablespoons extra-virgin olive oil
- 1 cup/250 ml white wine vinegar
- 1 small red chile pepper
- salt and freshly ground black pepper to taste

Rinse the zucchini thoroughly under cold running water and dry well. Cut the ends off and slice into rounds. • Heat the oil in a large deep skillet (frying pan) until very hot. • Fry the zucchini in batches for 6–8 minutes, or until golden brown all over. • Drain well on paper towels. • Transfer the zucchini to a deep serving dish. • Bring the vinegar and chile to a boil in a small saucepan. Pour over the zucchini. • Season with the salt and pepper. Cover and let marinate for 24 hours. • Serve at room temperature.

## Marinated bell peppers

*Serves: 8*
*Preparation: 20 minutes*
*Cooking: 3–5 minutes*
*Recipe grading: easy*

- $1^3/_4$ lb/800 g red and yellow bell peppers/ capsicums, seeded, cored, and cut into thin strips
- $3^1/_4$ cups/810 ml water
- 2 cups/500 ml white wine vinegar
- juice of 1 lemon
- $^1/_8$ teaspoon salt
- 10 black peppercorns
- 4 leaves fresh basil
- 1 teaspoon dried oregano
- 2 cloves garlic, thinly sliced
- extra-virgin olive oil to cover

Cook the bell peppers in the water, vinegar, lemon juice, salt, and peppercorns for 5 minutes. • Drain well and pat dry on a clean cloth. • Place in sterilized jars with the basil, oregano, garlic, and a sprinkling of salt. • Pour in enough oil to cover. Seal and store for at least a month before serving.

Marinated zucchini

## Roast potatoes with rosemary

*Serves: 4*
*Preparation: 10 minutes*
*Cooking: 30–35 minutes*
*Recipe grading: easy*

- 2 lb/1 kg potatoes, peeled and cut into small chunks
- $^1/_2$ cup/125 ml extra-virgin olive oil
- salt to taste
- freshly ground black pepper to taste
- 2–3 bunches rosemary
- 3 cloves garlic (optional)

Preheat the oven to 375°F/190°C/gas 5. • Rinse the potatoes thoroughly under cold running water and dry well. • Drizzle 4 tablespoons of oil into a baking dish. • Arrange the potatoes in the dish in one layer. Season with salt and pepper and sprinkle with the rosemary and garlic cloves, if using. • Drizzle with the remaining 4 tablespoons oil and mix well. • Bake for 30–35 minutes, or until the potatoes are tender, crisp, and golden brown all over, shaking the dish occasionally. • Season with extra salt, if liked. • Serve hot.

## Potatoes with sour cream and chives

*Serves: 4*
*Preparation: 20 minutes*
*Cooking: 15–20 minutes*
*Recipe grading: easy*

- 2 lb/1 kg small new potatoes, peeled
- $^3/_4$ cup/180 ml sour cream
- 2 tablespoons milk
- 2 tablespoons finely chopped chives
- $^1/_8$ teaspoon cayenne pepper

Cook the potatoes in a large pot of salted, boiling water for 15–20 minutes, or until tender. • Drain well and transfer to a deep serving dish. • Mix the sour cream, milk, and chives in a small bowl. • Drizzle over the potatoes. • Dust with pepper and serve.

## Spring vegetables

*Serves: 2–4*
*Preparation: 15 minutes*
*Cooking: 15 minutes*
*Recipe grading: easy*

- 2 lettuce hearts, cut in half
- 4 scallions/spring onions, coarsely chopped
- 8 snow peas/mangetouts, topped and tailed
- 3 oz/90 g asparagus tips, cut diagonally in half
- 7 oz/200 g peas
- 2 preserved artichokes, rinsed (optional)
- 1 tablespoon finely chopped flat-leaf parsley

- 1 tablespoon finely chopped mint
- 1 teaspoon finely grated lemon zest
- freshly ground black pepper to taste
- 2 tablespoons butter, cut up
- 5 tablespoons vegetable stock (bouillon cube) + more if needed
- 1 teaspoon fresh lemon juice

Rinse the lettuce hearts thoroughly under cold running water and dry well. • Place the lettuce in a large saucepan. Add the scallions, snow peas, asparagus tips, peas, and artichokes. Sprinkle with the parsley, mint, and lemon zest. Season with the pepper and dot with butter. • Add 5 tablespoons of vegetable stock. Bring to a boil and cook for 5–7 minutes. • If the cooking liquid begins to dry out, add a little more stock. The vegetables should be crunchy and the cooking liquid should be well-reduced. • Transfer the vegetables to a

heated serving dish. Drizzle with the lemon juice and serve with Greek yogurt.

## Potatoes Venetian-style

*Serves: 4*
*Preparation: 15 minutes*
*Cooking: 30–35 minutes*
*Recipe grading: easy*

- 1 onion, thinly sliced
- 6 tablespoons butter
- 6 tablespoons extra-virgin olive oil
- 2 lb/1 kg yellow waxy potatoes, peeled and cut into small chunks
- salt to taste
- 2 tablespoons finely chopped parsley

Sauté the onion in the butter and oil in a skillet (frying pan) until lightly browned. • Add the potatoes and cook for 30–35 minutes, or until

tender, stirring often. • Season with salt and sprinkle with the parsley. • Serve hot.

## Mashed potatoes

*Serves: 4*
*Preparation: 20 minutes*
*Cooking: 15–20 minutes*
*Recipe grading: easy*

- 2 lb/1 kg potatoes, peeled
- ³/₄ cup/180 ml heavy/double cream
- 2 tablespoons butter
- salt and freshly ground black pepper to taste

Cook the potatoes in a large pot of salted boiling water for 15–20 minutes, or until tender. • Drain well and transfer to a medium bowl. • Mash the potatoes. • Stir in the cream and butter until well blended. • Season with the salt and pepper. • Serve hot.

## Mushroom and tomato stew

*Serves: 4*
*Preparation: 20 minutes*
*Cooking: 25 minutes*
*Recipe grading: easy*

- 2 lb/1 kg fresh porcini or white mushrooms
- 2 cloves garlic, finely chopped
- 1 tablespoon finely chopped parsley
- 4 tablespoons extra-virgin olive oil
- salt and freshly ground black pepper to taste
- 1–2 tablespoons hot water
- 1 cup/250 ml tomato sauce (store-bought or homemade)

Rinse the mushrooms thoroughly under cold running water and dry well. • Detach the stems from the caps. • Slice the caps and chop the stalks coarsely. • Sauté the garlic and parsley in the oil in a large skillet (frying pan) for 3 minutes. Add the mushroom stems. Season with the salt and pepper and cook for 5 minutes. • Add the mushroom caps and mix well. Cook for 5 minutes. • Add enough water to moisten the mushrooms. • Stir in the tomato sauce and mix well. Simmer for 10–12 minutes. • Serve hot.

## Mushrooms in green sauce

*Serves: 8*
*Preparation: 20 minutes*
*Cooking: 20 minutes*
*Recipe grading: fairly easy*

Green sauce
- 1 clove garlic, finely chopped
- 1 teaspoon finely chopped mint
- 1 tablespoon finely chopped basil
- 1 bunch flat-leaf parsley, finely chopped
- 4 tablespoons dry white wine or sherry
- 3 tablespoons water
- 1 tablespoon capers (optional)

- 2 cloves garlic, finely chopped
- 4 tablespoons butter
- 4 tablespoons extra-virgin olive oil
- 2 lb/1 kg white button mushrooms, halved
- salt and freshly ground black pepper to taste
- 1 tablespoon all-purpose/plain flour
- juice of 1 lemon (optional)
- 1 tablespoon finely chopped parsley

Green sauce: Mix the garlic, mint, basil, parsley, wine, water, and capers, if using, in a small bowl until well blended. • Sauté the garlic in the butter in a large saucepan until pale gold, then add the oil. • Turn up the heat, and when it starts bubbling, add the mushrooms. • Cook, stirring constantly, until the juices are drawn out of the mushrooms. • Season with the salt and pepper and simmer over low heat for 8–10 minutes. Stir in the flour. • Remove from the heat and stir in the green sauce. • Return to the heat and bring to a boil. Cook and stir until the sauce thickens. Simmer for 5 minutes. Add a little water and the lemon juice if the sauce is too dry. Sprinkle with the parsley and serve hot.

## Mushrooms stuffed with goat's cheese and barley

*Serves: 4*
*Preparation: 25 minutes*
*Cooking: 20 minutes*
*Recipe grading: fairly easy*

- 12 large mushrooms
- 1 onion, finely chopped
- 2 cloves garlic, finely chopped
- 1 tablespoon finely chopped parsley
- 1 tablespoon finely chopped thyme
- 1 tablespoon finely chopped basil
- 2 tablespoons extra-virgin olive oil
- 2 oz/60 g pre-cooked barley
- 1 tablespoon Caprino cheese

Preheat the oven to 350°F/180°C/gas 4. • Rinse the mushrooms carefully under cold running water and dry well. • Detach the stems from the caps. • Chop the stalks coarsely. • Sauté the mushroom stalks, onion, garlic, parsley, thyme, and basil in the oil in a large skillet (frying pan) until the onion has softened. • Stir in the barley and goat's cheese. Cook for 2 minutes more. • Spoon the barley mixture into the mushroom caps. • Arrange in a large baking dish. • Cover with aluminum foil and bake for 12–15 minutes, or until tender. • Remove the foil and bake for 5 minutes more. • Serve warm.

Mushroom and Tomato stew

Baked potatoes with
bell pepper pesto

## Sautéed herbed zucchini

*Serves: 4*
*Preparation: 20 minutes*
*Cooking: 6–8 minutes*
*Recipe grading: easy*

- 1¹/₂ cloves garlic, 1 lightly crushed, ¹/₂ finely chopped
- 1 lb/500 g zucchini/courgettes, cut into thin rounds
- 4 tablespoons extra-virgin olive oil
- salt and freshly ground black pepper to taste
- 6 leaves fresh basil, finely chopped
- 2 leaves fresh mint, finely chopped

Sauté the crushed garlic and zucchini in 3 tablespoons of oil in a large deep skillet over high heat for 6–8 minutes, or until the zucchini are lightly browned. • Season with salt and pepper and discard the garlic. • Mix the basil, mint, and finely chopped garlic in a small bowl with the remaining oil. • Add to the zucchini and remove from heat. Mix well and serve hot.

## Baked potatoes with bell pepper pesto

*Serves: 4*
*Preparation: 45 minutes*
*Cooking: 35–45 minutes*
*Recipe grading: fairly easy*

- 8 potatoes, each weighing about 3 oz/90 g

Bell pepper pesto
- 1 red bell pepper/capsicum
- 1 tablespoon pine nuts
- 1 bunch basil
- 1 bunch parsley
- 1 clove garlic
- 5 tablespoons extra-virgin olive oil
- salt to taste
- 1 bunch arugula/rocket, to garnish

Preheat the oven to 300°F/150°C/gas 2. • Wrap each potato in aluminum foil. • Bake for 35–45 minutes, or until tender. • Bell pepper pesto: Place the bell pepper whole under the broiler (grill) at high heat, turning until the skin scorches and blackens. This will take about 20 minutes. When the pepper is black all over, wrap in foil and set aside for 10 minutes. When unwrapped, the skin will peel away easily. • Remove the seeds and white parts. Cut into small pieces. • Process the bell pepper, pine nuts, basil, parsley, garlic, and oil in a food processor until very finely chopped. Season with salt. • Cut the potatoes in half and arrange on a bed of arugula. • Place a tablespoonful of the

Sautéed herbed zucchini

bell pepper pesto in the center of each potato half. • Serve hot.

## Carrot purée

*Serves: 4*
*Preparation: 20 minutes*
*Cooking: 30 minutes*
*Recipe grading: easy*

- 15 oz/450 g carrots, peeled
- 1 sprig parsley
- 1 sprig thyme
- 2 bay leaves
- 5 black peppercorns
- 2 cloves garlic, 1 unpeeled, 1 peeled and lightly crushed
- 4 tablespoons vegetable stock (bouillon cube) + more as needed
- 2 tablespoons Mascarpone cheese

- 1 tablespoon freshly grated Parmesan cheese
- $^1/_2$ teaspoon ground nutmeg
- salt and freshly ground black pepper to taste

Preheat the oven to 300°F/150°C/gas 2. • Grease a large baking sheet with oil. • Cook the carrots in a large pot of salted, boiling water with the parsley, thyme, bay leaves, peppercorns, and unpeeled garlic for 15–20 minutes, or until tender. • Drain well and spread out on the baking sheet. • Bake for 8–10 minutes to dry the carrots out. • Process the carrots, crushed garlic, and 4 tablespoons of vegetable stock in a food processor until puréed. • Transfer the purée to a small saucepan and place over low heat, stirring constantly, until thick and smooth, adding more stock if needed. • Cool for 15 minutes, then stir in the Mascarpone

and Parmesan. Season with the nutmeg, salt, and pepper. • Serve hot.

## Caramelized parsnips

*Serves: 4*
*Preparation: 20 minutes*
*Cooking: 1 hour*
*Recipe grading: easy*

- 2 lb/1 kg parsnips, peeled and cut in 4
- $^1/_4$ cup/50 g firmly packed light brown sugar
- 2 tablespoons vegetable stock (bouillon cube)

Preheat the oven to 375°F/190°C/gas 5. • Cook the parsnips in a large pot of salted, boiling water for 5 minutes. • Drain well and arrange in a large baking dish. • Sprinkle with the sugar and drizzle with the vegetable stock. • Bake for 55 minutes, or until caramelized. • Serve hot.

salt and sprinkle with the dill. Let marinate for 1 hour. • Place the bell peppers in a large saucepan with the water, vinegar, wine, sugar, and garlic. Bring to a boil and cook for 5 minutes. • Remove from heat and let cool completely. • Transfer to the bowl with the cucumbers and mix well. • Sprinkle with the savory and drizzle with the oil. • Season with the salt and pepper and serve.

## Broiled bell pepper relish

*Serves: 2–4*
*Preparation: 20 minutes*
*Cooking: 8–10 minutes*
*Recipe grading: easy*

• 1 red bell pepper/capsicum
• 1 yellow bell pepper/capsicum
• 2 firm-ripe tomatoes
• 2 scallions/spring onions, finely chopped
• 2 cloves garlic, finely chopped
• $1/4$ teaspoon ground cumin seeds
• $1/2$ teaspoon sugar
• 1 tablespoon balsamic vinegar
• 1 tablespoon extra-virgin olive oil
• salt and freshly ground black pepper to taste
• 2 tablespoons finely chopped cilantro/coriander

Turn on the broiler (grill). • Broil the bell peppers and tomatoes 4–6 inches (10–15 cm) from the heat source, turning them often until the skins turn black. When black all over, wrap in foil and set aside for 10 minutes. When unwrapped, the skins will peel away easily. • Cut the bell peppers in half and remove the stems and seeds. Cut the soft flesh of the bell peppers and the tomatoes into bite-sized pieces. • Mix the bell peppers, tomatoes, scallions, garlic, cumin, sugar, vinegar, and oil in a large bowl. • Season with the salt and pepper and sprinkle with the cilantro. • Serve with freshly baked bread or with boiled basmati rice.

Sweet and sour bell peppers with cucumber

## Sweet and sour bell peppers with cucumber

*Serves: 6*
*Preparation: 15 minutes*
*  + 1 hour to marinate*
*Cooking: 5 minutes*
*Recipe grading: easy*

• 3 cucumbers, peeled and cut in half lengthwise
• salt and freshly ground black pepper to taste
• 1 tablespoon finely chopped dill
• 1 red, 1 yellow, and 1 green bell pepper/capsicum, seeded, cored, and cut into small chunks
• 2 cups/500 ml water
• 2 cups/500 ml white wine vinegar
• 1 cup/250 ml dry white wine
• 1 teaspoon sugar
• 2 cloves garlic
• 1 tablespoon finely chopped savory
• 1 tablespoon extra-virgin olive oil

Use a teaspoon to scrape the seeds from the cucumbers. Cut into small sticks and place in a large bowl. • Season with the

## Mixed braised bell peppers

*Serves: 4–6*
*Preparation: 15 minutes*
*Cooking: 25 minutes*
*Recipe grading: easy*

- 4–6 bell peppers/capsicums, mixed colors, cut into thin strips
- 2 large onions, thinly sliced
- 2 cups/500 g peeled and chopped tomatoes
- 4 tablespoons extra-virgin olive oil
- 3 cloves garlic, finely chopped
- salt and freshly ground black pepper to taste
- 6 leaves fresh basil, torn

Place the bell peppers, onions, and tomatoes in a large saucepan. Add the oil and garlic and season with salt and pepper. • Cover and cook over medium heat for 15 minutes. • Uncover and cook over high heat for 5 more minutes, to allow some of the cooking liquid to evaporate. Continue cooking for 5 minutes more, or until the bell peppers are tender. • Serve hot or at room temperature, garnished with the basil.

## Bell peppers with leeks

*Serves: 4*
*Preparation: 10 minutes*
*Cooking: 15 minutes*
*Recipe grading: easy*

- whites of 3 leeks, thinly sliced
- 1 red, 1 yellow, and 1 green bell pepper/capsicum, seeded, cored, and cut into thin strips
- 3 tablespoons extra-virgin olive oil
- ½ teaspoon dried oregano
- salt and freshly ground black pepper to taste

Sauté the leeks and bell peppers in the oil in a large skillet (frying pan) over medium heat for 10 minutes, or until the vegetables are almost tender. • Sprinkle with the oregano and cook until the vegetables are cooked. • Season with salt and pepper and serve hot.

Mixed braised bell peppers

## Zucchini and bell pepper mix

*Serves: 4*
*Preparation: 10 minutes*
*Cooking: 15 minutes*
*Recipe grading: easy*

- 12 oz/350 g zucchini/courgettes, cut in 4 lengthwise
- 1 red and 1 yellow bell pepper/capsicum, seeds removed and cut into small cubes
- 4 tablespoons extra-virgin olive oil
- salt and freshly ground black pepper to taste
- 1 tablespoon finely chopped parsley
- 1 tablespoon finely chopped mint

Use a teaspoon to scoop out the seeds in the center of the zucchini. • Cut into small cubes. • Sauté the zucchini and bell peppers in the oil in a large skillet over medium heat. • Season with the salt and pepper and cook for 15 minutes, or until the zucchini and bell peppers are tender. • Sprinkle with the parsley and mint. • Transfer to a large heated serving plate and serve hot.

*Radicchio, or red chicory, can be used in salads or baked like a vegetable. Treviso radicchio is long and tapered, whereas Verona radicchio is smaller and round. Both have a slightly bitter taste.*

## Radicchio Treviso-style

*Serves: 6*
*Preparation: 20 minutes*
*Cooking: 15–20 minutes*
*Recipe grading: easy*

- 6 heads Treviso radicchio or red chicory
- 3–4 tablespoons extra-virgin olive oil
- salt and freshly ground black pepper to taste

Rinse the radicchio heads thoroughly under cold running water and dry well. • Trim off the end of the stalk and cut each head lengthwise into quarters. • Grease a large skillet (frying pan) with 1 tablespoon of oil. • Place the radicchio pieces in the skillet in a single layer. Drizzle with the remaining oil and season with the salt and pepper. • Cook over low heat for 15–20 minutes, or until the radicchio is tender but still crisp. • Serve hot.

# Pumpkin and potato bake

*Serves: 4*
*Preparation: 30 minutes*
*Cooking: 1 hour*
*Recipe grading: easy*

- 1 lb/500 g potatoes
- 1 lb/500 g pumpkin flesh, cut into small cubes
- 4 tablespoons butter
- 4 tablespoons finely chopped parsley
- 4 eggs, separated
- 1 cup/125 g freshly grated Parmesan cheese
- salt and freshly ground black pepper to taste
- 8 oz/250 g Mozzarella cheese, thinly sliced
- 1/2 cup/60 g fine dry bread crumbs

Preheat the oven to 350°F/180°C/gas 4. • Butter a large baking dish. • Cook the potatoes in their skins in salted, boiling water for 15–20 minutes, or until tender. Drain well and peel. • Place the pumpkin in the prepared baking dish. Cover with aluminum foil and bake for 15–20 minutes, or until softened. • Process the potatoes and pumpkin in a food processor until puréed. • Place in a large bowl and stir in 2 tablespoons of butter, the parsley, egg yolks, and 1/2 cup (60 g) of Parmesan. Season with salt and pepper. • Beat the egg whites in a large bowl with an electric mixer at high speed until stiff peaks form. Use a large rubber spatula to fold them into the pumpkin mixture. • Butter a baking dish. • Spoon in half the pumpkin mixture. Cover with the Mozzarella and top with the remaining pumpkin mixture. • Sprinkle with the bread crumbs and remaining Parmesan. Dot with the remaining. • Bake for 45 minutes. • Serve hot.

Radicchio Treviso-style

# Braised Belgian endives with black olives

*Serves: 4*
*Preparation: 20 minutes*
*Cooking: 25–30 minutes*
*Recipe grading: easy*

- 4 heads Belgian endives, cut in half
- 3 oz/90 g celery stalks, finely chopped
- 1 onion, finely chopped
- 1/2 cup/50 g black olives, pitted
- 1 teaspoon sugar
- finely shredded zest of 1/2 lemon
- 3 tablespoons vinegar
- 3 tablespoons extra-virgin olive oil
- salt and freshly ground black pepper to taste
- 1 cup/250 ml vegetable stock (bouillon cube)

Preheat the oven to 400°F/200°C/gas 6. • Place the Belgian endives in a large baking dish. • Sauté the celery, onion, olives, sugar, lemon zest, vinegar, and oil in a large deep skillet for 5–10 minutes. Season with salt and pepper. • Spoon the mixture over the endives and pour in the vegetable stock. • Bake for 25–30 minutes, or until the endives are tender. • Serve hot.

# Baked cabbage, rice, and tomato

*Serves: 4*
*Preparation: 30 minutes*
*Cooking: 25–30 minutes*
*Recipe grading: easy*

- 1 small Savoy cabbage
- 2 onions, finely chopped
- 2 cloves garlic, finely chopped
- 3 tablespoons extra-virgin olive oil
- 1 1/3 cups/270 g parboiled short-grain rice
- salt and freshly ground black pepper to taste
- 2 cups/500 g chopped tomatoes
- 2 cups/250 g freshly grated Gruyère cheese
- 1 quantity Béchamel sauce (see Mushroom soup with sherry, page 56)
- 1 tablespoon butter

Preheat the oven to 350°F/180°C/gas 4. • Butter a baking dish. • Clean the cabbage by discarding the tough outer leaves and trimming the stalk. Cut in half, discard the hard core, and chop the leaves into strips. • Blanch the cabbage in salted, boiling water for 1 minute. Drain well and spread out on a clean cloth to dry. • Sauté the onions and garlic in the oil in a large skillet (frying pan) until the onions are transparent. • Add the rice and season with the salt and pepper. Cook over high heat for 2–3 minutes, stirring constantly. • Add the tomatoes and cook for 15 minutes, or until the rice is tender. • Stir 1 cup (125 g) of Gruyère into the Béchamel sauce. • Place alternate layers of the cabbage and rice mixture in the prepared baking dish. • Pour the Béchamel sauce over the top and sprinkle with the remaining Gruyère. Dot with the butter. • Bake for 25–30 minutes, or until the cheese is bubbling and golden brown. • Serve hot.

## Spinach mold

*Serves: 4*
*Preparation: 40 minutes*
*Cooking: 45 minutes*
*Recipe grading: fairly easy*

- 2 tablespoons butter
- 1¹/₂ lb/750 g fresh spinach leaves, stalks removed
- 4 tablespoons heavy/double cream
- 1 quantity Béchamel sauce (see Mushroom cream with sherry, page 56)
- ¹/₂ cup/60 g freshly grated Parmesan cheese
- ¹/₂ teaspoon ground nutmeg
- 2 eggs, separated
- salt and freshly ground black pepper to taste

Preheat the oven to 350°F/180°C/gas 4. • Butter and flour a 10-inch (25-cm) ring mold. • Cook the spinach in a large pot of salted, boiling water for 5 minutes, or until tender. Drain well and cool under cold running water, squeezing out the excess moisture. Place in a food processor and process until finely chopped. • Transfer to a large saucepan with the cream. • Cook, stirring constantly, over medium heat until all the moisture has been absorbed. • Remove from heat. Stir in the Béchamel sauce and add the Parmesan, nutmeg, and egg yolks. Season with salt and pepper. • Beat the egg whites in a medium bowl with an electric mixer at high speed until stiff peaks form. • Use a large rubber spatula to fold them into the spinach mixture. • Pour the mixture into the prepared mold. • Half fill a large roasting pan with hot water and place the mold in the waterbath. • Bake for 45 minutes. • Cool for 10 minutes. Carefully invert the mold and turn out onto a serving plate. • Serve hot with a tomato sauce.

## Spinach with mushrooms in Madeira cream sauce

*Serves: 4*
*Preparation: 20 minutes*
*Cooking: 15 minutes*
*Recipe grading: easy*

- 2 lb/1 kg fresh spinach leaves, stalks removed
- 4 oz/125 g mushrooms, finely chopped
- 4 tablespoons butter
- 1 teaspoon salt
- ¹/₂ teaspoon ground nutmeg
- 1 tablespoon all-purpose/plain flour
- 6 tablespoons Madeira wine
- 4 tablespoons heavy/double cream
- 1 tablespoon finely chopped parsley

Wash the spinach under cold running water. Do not drain but place in a saucepan and cook, with just the water clinging to its leaves, for 3 minutes. Drain, press out excess water, chop coarsely, and set aside. • Sauté the mushrooms in 1 tablespoon of butter in a skillet (frying pan) for 5 minutes. • Add the mushrooms to the spinach with the remaining butter, salt, and nutmeg. Sprinkle with the flour and drizzle with the Madeira and cream. • Transfer to a serving dish and sprinkle with the parsley.

## Spinach bites

*Serves: 6*
*Preparation: 20 minutes*
*Cooking: 12–15 minutes*
*Recipe grading: easy*

- 6 slices firm-textured bread, cut into small cubes
- 2 tablespoons freshly grated Parmesan cheese
- 2 scallions/spring onions, finely chopped
- 2 cloves garlic, finely chopped
- 10 oz/300 g frozen spinach leaves, thawed
- 4 tablespoons vegetable stock (bouillon stock)
- 2 tablespoons butter, melted
- salt and freshly ground black pepper to taste
- 2 egg whites

Preheat the oven to 350°F/180°C/gas 4. • Mix the bread cubes, Parmesan, scallions, and garlic in a large bowl. Add the spinach, stock, and butter. • Season with salt and pepper. • Beat the egg whites in a small bowl with an electric mixer at high speed until stiff peaks form. • Use a large rubber spatula to fold them into the spinach mixture. • Shape the spinach mixture into balls the size of walnuts. • Arrange the balls on a large baking sheet. • Bake for 12–15 minutes, or until crisp and lightly browned. • Serve hot.

*Spinach mold*

## Pea mousse

*Serves: 4*
*Preparation: 30 minutes + 2 hours to chill*
*Cooking: 15 minutes*
*Recipe grading: fairly easy*

- 1 lb/500 g fresh or frozen peas
- 1 onion, cut in half
- 2 cups/500 g fresh, creamy goat's cheese
- 3 tablespoons extra-virgin olive oil
- salt and freshly ground black pepper to taste
- 8 cherry tomatoes, cut in quarters
- 2 tablespoons finely chopped parsley

Cook the peas and onion in a large pot of salted, boiling water for 15 minutes. • Drain well and set aside to cool. • Process the goat's cheese, peas, onion, and oil in a food processor or blender until creamy. Season with salt and pepper. • Line a 1 quart (1 liter) pudding mold with plastic wrap (cling film). • Pour in the pea mixture, pressing with a spoon to eliminate air pockets. Knock the mold against the work bench to eliminate air bubbles. • Refrigerate for at least 2 hours. • Invert the mousse and turn out onto a serving dish. Garnish with the cherry tomatoes and parsley and serve.

## Petits pois with baby onions

*Serves: 6*
*Preparation: 15 minutes*
*Cooking: 8–10 minutes*
*Recipe grading: easy*

- 8 oz/250 g frozen petits pois
- 8 oz/250 g baby onions
- 4 tablespoons water
- 1 tablespoon butter
- 1 teaspoon dried mint
- salt and freshly ground black pepper to taste
- salt and freshly ground black pepper to taste

Place the petits pois, onions, and water in a medium saucepan over medium heat. Bring to a boil and simmer for 8–10 minutes, or until the petits pois and onions are tender. • Drain well and stir in the butter and mint. • Season with salt and pepper. Transfer to a heated serving bowl and serve hot.

## Eggplant with basil

*Serves: 6*
*Preparation: 15 minutes + 1 hour to degorge the eggplants*
*Cooking: 20 minutes*
*Recipe grading: easy*

- 1 lb/500 g eggplants/aubergines, cut into bite-sized chunks
- 1–2 tablespoons coarse sea salt
- 3 tablespoons extra-virgin olive oil
- 1 teaspoon finely chopped garlic
- 1 teaspoon finely chopped red chile pepper
- 2 tablespoons soy sauce
- 1 1/2 tablespoons sugar
- 1 tablespoon white wine vinegar
- 1/2 teaspoon salt
- large bunch fresh basil
- 1 tablespoon sesame oil

Place the eggplant in a colander. Sprinkle with salt and degorge for 1 hour. • Heat the olive oil in a large wok or skillet (frying pan) over medium heat. • Sauté the garlic and chile for 1–2 minutes. • Add the eggplant and sauté for 10 minutes, or until tender. • Add the soy sauce, sugar, vinegar, salt, and basil and mix well. • Drizzle with the sesame oil and serve hot.

## Eggplant with Pecorino cheese

*Serves: 4*
*Preparation: 15 minutes + 1 hour to degorge the eggplants*
*Cooking: 30 minutes*
*Recipe grading: fairly easy*

- 4 medium eggplants, cut into $^1/_4$-inch/5-mm slices
- 1–2 tablespoons coarse sea salt
- 2 eggs
- freshly ground black pepper to taste
- 4 oz/125 g hard Pecorino cheese, cut into short thin strips
- 20 fresh basil leaves, torn
- $^3/_4$ cup/90 g bread crumbs
- 2 cups/500 ml extra-virgin olive oil, for frying

Place the eggplant slices in a colander. Sprinkle with salt and degorge for 1 hour. • Beat the eggs in a small bowl until frothy. Season with pepper. • Fill pairs of eggplant slices with the Pecorino and basil. • Press the slices firmly together, carefully dip them in the egg, and then in the bread crumbs. • Heat the oil in a deep fryer or skillet (frying pan) until very hot. • Fry 2–3 sandwiches at a time for 5–7 minutes, or until golden brown on both sides. • Serve hot.

## Spicy grilled eggplants

*Serves: 6*
*Preparation: 15 minutes + 1 hour to degorge the eggplants*
*Cooking: 20 minutes*
*Recipe grading: easy*

- 3 large eggplants, cut into $^1/_2$-inch/1-cm thick slices
- 1–2 tablespoons coarse sea salt
- 1–2 hot chile peppers, finely chopped
- $^1/_2$ cup/120 ml extra-virgin olive oil
- salt and freshly ground black pepper to taste
- 10 fresh basil leaves, torn

Place the eggplant slices in a colander. Sprinkle with salt and degorge for 1 hour. • Heat a grill pan to very hot and place the slices on it, pressing them down with a fork so that they press against the grill pan. Turn the slices often. • As soon as the pulp is soft, remove from the grill pan and arrange on a serving dish. • If you do not have a grill pan, cook the eggplants under a broiler (grill). • Mix the chilies and oil until well blended. Season with salt and pepper. Cover and set aside. • When the eggplants are cooked, pour the spicy oil over the top and sprinkle with the basil. • Serve at room temperature.

## Eggplant cooked with tomato and garlic

*Serves: 4*
*Preparation: 15 minutes*
*Cooking: 20 minutes*
*Recipe grading: easy*

- 6 eggplants/aubergines, cut in 4 lengthwise
- 4 cloves garlic, finely chopped
- 3 tablespoons extra-virgin olive oil
- salt and freshly ground black pepper to taste
- 3 firm-ripe tomatoes, peeled and finely chopped
- 2 tablespoons finely chopped parsley

Slice the eggplants into 1-inch (2.5-cm) long pieces. • Sauté the garlic in the oil in a large skillet (frying pan) for 2–3 minutes. • Add the eggplant and season with salt and pepper. Cook over medium heat for 15 minutes. • Add the tomatoes and cook for 10 minutes more, or until the water released by the tomatoes has reduced. • Sprinkle with the parsley. • Serve hot as a side dish or pasta sauce.

## Mixed fried summer vegetables

*Serves: 4–6*
*Preparation: 20 minutes*
*Cooking: 25 minutes*
*Recipe grading: easy*

- 4 zucchini/courgettes
- 4 eggplants/aubergines
- 12 large zucchini flowers
- 2 cups/300 g all-purpose/plain flour
- 4 eggs, lightly beaten
- 6 tablespoons beer
- 3 cups/750 ml extra-virgin olive oil, for frying
- 1/8 teaspoon salt

Cut the zucchini in half crosswise and cut each half in quarters lengthwise. • If using long eggplants, cut into 1/4-inch (5-mm) rounds. If using the larger, pear-shaped eggplants, cut in 1/4-inch (5-mm) thick slices and cut each slice in halves or quarters (depending on how big they are). • Trim the stems of the zucchini flowers and wash carefully. Pat dry with paper towels. • Sift the flour into a large bowl. • Beat the eggs and beer in a medium bowl until well blended. • Heat the oil in a deep fryer or skillet (frying pan) until very hot. • Dip the vegetables in the flour, shaking off any excess, followed by the egg. • Fry the vegetables in batches for 5–7 minutes, or until golden brown all over. • Drain well on paper towels. • Sprinkle with the salt and serve hot.

## Eggplant rolls with Parmesan and basil

*Serves: 6*
*Preparation: 30 minutes + 1 hour to degorge the eggplants*
*Cooking: 15–20 minutes*
*Recipe grading: fairly easy*

- 2 eggplants/aubergines, cut into 12–16 thin slices
- 1–2 tablespoons coarse sea salt
- 5 oz/150 g zucchini/courgettes, chopped
- 1 red bell pepper/capsicum, seeded, cored, and chopped
- 1 onion, finely chopped
- 4 tablespoons extra-virgin olive oil
- salt and freshly ground black pepper to taste
- 1/2 cup/60 g freshly grated Parmesan cheese
- 2 firm-ripe tomatoes, peeled and finely chopped
- 1/2 cup/50 g green olives, pitted
- 1 tablespoon finely chopped basil

Place the eggplant slices in a colander. Sprinkle with salt and degorge for 1 hour. • Preheat the oven to 400°F/200°C/gas 6. • Process the zucchini, bell pepper, and onion in a food processor until finely chopped. • Sauté the zucchini mixture in 2 tablespoons of oil in a large skillet (frying pan) over high heat until lightly browned. • Transfer to a large bowl and season with salt and pepper. Stir in the Parmesan. • Spoon some of the filling mixture onto each eggplant slice. Carefully roll the slices up and place them seam-side down in a large baking dish. • Sprinkle with the tomatoes, olives, and basil. Season with salt and pepper and drizzle with the remaining oil. • Bake for 15–20 minutes, or until the eggplants are tender. • Serve hot.

## Eggplant chutney

*Serves: 6*
*Preparation: 20 minutes + 12 hours to chill*
*Cooking: 1 hour*
*Recipe grading: fairly easy*

- 2 eggplants/aubergines, cut into 1/4-inch/5-mm cubes
- 1 onion, coarsely chopped
- 1 clove garlic, finely chopped
- 2 tablespoons finely chopped fresh ginger root
- 3 tablespoons brown sugar
- 1 teaspoon lightly crushed fennel seeds
- 2 tablespoons red wine vinegar
- 2 teaspoons sesame oil
- 1 tablespoon golden raisins/sultanas
- 6 tablespoons vegetable stock (bouillon cube)
- 2 tablespoons pine nuts, toasted

Preheat the oven to 350°F/180°C/gas 4. • Line a baking sheet with aluminum foil. • Mix the eggplant cubes, onion, garlic, ginger, sugar, and fennel seeds in a large bowl until well blended. • Spoon the mixture onto the prepared baking sheet. Drizzle with the red wine vinegar and sesame oil. • Bake for 45–50 minutes, or until the eggplant is tender. • Sprinkle with the raisins and drizzle with the vegetable stock. • Bake for 10–15 minutes more, or until the stock has been absorbed. • Transfer to a serving dish and sprinkle with the pine nuts. • Refrigerate for at least 12 hours before serving.

*Eggplant cooked with tomato and garlic*

## Artichoke stew

*Serves: 4*
*Preparation: 30 minutes*
*Cooking: 25 minutes*
*Recipe grading: easy*

- 8 artichokes
- juice of 1 lemon
- 3 cloves garlic, finely chopped
- 4 tablespoons extra-virgin olive oil
- 1 cup/250 ml dry white wine
- salt and freshly ground black pepper to taste
- 3 tablespoons finely chopped parsley

Clean the artichokes, removing all but the tender, inner leaves. Peel the stems and cut into wheels. • Place the artichokes and stems in a bowl of cold water with the lemon juice for 10 minutes. • Drain the artichokes and cut into quarters. • Place the artichoke quarters and stems, garlic, oil, wine, salt, and pepper in a large saucepan. Cover and cook for 20 minutes. Sprinkle with the parsley and cook for 5 minutes more. • Serve hot with a platter of fresh, creamy cheeses, such as Mozzarella, Ricotta, or Caprino.

## Curried Brussels sprouts

*Serves: 4–6*
*Preparation: 20 minutes*
*Cooking: 35 minutes*
*Recipe grading: easy*

- 1 onion, finely chopped
- 2 tablespoons butter
- 1 tablespoon all-purpose/plain flour
- 2 cups/500 ml vegetable stock (bouillon cube)
- 1 Golden Delicious apple, peeled and thinly sliced
- 1 cup/250 ml light/single cream
- 1¹/₂ tablespoons curry powder
- salt and freshly ground black pepper to taste
- 2 lb/1 kg Brussels sprouts

Sauté the onion in the butter in a large skillet (frying pan) over medium heat until transparent. • Stir in the flour. • Pour in 1 cup (250 ml) of vegetable stock, stirring constantly. • Add the apple and remaining stock. Simmer over low heat for 20 minutes, or until the apple breaks down and the sauce is thick and creamy. • Stir in the cream and curry powder and season with salt and pepper. Simmer for 5 minutes more, stirring constantly. • Cook the Brussels sprouts in a large pot of salted, boiling water for 10 minutes. • Drain well and arrange on a serving plate. • Pour the sauce over the top and serve.

## Brussels sprouts with nutmeg

*Serves: 4–6*
*Preparation: 5 minutes*
*Cooking: 10 minutes*
*Recipe grading: easy*

- 2 lb/1 kg Brussels sprouts
- 4 tablespoons butter
- ¹/₂ teaspoon ground nutmeg

Cook the Brussels sprouts in a large pot of salted, boiling water for 10 minutes, or until tender. • Drain well and transfer to a serving dish. • Toss with the butter and nutmeg and serve hot.

## Brussels sprouts with onions

*Serves: 4*
*Preparation: 15 minutes*
*Cooking: 20 minutes*
*Recipe grading: easy*

- 8 oz/250 g Brussels sprouts
- 8 oz/250 g baby onions
- 1 tablespoon butter
- 4 tablespoons sugar
- salt and freshly ground white pepper to taste

Cook the Brussels sprouts in a large pot of salted boiling water for 10 minutes, or until tender. • Drain well and transfer to a serving dish. • Cook the onions in a large pot of salted, boiling water for 8–10 minutes, or until tender. • Drain well and add to the Brussels sprouts. • Melt the butter in a large skillet over medium heat and stir in the sugar. Cook until golden. • Add the Brussels sprouts and onions and toss until well coated. Season with salt and pepper. • Serve hot.

## Cauliflower cheese

*Serves: 4–6*
*Preparation: 20 minutes*
*Cooking: 15–20 minutes*
*Recipe grading: fairly easy*

- 6 tablespoons butter
- 4 tablespoons all-purpose/plain flour
- 2 cups/500 ml milk
- grated zest and juice of 1 lemon
- 1 cup/125 g freshly grated Cheddar cheese
- salt and freshly ground black pepper to taste
- 1 cauliflower, weighing about 1 lb/500 g, cut into florets
- 4 slices white sandwich bread, cut into small cubes

Melt 2 tablespoons of butter in a medium saucepan. Stir in the flour. • Add the milk and stir until well blended. • Bring to a boil, stirring constantly, and cook for 1 minute. • Add the lemon zest and Cheddar and season with salt and pepper. • Stir in the lemon juice and simmer for 5 minutes. • Cook the cauliflower in a large pot of salted, boiling water for 10 minutes, or until tender. • Drain well and set aside. • Melt the remaining butter in a skillet (frying pan) over medium heat. Add the bread and sauté until lightly browned. • Place half the cauliflower in a baking dish and cover with half the sauce. • Sprinkle with half the bread cubes. Place the remaining cauliflower on top and cover with the remaining sauce. • Sprinkle with the remaining bread cubes and serve hot.

*Curried Brussels sprouts*

Carrots in caramel sauce with parsley

Transfer to a food processor and process until smooth. • Stir the Parmesan, eggs, mint, and carrot mixture into the Béchamel sauce. Season with salt and pepper and mix well. • Spoon the carrot mixture carefully into the mold, taking care not to knock any of the pieces of carrot off the sides. • Half fill a roasting pan with hot water and place the mold in the waterbath. Bake for 50 minutes. • Cool for 10 minutes, then invert the mold onto a serving dish. • Serve at room temperature.

## Carrots in caramel sauce with parsley

*Serves: 6–8*
*Preparation: 10 minutes*
*Cooking: 20 minutes*
*Recipe grading: easy*

- 3 lb/1.5 kg carrots
- 1 cup/250 ml water
- ¹/₂ cup/125 g butter
- salt to taste
- freshly ground black pepper to taste
- 2 tablespoons sugar
- 3 tablespoons finely chopped parsley

Use a peeler to scrape the carrots and rinse thoroughly under cold running water. • Cut the carrots into 2-inch (5-cm) sticks. • Place the carrots and water in a large deep skillet (frying pan). Add 4 tablespoons of butter and cook over high heat until the water has evaporated. • Season with salt and pepper, add the remaining butter, and sprinkle with the sugar. • Sauté the carrots until caramelized. • Sprinkle with the parsley and serve hot.

## Carrot and onion mold

*Serves: 6*
*Preparation: 40 minutes*
*Cooking: 50 minutes*
*Recipe grading: fairly easy*

- 2 tablespoons butter
- ¹/₂ cup/70 g fine dry bread crumbs
- 1¹/₂ lb/750 g carrots, cut in rounds
- 4 tablespoons extra-virgin olive oil
- 4 onions, finely grated
- ¹/₂ cup/60 g freshly grated Parmesan cheese
- 2 eggs, lightly beaten
- 2 tablespoons finely chopped fresh mint
- 1 quantity Béchamel sauce (see Mushroom soup with sherry, page 56)
- salt and freshly ground black pepper to taste

Preheat the oven to 400°F/200°C/gas 6. • Butter a 12-inch (30-cm) ring mold and sprinkle with bread crumbs. • Sauté half the carrots in 1 tablespoon of oil in a large skillet (frying pan) over medium heat for 5 minutes. Remove from heat and set aside. • Line the mold with the carrot rounds by sticking them one by one to the butter and bread crumbs until the entire mold is covered. • Sauté the onions in the remaining oil for 5 minutes. • Add the remaining carrots. Cook, covered, for 20 minutes, or until the carrots are tender.

# Green bean mold

Serves: 4
Preparation: 40 minutes
Cooking: 1 hour
Recipe grading: complicated

- 4 tablespoons butter
- ¹/₂ cup/70 g fine dry bread crumbs
- 14 oz/400 g green beans, topped and tailed
- ¹/₂ onion, finely chopped
- 1 stalk celery, finely chopped
- 1 tablespoon finely chopped parsley
- 2 tablespoons extra-virgin olive oil
- ¹¹/₂ cup/125 ml vegetable stock (bouillon cube)
- ¹/₄ cup/30 g freshly grated Parmesan cheese
- ¹/₂ quantity Béchamel sauce (see Mushroom soup with sherry, page 56)
- salt and freshly ground black pepper to taste
- 2 eggs, lightly beaten
- 2 tablespoons fine dry bread crumbs

Preheat the oven to 350°F/180°C/gas 4. • Butter a 10-inch (25-cm) ring mold and sprinkle with the bread crumbs. • Cook the beans in a large pot of salted, boiling water for 8–10 minutes, or until tender. Drain well and dry on a clean cloth. • Sauté the onion, celery, and parsley in the oil and 2 tablespoons of butter in a large skillet (frying pan). When the onion begins to color, add the beans. • Sauté for 5 minutes. • Pour in the stock, cover, and cook for 20 minutes. • Stir the Parmesan into the Béchamel sauce and season with salt and pepper. • Drain the beans and transfer to a large bowl. • Add half the Béchamel sauce and the eggs, mixing well. • Arrange the beans in the mold and cover with the remaining Béchamel sauce. • Half fill a large roasting pan with hot water and place the mold in the waterbath. • Bake for 40 minutes, or until the mold is set. •

Zucchini with green beans

Invert the mold and turn out onto a serving dish. • Serve hot or at room temperature.

# Zucchini with green beans

Serves: 6
Preparation: 15 minutes
Cooking: 10 minutes
Recipe grading: easy

- 2 cloves garlic, lightly crushed
- 4 tablespoons extra-virgin olive oil
- 14 oz/400 g zucchini/courgettes, cut into thin sticks
- 10 oz/300 g green beans, topped and tailed
- 6 scallions/spring onions, finely chopped
- salt to taste
- 4 tablespoons cider vinegar
- 4 tablespoons water
- 1 bunch mint

Sauté the garlic in the oil in a large skillet (frying pan) over high heat for 2–3 minutes. • Discard the garlic. • Add the zucchini, green beans, and scallions and cook for 3 minutes over medium heat. • Season with salt and add the vinegar and water. • Cover and cook for 10 minutes, or until the vegetables are tender, stirring occasionally. • Uncover and cook over high heat for 2 minutes, or until the vinegar has evaporated. • Transfer to a heated serving plate, sprinkle with the mint, and serve.

# DESSERTS

Fresh fruit salads, nutty brownies, fruit poached in wine, crisp fruit fritters—an endless array of desserts can be created using healthy, natural ingredients. In this chapter we have tapped into the Italian tradition of fruit, or fruit and rice fritters. Serve them as a dessert after a family meal or dinner party, or with tea or coffee at morning or afternoon tea.

*Choose the freshest fruit available to create the melt-in-your-mouth fritters in this chapter. For economy and taste, always use in-season firm-textured fruit. Healthwise, when frying always ensure that the oil is very hot. About 325–350°F (160–175°C) is the ideal temperature for fritters. Always add just a few fritters to the pan at a time. The batter should seal on impact with the oil, forming a delicious crisp outer layer which will prevent the fritter from absorbing large amounts of oil.*

Battered fresh fruit (see page 222)
Sliced apple fritters (see page 222)

*Bananas are nature's ultimate fast food—just peel and eat! They are a healthy food choice, supplying impressive amounts of potassium, a full range of B vitamins, and smaller amounts of vitamins A and C. Bananas also provide protein and dietary fiber.*

## Dried fruit and nut gnocchi

*Serves: 4–6*
*Preparation: 15 minutes + 1 hour to rest the batter*
*Cooking: 25–30 minutes*
*Recipe grading: fairly easy*

- 1²/₃ cups/250 g all-purpose/plain flour
- ³/₄ cup/180 ml milk
- ¹/₃ cup/70 g sugar
- 3 tablespoons butter, melted
- 3 egg yolks
- 1 teaspoon baking powder
- 1 tablespoon Marsala wine
- 1 teaspoon ground cinnamon
- ¹/₈ teaspoon salt
- 10 oz/300 g dried fruit and nuts, such as prunes, pineapple, papaya, pear, apricots, peanuts, hazelnuts, pecans, walnuts, or figs
- 2 cups/500 ml olive oil, for frying
- ¹/₃ cup/50 g confectioners'/icing sugar

Beat the flour, milk, sugar, butter, egg yolks, baking powder, Marsala, cinnamon, and salt in a large bowl with an electric mixer at medium speed until smooth. • Cover with a clean cloth and let stand in a warm place for 1 hour. • Chop the dried fruit and nuts in a food process or until very finely chopped. • Shape the fruit and nut mixture into balls the size of walnuts. • Dip the balls into the batter, turning to coat well. • Heat the oil in a deep fryer or skillet (frying pan)

until very hot. • Fry the gnocchi in batches for 5–7 minutes, or until crisp and golden brown all over. • Drain well on paper towels. • Dust with the confectioners' sugar and serve hot.

## Battered fresh fruit

*Serves: 4–6*
*Preparation: 20 minutes + 1 hour to rest the batter*
*Cooking: 5–7 minutes*
*Recipe grading: fairly easy*

- 3 eggs
- 4 tablespoons all-purpose/plain flour
- 1 quart/1 liter milk
- 1 small pineapple
- 2 firm-ripe bananas
- 2 tart apples, cut into wedges
- ¹/₂ teaspoon baking powder
- 1 teaspoon vanilla extract/essence
- 2 cups/500 ml olive oil, for frying
- ¹/₃ cup/50 g confectioners'/icing sugar

Beat the eggs in a large bowl with an electric mixer at high speed until pale. • With mixer at medium speed, beat in 2 tablespoons of flour and the milk. • Cover with a clean cloth and let stand in a warm place for 1 hour. • Peel the pineapple and cut the flesh into ¹/₂-inch (1-cm) thick slices. Cut each slice in 4. • Peel the bananas and cut in 4. •

Stir the baking powder and vanilla into the batter. • Dip the pineapple, bananas, and apples in the batter, turning to coat well. • Heat the oil in a deep fryer or skillet (frying pan) until very hot. • Fry the fruit in batches for 5–7 minutes, or until crisp golden brown all over. • Drain well on paper towels. • Dust with the confectioners' sugar and serve hot.

## Sliced apple fritters

*Serves: 4–6*
*Preparation: 20 minutes + 1 hour to rest the batter*
*Cooking: 5–7 minutes*
*Recipe grading: fairly easy*

- 2 eggs, separated
- ³/₄ cup/125 g all-purpose/plain flour
- ¹/₂ cup/125 ml dry white wine
- 2 tablespoons extra-virgin olive oil
- ¹/₈ teaspoon salt
- 6 tart apples, peeled and cored
- juice of 1 lemon
- 2 cups/500 ml olive oil, for frying
- ¹/₃ cup/50 g confectioners'/icing sugar

Beat the egg yolks in a large bowl with an electric mixer at high speed until pale. • With mixer at medium speed, beat in the flour, wine, extra-virgin oil, and salt. • Cover with a clean cloth and let stand for 1 hour. • Slice the apples and slice crosswise. Drizzle with the lemon juice to prevent them from turning brown. • With mixer at high speed, beat the egg whites in a large bowl until stiff peaks form. Use a large rubber spatula to fold them into the batter. • Dip the apple slices in the batter, turning to coat well. • Heat the oil in a deep fryer or skillet (frying pan) until very hot. • Fry the apple slices in batches for 5–7 minutes, or until lightly browned all over. • Drain well on paper towels. • Dust with the confectioners' sugar and serve hot.

*Dried fruit and nut gnocchi*

Orange rice fritters

## Orange rice fritters

*Serves: 6*
*Preparation: 20 minutes + 30 minutes to stand*
*Cooking: 1 hour*
*Recipe grading: fairly easy*

- 2 cups/500 ml milk
- 1¼ cups/310 ml water
- 1 cup/200 g short-grain rice
- ⅛ teaspoon salt
- 3 egg yolks
- ¾ cup/150 g sugar
- ¾ cup/125 g all-purpose/plain flour
- 6 oz/180 g oranges, cut into small pieces
- 1 teaspoon vanilla extract/essence
- 1 tablespoon orange liqueur
- 2 cups/500 ml olive oil, for frying

Mix the milk and water in a large saucepan. Add the rice and salt. • Bring to a boil over medium heat and simmer until all the liquid has been absorbed, about 40 minutes. •

Remove from heat and stir in the egg yolks, ½ cup (100 g) of sugar, the flour, orange, vanilla, and orange liqueur until well blended. • Let stand for 30 minutes. • Heat the oil in a deep fryer or skillet (frying pan) until very hot. • Drop scant tablespoons of the batter into the oil and fry in batches for 5–7 minutes, or until crisp and golden brown all over. • Drain well on paper towels. • Dust with the remaining sugar and serve hot.

## Apple fritters

*Serves: 6*
*Preparation: 20 minutes*
*Cooking: 30 minutes*
*Recipe grading: fairly easy*

- 2⅔ cups/400 g all-purpose/plain flour
- 1 teaspoon baking powder
- ⅛ teaspoon salt
- ⅔ cup/140 g superfine/caster sugar

- grated zest of 1 lemon
- juice of ½ orange
- 2 teaspoons dark rum
- 2 eggs
- ⅔ cup/150 ml milk
- ½ cup/90 g golden raisins/sultanas, soaked in warm water for 10 minutes and drained
- 1½ lb/750 g apples, peeled, cored, and cut into small sticks
- 2 cups/500 ml olive oil, for frying
- ⅓ cup/50 g confectioners'/icing sugar

Sift the flour, baking powder, and salt into a large bowl. Beat in the sugar, lemon zest, orange juice, rum, and eggs. Add the milk gradually and stir until smooth. • Stir in the raisins and apples. • Heat the oil in a deep fryer or skillet (frying pan) until very hot. • Drop scant tablespoons of the batter into the oil and fry in batches for 5–7 minutes, or until crisp and golden brown all over. • Drain well on paper towels. • Dust with the confectioners' sugar and serve hot.

# Fried carnival cookies

*Serves: 4*
*Preparation: 20 minutes + 30 minutes to stand*
*Cooking: 30 minutes*
*Recipe grading: fairly easy*

- 2 cups/300 g all-purpose/plain flour
- 2 tablespoons butter, softened
- 2 eggs
- $^{1}/_{4}$ cup/50 g sugar
- 1$^{1}/_{2}$ tablespoons Vin Santo or other good quality sweet dessert wine
- 1$^{1}/_{2}$ tablespoons finely grated orange zest
- $^{1}/_{8}$ teaspoon salt
- 2 cups/500 ml olive oil, for frying
- $^{1}/_{3}$ cup/50 g confectioners'/icing sugar

Sift the flour into a bowl and make a well in the center. Stir in the butter, eggs, sugar, Vin Santo, orange zest, and salt to obtain a firm dough. • Shape into a ball, cover with a clean cloth and let stand for 30 minutes. • Roll the dough out into a thin sheet. • Cut into diamonds, rectangles, and into broad rectangular strips that can be tied loosely into a knot if wished. • Heat the oil in a deep fryer or skillet (frying pan) until very hot. Fry the cookies in batches for 5–7 minutes, or until light golden all over. • Drain well on paper towels. • Dust with the confectioners' sugar and serve hot or at room temperature.

# Lemon rice fritters

*Serves: 4–6*
*Preparation: 30 minutes + 1 hour to chill*
*Cooking: 5–7 minutes*
*Recipe grading: easy*

- 1 cup/200 g short-grain rice
- 2 cups/500 ml milk
- 1 tablespoon butter
- 3 tablespoons sugar
- finely grated zest of $^{1}/_{2}$ lemon
- 2 eggs
- $^{1}/_{8}$ teaspoon salt
- $^{1}/_{3}$ cup/50 g all-purpose/plain flour
- $^{1}/_{3}$ cup/60 g golden raisins/sultanas, soaked in warm water for 10 minutes and drained
- 4 tablespoons dark rum
- 2 cups/500 ml olive oil, for frying
- $^{2}/_{3}$ cup/100 g confectioners'/icing sugar

Cook the rice in the milk for 1 hour, or until the grains have almost disintegrated. • Remove from heat and stir in the butter, sugar, and lemon zest. • Add the eggs one at a time, beating until just blended. • Add the salt, flour, raisins, and rum. • Refrigerate for 1 hour. • Heat the oil in a deep fryer or skillet (frying pan) until very hot. • Drop scant tablespoons of the batter into the oil and fry in batches for 5–7 minutes, or until crisp and golden brown all over. • Drain well on paper towels. • Dust with the confectioners' sugar and serve hot.

Banana fritters

## Scotch pancakes

*Serves: 4*
*Preparation: 10 minutes*
*Cooking: 25 minutes*
*Recipe grading: easy*

- 1¹/₃ cups/200 g all-purpose/plain flour
- 1 teaspoon baking powder
- ¹/₈ teaspoon salt
- 2 eggs
- 1¹/₄ cups/310 ml milk
- 4 tablespoons butter, melted

Sift the flour, baking powder, and salt into a large bowl and make a well in the center. • Add the eggs one at a time, beating until just blended. • Gradually pour in the milk, followed by the butter. Beat until smooth. • Grease a small skillet (frying pan) with butter. • Heat the skillet to very hot and drop in tablespoons of the batter. • Cook the pancakes for 1–2 minutes, or until holes begin to show and the underside is brown. • Flip the pancakes over with the help of a spatula and cook the other side until nicely browned. Repeat with the remaining batter. • Serve hot with warmed fruit jelly (jam), chopped fresh fruit, ice cream, or whipped cream.

## Banana fritters

*Serves: 6*
*Preparation: 15 minutes*
*Cooking: 25 minutes*
*Recipe grading: easy*

- 6 firm-ripe bananas, peeled
- 1 tablespoon sugar
- 1 tablespoon all-purpose/plain flour
- 1 teaspoon ground ginger
- ¹/₂ teaspoon ground cinnamon
- 2 cups/500 ml olive oil, for frying

Mash the bananas in a medium bowl. • Stir in the sugar, flour, ginger, and cinnamon, mixing well. • Heat the oil in a deep fryer or skillet (frying pan) until very hot. • Drop tablespoons of the batter into the oil and fry the fritters in batches for 5–7 minutes, or until crisp and golden brown all over. • Drain well on paper towels. • Serve hot.

## Blinis

*Serves: 6–8*
*Preparation: 30 minutes + 1 hour 45 minutes to stand*
*Cooking: 1–2 minute(s)*
*Recipe grading: complicated*

- ¹/₂ oz/15 g fresh yeast or 1 package (¹/₄ oz/7 g) active dry yeast
- 6 tablespoons warm water
- ¹/₂ teaspoon sugar
- 1 cup/150 g buckwheat flour
- 1 cup/150 g unbleached white bread flour
- ¹/₂ teaspoon salt
- 1¹/₄ cups/310 ml milk
- 4 tablespoons sour cream

DESSERTS

- 4 tablespoons unsalted butter
- 3 eggs, separated

Mix the yeast, water, and sugar in a small bowl. Set aside for 5 minutes, or until foamy. • Sift the flours and salt into a large slightly warm bowl. • Beat the milk and sour cream in a measuring container, adding enough water to make up 2 cups (500 ml) of liquid. • Pour the milk mixture into a medium saucepan. Add the butter and cook over low heat until the butter has melted. • Remove from heat and let cool to warm. • Add the egg yolks, beating until just blended. • Pour the milk and yeast mixtures into the dry ingredients, beating until smooth. • Cover with a damp clean cloth and let rest for 1 hour and 30 minutes. • Beat the egg whites in a large bowl with an electric mixer at high speed until stiff peaks form. Use a large rubber spatula to fold them into the mixture. • Cover with a clean cloth and let rest for 10 minutes. • Grease two large skillets (frying pans) with oil. • Heat the

skillets to very hot and drop tablespoons of the batter onto them. • Cook the blinis for 1–2 minutes, or until the batter bubbles and the underside is lightly browned. • Turn the blinis over and cook until very thin and full of holes. If the batter is too thick, carefully add a little more warm milk. • Serve hot with butter.

## Sweet coconut treats

*Serves: 4*
*Preparation: 40 minutes + 3 hours to chill*
*Cooking: 15–20 minutes*
*Recipe grading: fairly easy*

- 1¼ cups/190 g pistachios, shelled
- 1⅓ cups/200 g all-purpose/plain flour
- 6 tablespoons butter, softened
- 2 tablespoons freshly grated coconut
- ⅓ cup/50 g confectioners'/icing sugar
- 1 egg + 1 egg yolk
- ½ cup/100 g sugar

Blanch the pistachios in a pot of boiling water for 1 minute. Drain well and use a clean cloth to rub off the skins. • Let cool, then transfer to a food processor and process until very finely chopped. • Sift the flour onto a work surface and make a well in the center. • Use your fingertips to rub in the butter, coconut, confectioners' sugar, and the egg and egg yolk, working to obtain a smooth dough. • Shape into a ball, wrap in plastic wrap (cling film), and refrigerate for at least 2 hours. • Discard the plastic wrap and divide the dough into balls the size of walnuts. Form into crescent shapes, wrap individually in plastic wrap, and refrigerate for 1 hour more. • Preheat the oven to 350°F/ 180°C/gas 4. • Butter and flour a large baking sheet. • Discard the plastic wrap and sprinkle the cookies with the sugar. Dip in the finely chopped pistachios until well coated. • Arrange on the prepared baking sheet. • Bake for 15–20 minutes, or until firm to the touch. • Cool the cookies completely on the baking sheet.

*Strawberries contain powerful antioxidents which some experts claim can halt cancerous tumor growth. Strawberries are also believed to have anti-bacterial properties that detoxify the digestive system. In any case, these delicious berries are good sources of vitamins A and C and provide fiber, iron, calcium, and potassium.*

## Fresh fruit chocolate fondue

*Serves: 8*
*Preparation: 15 minutes*
*Cooking: 15 minutes*
*Recipe grading: fairly easy*

- 2 lb/1 kg fresh fruit, such as grapes, figs, strawberries, bananas, apples, apricots, plums, or peaches
- 2 cups/500 ml water
- juice of 1 lemon
- 1 lb/500 ml semisweet/dark chocolate, coarsely chopped
- 1 cup/250 ml heavy/double cream
- 4 tablespoons butter
- ¼ cup/50 g sugar
- ½ cup/50 g finely chopped almonds, toasted
- ½ cup/50 g finely chopped hazelnuts, toasted
- ½ cup/60 g shredded coconut

Rinse the fruit thoroughly under cold running water and dry well. Cut the larger pieces into bite-sized chunks. • If using apples, pears, or bananas, soak the chunks in water and lemon juice for a few minutes to prevent the flesh from turning brown. Drain well. • Place the fruit in a serving dish. • Melt the chocolate in a double boiler over barely simmering water. Stir in the cream, butter, and sugar until well blended. • Pour the chocolate mixture into a fondue bowl and keep warm over the flame. • Place bowls filled with the almonds, hazelnuts, and coconut on the table, so that your guests can dip pieces of fruit into them, after dipping them in the chocolate sauce.

## Broiled bananas with strawberry coulis

*Serves: 2–4*
*Preparation: 20 minutes*
*Cooking: 5–10 minutes*
*Recipe grading: easy*

- 12 oz/350 g strawberries
- 2 tablespoons sugar
- 5 firm-ripe bananas, peeled
- 2 tablespoons butter, melted
- 1 bunch mint, separated into leaves

Rinse the strawberries thoroughly under cold running water and dry well. Remove the leaves. • Process all but 4 strawberries with the sugar in a food processor or blender until puréed. • Slice 4 bananas in half lengthwise and brush with the butter. • Turn on the broiler (grill). Broil the bananas 4–6 inches (10–15 cm) from the heat source, turning often, until lightly browned. • Arrange on a serving plate and spoon the strawberry coulis over the top. • Slice the reserved strawberries and banana into rounds. Place around the outside edge of the plate and garnish with the mint leaves.

## Citrus fruit with caramelized topping

*Serves: 6*
*Preparation: 20 minutes*
*Cooking: 15 minutes*
*Recipe grading: easy*

- 3 bananas, peeled
- 2 tablespoons fresh lemon juice
- 2 tablespoons water
- 3 pink grapefruit, peeled
- 3 oranges, peeled
- 3 tangerines, peeled
- 2 tablespoons brown sugar

Slice the bananas and place in a medium bowl. Drizzle with the lemon juice and water and set aside for 5 minutes. • Slice the grapefruit, oranges, and tangerines, discarding the pips. • Drain the bananas well and mix with the citrus fruit. • Spoon the fruit into individual heatproof serving dishes. • Sprinkle with the brown sugar. • Turn on the broiler (grill). Broil the fruit 4–6 inches (10–15 cm) from the heat source until the sugar has caramelized. • Serve hot.

Broiled bananas with strawberry coulis

Fruit baskets with balsamic vinegar

## Summer fruit compôte

*Serves: 6*
*Preparation: 10 minutes*
*Cooking: 12 minutes*
*Recipe grading: easy*

• 8 oz/250 g peaches, pitted
• 8 oz/250 g apricots, pitted
• 3$^1$/$_2$ oz/100 g seedless white grapes, cut in half
• 3 tablespoons butter
• $^1$/$_2$ cup/100 g superfine/caster sugar
• 1 cup/250 ml fruity white wine
• 3$^1$/$_2$ oz/100 g strawberries
• $^3$/$_4$ cup/180 ml heavy/double cream
• $^1$/$_2$ cup/50 g finely chopped hazelnuts, toasted

Cut the peaches and apricots into small bite-sized pieces. • Sauté the fruit in the butter in a small saucepan for 2 minutes. Add the sugar and wine and cook for 10 minutes. • Remove from heat and let cool completely. • Add the strawberries. • Beat the cream in a medium bowl with an electric mixer at high speed until stiff. • Serve the fruit, topped with the cream and sprinkled with the hazelnuts.

## Fruit baskets with balsamic vinegar

*Serves: 6*
*Preparation: 25 minutes*
*Cooking: 8–10 minutes*
*Recipe grading: easy*

• 7 oz/200 g frozen puff pastry, thawed
• 1 small cantaloupe/rock melon, weighing about 1 lb/500 g
• 4 apricots, pitted
• 6 oz/180 g strawberries, hulled
• 2 peaches, pitted
• 2–4 red plums, pitted
• 1 watermelon, weighing about 12 oz/400 g
• 2 tablespoons sugar
• 2 tablespoons balsamic vinegar
• 4 leaves fresh mint

Preheat the oven to 400°F/200°C/gas 6. • Butter six small ovenproof ramekins. • Unroll or unfold the pastry on a lightly floured surface. Use a sharp knife to cut the pastry into 6 squares. • Line the bottom and sides of each prepared mold with a pastry square, trimming the edges to fit. Prick the pastry well with a fork. • Bake for 8–10 minutes, or until lightly browned. • Rinse the fruit thoroughly under cold running water and dry well. Cut into bite-sized pieces. • Place the fruit in a large bowl with the sugar and balsamic vinegar, mixing well. • Spoon the fruit into the baked pastry shells, decorate with the mint leaves, and serve immediately.

DESSERTS

# Pears
## with fruits of the forest sauce

*Serves: 6*
*Preparation: 20 minutes*
*Cooking: 20–25 minutes*
*Recipe grading: fairly easy*

- 3 pears, peeled, cored, and cut in half
- juice of 1¹/₂ lemons
- 4 tablespoons water + extra to cover the pears
- 1³/₄ cups/350 g sugar
- 1 stick cinnamon
- 1¹/₄ cups/310 g mixed fruits of the forest, such as raspberries, blackcurrants, blueberries, or strawberries
- ¹/₂ cup/125 ml sweet dessert wine
- ¹/₃ cup/50 g confectioners'/icing sugar

Drizzle the pears with the juice of ¹/₂ lemon to prevent them from turning brown. • Place in a small saucepan and add enough water to just cover the pears, 1 cup (200 g) of sugar, juice of ¹/₂ lemon, and the cinnamon. Cook for 12–15 minutes, or until the pears are tender but still firm. • Remove from heat and let cool in the syrup. • Place the fruits of the forest (reserving a few for decoration) in a medium saucepan. Add the remaining sugar, 4 tablespoons of water, the wine, and the remaining lemon juice. Place over low heat and cook until the mixture starts to thicken. • Transfer to a food processor or blender and process until puréed. Strain to remove the seeds. • Drain the pears and place one pear half in each of six individual serving dishes. Cut into thin slices and spoon the fruits of the forest sauce over the top. • Decorate with the reserved fruit, dust with the confectioners' sugar, and serve.

# Tropical fruit baskets

*Serves: 6–8*
*Preparation: 20 minutes*
*Cooking: 8–10 minutes*
*Recipe grading: fairly easy*

- ¹/₂ cup/125 g butter
- 8 tablespoons corn/golden syrup
- ¹/₂ cup/50 g sugar
- ¹/₂ teaspoon cream of tartar
- ³/₄ cup/125 g all-purpose/plain flour
- 2 teaspoon ground ginger
- fresh fruit salad, made with fruits of the season, sliced and marinated with lemon juice and sugar

Preheat the oven to 350°F/180°C/gas 4. • Butter a large baking sheet. • Heat the butter, corn syrup, and sugar over low heat in a small saucepan until melted. • Remove from heat and stir in the cream of tartar, flour, and ginger. • Drop tablespoons of the mixture onto the prepared baking sheet. Shape into 2-inch (5-cm) rounds, spacing well apart. • Bake for 8–10 minutes, or until golden brown. • Cool the cookies on the sheet for 5 minutes, or until pliable. • Use a thin metal spatula to remove them from the sheet. • Shape into small baskets, fluting the edges with your fingertips. • Let cool completely, then fill with fresh fruit salad just before serving.

Tropical fruit baskets

to cook evenly. • Beat the egg yolks, the remaining sugar, rusks, Amaretti cookies, and rum in a large bowl with an electric mixer at medium speed until well blended. • Beat the egg whites and salt in a large bowl until stiff peaks form. • Use a large rubber spatula to fold them into the mixture. • Arrange the figs and peaches in the prepared baking dish. • Pour the egg mixture over the top. • Bake for 25–30 minutes, or until lightly browned on top. • Serve hot.

## Peach and Ricotta pie

*Serves: 4*
*Preparation: 20 minutes*
*Cooking: 55–60 minutes*
*Recipe grading: easy*

- 5 tablespoons butter
- 2 tablespoons dry bread crumbs
- $^1/_2$ cup/100 g granulated sugar
- $^1/_8$ teaspoon salt
- 8 oz/250 g Ricotta cheese
- 2 eggs, separated
- $^1/_3$ cup/50 g cornstarch/cornflour
- zest and juice of 1 lemon
- 2 tablespoons finely ground almonds, toasted
- 3 yellow peaches, pitted and sliced
- 2 tablespoons confectioners'/icing sugar

Preheat the oven to 325°F/170°C/gas 3. • Butter an 8-inch (20-cm) pie pan and sprinkle with the bread crumbs. • Beat the butter, sugar, and salt in a large bowl with an electric mixer at high speed until creamy. • With mixer at medium speed, add the Ricotta and egg yolks, beating until just blended. • Stir in the cornstarch, lemon juice and zest, and almonds. • With mixer at high speed, beat the egg whites in a medium bowl until stiff peaks form. • Use a large rubber spatula to fold them into the mixture. • Stir in the peaches. • Pour the mixture into the prepared pan. • Bake for 55–60 minutes, or until a toothpick inserted into the center comes out clean. •

## Broiled fruit skewers

*Serves: 4*
*Preparation: 20 minutes*
*Cooking: 10 minutes*
*Recipe grading: easy*

- 1 small pineapple, peeled and tough inner core removed
- 2 large Granny Smith apples, peeled and cored
- 1–2 mangoes, peeled
- 4 kiwifruit, peeled
- 3–4 bananas, peeled
- 4 tablespoons honey
- 3 tablespoons dark rum
- 2 tablespoons fresh lemon juice
- $1^1/_2$ cups/375 ml heavy/double cream
- pulp of 2 passion fruit
- 2 tablespoons sugar

Chop the fruit into bite-sized chunks. • Thread the fruit alternately onto 8 long skewers. If using wooden skewers, dip them in cold water to prevent them from burning. • Mix the honey, rum, and lemon juice in a small bowl. • Brush half the mixture over the fruit. • Turn on the broiler (grill). • Broil the skewers 4–6 inches (10–15 cm) from the heat source. Cook, turning and basting

often with the remaining honey mixture, until the fruit is lightly browned. • Beat the cream, passion fruit pulp, and sugar in a small bowl with an electric mixer at high speed until stiff. Serve with the grilled fruit.

## Peach and fig bake

*Serves: 8*
*Preparation: 30 minutes*
*Cooking: 35–40 minutes*
*Recipe grading: easy*

- 12 figs
- 6 peaches
- $^1/_2$ cup/100 g sugar
- 3 eggs, separated + 3 egg yolks
- 10 rusks/Zwieback, crumbled
- 3 Amaretti cookies/macaroons, store-bought and crumbled
- 4 tablespoons dark rum
- $^1/_8$ teaspoon salt

Preheat the oven to 350°F/180°C/gas 4. • Butter a large baking dish. • Cut the figs and peaches into segments. • Sprinkle with a little of the sugar. • Turn on the broiler (grill). • Broil the fruit for 10 minutes, turning often

Dust with the confectioners' sugar and serve hot or at room temperature.

## Pineapple glacé

*Serves: 4*
*Preparation: 25 minutes + 6 hours to chill*
*Recipe grading: easy*

- 2 small pineapples
- 6 tablespoons orange liqueur
- 2 tablespoons sugar
- 1 quart/1 liter vanilla ice cream

Rinse the pineapples thoroughly under cold running water and dry well. Slice in half lengthwise, leaving the tops attached. • Use a knife and spoon to scoop out the flesh, leaving a shell about $^1/_2$-inch (1-cm) thick. Reserve the flesh. • Sprinkle the shell with the sugar and drizzle each half with $^1/_2$ tablespoon orange liqueur. • Refrigerate for at least 4 hours. • Leave the ice cream out at room temperature for 10 minutes to soften. • Chop the pineapple flesh finely and stir it into the ice cream with the remaining orange liqueur. • Spoon the ice cream into the shells and freeze for 2 hours before serving.

## Baked cinnamon apricots

*Serves: 6*
*Preparation: 30 minutes*
*Cooking: 10–15 minutes*
*Recipe grading: easy*

- 1 cup/250 ml dry white wine
- $^1/_2$ cup/100 g firmly packed light brown sugar
- 1 teaspoon ground cinnamon
- 12 large apricots, pitted and cut in half
- 12 Amaretti cookies/macaroons, crushed
- $^1/_4$ cup/45 g pine nuts
- $^1/_4$ cup/45 g raisins

Preheat the oven to 400°F/200°C/gas 6. • Butter a large baking dish. • Mix the wine, brown sugar, and cinnamon in a small saucepan. Cook over high heat for 15 minutes, or until syrupy. • Use a teaspoon to scoop out a little of the flesh from each apricot half. Chop finely. • Arrange the apricot halves in the prepared baking dish. • Drizzle with the syrup and sprinkle with the Amaretti cookies, chopped apricots, pine nuts, and raisins. • Bake for 10–15 minutes, or until lightly browned. • Serve hot or at room temperature.

## Apricot pockets

*Serves: 6*
*Preparation: 20 minutes*
*Cooking: 12–15 minutes*
*Recipe grading: easy*

- 1 cup/250 ml dry white wine
- 6 tablespoons brown sugar
- 2 tablespoons honey
- 1 teaspoon ground cinnamon
- 12 apricots, cut in half and pitted
- 10 Amaretti cookies/macaroons, crushed
- 2 tablespoons pine nuts
- 2 tablespoons raisins

Preheat the oven to 400°F/200°C/gas 6. • Cook the wine, brown sugar, honey, and cinnamon in a medium saucepan over high heat until syrupy. • Cut out 6 pieces of nonstick parchment paper to make the "pockets." • Place two apricots in each pocket and pour over a little of the syrup. Sprinkle with the Amaretti cookies and decorate with the pine nuts and raisins. • Tie up the pockets with kitchen string. • Bake for 12–15 minutes, or until the apricots have softened. • Serve warm.

Pineapple glacé

Peanut brownies

## Peanut brownies

*Serves: 4*
*Preparation: 25 minutes*
*Cooking: 35–40 minutes*
*Recipe grading: fairly easy*

- $^3/_4$ cup/180 g butter
- 1 egg
- $^2/_3$ cup/140 g firmly packed light brown sugar
- $^1/_2$ teaspoon baking powder
- $1^1/_3$ cups/200 g all-purpose/plain flour
- $1^3/_4$ cups/430 ml sweetened condensed milk
- $^1/_8$ teaspoon salt
- 1 cup/100 g finely chopped peanuts

Preheat the oven to 350°F/180°C/gas 4. • Line a baking sheet with parchment paper. • Beat $^2/_3$ cup (150 g) of butter, the egg, $^1/_3$ cup (70 g) brown sugar, and the baking powder in a large bowl with an electric mixer at medium speed until creamy. • With mixer at low speed, gradually beat in the flour. • Pour the mixture onto the prepared baking sheet, spreading it out. • Bake for 20–25 minutes, or until a toothpick inserted into the center comes out clean. • Lower the oven temperature to 300°F/150°C/gas 2. • Cook the remaining butter, remaining sugar, condensed milk, and salt in a small saucepan over low heat, stirring constantly, until well blended. • Remove from heat and stir in the peanuts. • Pour the peanut mixture over the baked cake. • Bake for 15 minutes more. • Turn off the oven and let the brownies cool in the oven with the door slightly ajar. • Cut into squares, peel off the parchment paper, and serve.

## Almond cookies

*Serves: 6*
*Preparation: 30 minutes*
*Cooking: 40–45 minutes*
*Recipe grading: easy*

- 6 egg whites
- 6 cups/600 g finely ground almonds
- $2^1/_2$ cups/500 g sugar
- 1 tablespoon butter
- 4 tablespoons all-purpose/plain flour

Preheat the oven to 350°F/180°C/gas 4. • Butter and flour a baking sheet. • Beat the egg whites in a large bowl with an electric mixer at high speed until stiff peaks form. • Use a large rubber spatula to fold in the almonds and sugar. • Transfer to a large bowl over barely simmering water and cook for 20 minutes, stirring constantly. • Fold in the flour. • Drop tablespoons of the mixture onto the prepared baking sheet. • Bake for 40–45 minutes, or until golden brown. • Cool the cookies completely on the baking sheet.

## Chocolate truffles

*Serves: 6*
*Preparation: 20 minutes + 2 hours to chill*
*Recipe grading: easy*

- 4 tablespoons butter
- $^1/_2$ cup/75 g confectioners'/icing sugar
- 2 egg yolks
- $^1/_2$ cup/125 ml light/single cream
- $^1/_2$ teaspoon vanilla extract/essence
- 10 oz/300 g semisweet/dark chocolate, coarsely grated
- 4 tablespoons unsweetened cocoa powder

Beat the butter and confectioners' sugar in a large bowl with an electric mixer at high speed until creamy. • With mixer at medium speed, add the egg yolks, beating until just blended. • Bring the cream to a boil over medium heat. • Remove from heat and add the vanilla. • Pour the cream into the butter mixture. Stir in the chocolate and let cool • Refrigerate for at least 2 hours. • Use a tablespoon to form the mixture into balls the size of walnuts. Roll in the cocoa. • Refrigerate until ready to serve.

## Rice pudding with raspberry sauce

*Serves: 8*
*Preparation: 20 minutes + 2 hours to chill*
*Cooking: 45 minutes*
*Recipe grading: fairly easy*

- 1 tablespoon almond oil
- 1 quart/1 liter milk
- finely grated zest of $^1/_2$ lemon
- $^1/_8$ teaspoon salt
- 1 cup/200 g short-grain rice
- 1 firm-ripe pear, weighing about 5 oz/150 g, peeled, cored, and cubed
- $^2/_3$ cup/140 g sugar
- 1 tablespoon almond liqueur
- $^1/_2$ cup/125 g raspberries, washed
- $^1/_3$ cup/110 g raspberry preserves

Grease a $1^1/_2$ quart (1.5 liter) pudding mold with the almond oil. • Bring the milk, lemon zest, and salt to a boil in a large saucepan. • Stir in the rice and simmer for 10 minutes. • Add the pear to the rice mixture. • Cook, stirring constantly, until thick, creamy, and dense, about 35 minutes. • Remove from heat and stir in the sugar and almond liqueur. • Pour the mixture into the prepared mold and let cool to room temperature. • Refrigerate for at least 2 hours. • Dip the mold in warm water, invert, and turn out onto a serving plate. • Arrange the raspberries on top of the pudding. • Heat the raspberry preserves in a small saucepan over low heat until liquid. • Spoon the preserves over the raspberries and serve.

## Sticky raisin puddings with caramel sauce

*Serves: 6–10*
*Preparation: 40 minutes*
*Cooking: 15–20 minutes*
*Recipe grading: fairly easy*

### Dough

- 1 cup/180 g golden raisins/sultanas
- 4 tablespoons cherry liqueur
- 4 tablespoons water
- 1⅓ cups/200 g all-purpose/plain flour
- ⅓ cup/50 g cornstarch/cornflour
- ½ teaspoon baking powder
- ½ cup/80 g almonds
- 1¼ cups/250 g sugar
- 1 cup/250 g butter, softened
- ⅛ teaspoon salt
- 4 eggs, separated
- ¾ cup/180 ml milk
- 2 teaspoons dark rum

### Caramel sauce

- 6 tablespoons butter
- ½ cup/100 g firmly packed light brown sugar
- 1⅔ cups/400 ml heavy/double cream

Preheat the oven to 350°F/180°C/gas 4. • Butter 10 individual soufflé molds. • Soak the raisins in the cherry liqueur and water in a small bowl for 10 minutes. Drain and set aside. • Sift the flour, cornstarch, and baking powder into a large bowl. • Process the almonds and ¼ cup (50 g) sugar in a food processor until finely ground. • Stir the almond mixture into the dry ingredients. • Beat the butter, remaining sugar, and salt in a large bowl with an electric mixer at high speed until creamy. • With mixer at medium speed, add the egg yolks, beating until just blended. • With mixer at low speed, gradually beat in the dry ingredients, followed by the milk and rum. • With mixer at high speed, beat the egg whites in a large bowl until stiff peaks form. • Use a large rubber spatula to fold them into the mixture. • Stir in the raisins. • Divide the mixture evenly among the prepared molds. • Place the molds on a baking sheet. • Bake for 15–20 minutes, or until golden brown. • Cool the puddings completely in the molds. • Turn out onto individual serving plates. • Caramel sauce: Cook the butter and brown sugar in a small saucepan over low heat, stirring constantly, until melted. • Stir in ¾ cup (180 ml) of cream. Bring to a boil and cook for 5 minutes, or until the sauce has thickened. • Spoon the sauce over the puddings. • With mixer at high speed, beat the cream in a large bowl until stiff. • Decorate each pudding with a little cream and serve.

## Poor man's cake

*Serves: 6*
*Preparation: 30 minutes + 40 minutes to soak*
*Cooking: 25–30 minutes*
*Recipe grading: easy*

- 1 cup/180 g golden raisins/sultanas
- ½ cup/125 ml dark rum
- 12 oz/350 g stale white bread
- 1 quart/1 liter milk
- 6 tablespoons butter
- 1¼ cups/250 g sugar
- 5 eggs, lightly beaten
- grated zest of 1 lemon

Soak the raisins in the rum in a small bowl for 10 minutes. Drain and set aside. • Cut the bread into small pieces and place in a large bowl. • Bring the milk to a boil in a small saucepan. • Stir in the butter and sugar and pour over the bread. • Set aside

*Sticky raisin puddings with caramel sauce*

for 30 minutes, or until the bread has absorbed all the milk. • Preheat the oven to 350°F/180°C/gas 4. • Butter a 10-inch (25-cm) round baking pan and sprinkle with bread crumbs. • Add the eggs, raisins, and lemon zest to the bread mixture. • Pour the mixture into the prepared pan. • Bake for 25–30 minutes, or until lightly browned and a toothpick inserted into the center comes out clean. • Cool the cake in the pan for 15 minutes. • Turn out onto a rack and serve warm.

## Chocolate mold

*Serves: 6*
*Preparation: 30 minutes*
*Cooking: 20–25 minutes*
*Recipe grading: fairly easy*

- ½ cup/75 g all-purpose/plain flour
- 1 cup/250 ml milk
- ½ cup/100 g sugar
- 4 tablespoons butter
- 4 eggs, separated
- 5 tablespoons unsweetened cocoa powder

Preheat the oven to 375°F/190°C/gas 5. • Butter and flour a 10-inch (25-cm) ring mold. • Mix the flour with 2 tablespoons milk in a small bowl until smooth. • Bring the remaining milk to a boil in a small saucepan with the sugar and butter. • Stir in the flour mixture and mix well. • Remove from heat and let cool completely. • Beat the egg yolks in a large bowl with an electric mixer at high speed until pale. • Beat the egg whites in a large bowl until stiff peaks form. • Use a large rubber spatula to fold the cocoa into the cooled milk mixture, followed by the beaten yolks and beaten whites. • Pour the mixture into the prepared mold. • Bake for 20–25 minutes, or until a toothpick inserted into the center comes out clean. • Cool the cake completely in the mold. • Invert the mold and turn out onto a serving plate.

Strawberries in red wine

deep flameproof casserole into which they fit snugly, standing upright, stalks uppermost. • Sprinkle with $^1/_2$ cup (100 g) sugar. Pour in the wine and add the cloves, lemon zest, and cinnamon, if using. • Bake for 50–60 minutes, or until tender and an attractive russet color. • Lift the pears carefully out of the wine and place upright in a serving dish or in individual glass dishes. • Pour the cooking liquid into a small saucepan and cook over medium heat until reduced to a pouring syrup. • Discard the cloves, lemon zest, and cinnamon. • Pour the syrup over the pears. • Serve at room temperature.

## Strawberries in red wine

*Serves: 4*
*Preparation: 10 minutes*
*Recipe grading: easy*

- 1$^1/_4$ cups/300 g strawberries, washed and hulled
- 3 tablespoons sugar
- 4 tablespoons dry red wine

Cut the strawberries into small pieces. Place in individual serving bowls and sprinkle with the sugar. • Drizzle with the wine and serve.

## Sautéed pineapple slices with Ricotta cream

*Serves: 4*
*Preparation: 15minutes*
*Cooking: 10–15 minutes*
*Recipe grading: easy*

- $^3/_4$ cup/180 g Ricotta cheese
- 4 tablespoons sugar
- 2 tablespoons heavy/double cream
- juice of 1 lemon
- 1 medium pineapple, peeled and tough inner core removed
- 2 tablespoons butter
- $^1/_4$ teaspoon ground cinnamon

## Cherries cooked in red wine

*Serves: 4*
*Preparation: 15 minutes*
*Cooking: 25–30 minutes*
*Recipe grading: easy*

- 1$^1/_2$ lb/750 g cherries, pitted
- 1$^1/_4$ cups/250 g sugar
- 2 cups/500 ml full-bodied, dry red wine
- 1$^1/_4$ -inch/3-cm stick cinnamon
- 2–3 pieces shredded orange zest
- 2 tablespoons redcurrant jelly

Cook the cherries, sugar, wine, cinnamon, and orange zest in a large saucepan over low heat for 25–30 minutes, stirring occasionally. • Use a slotted spoon to remove the cherries from the liquid, draining them briefly. Transfer the cherries to a serving dish. • Discard the cinnamon. • Add the redcurrant

jelly to the cooking liquid and cook over medium heat until the jelly has melted. • Pour the liquid over the cherries and serve.

## Pears in red wine

*Serves: 4*
*Preparation: 15 minutes*
*Cooking: 50–60 minutes*
*Recipe grading: easy*

- 4 large firm-ripe cooking pears
- 1$^1/_4$ cups/250 g sugar
- 2 cups/500 ml full-bodied, dry red wine (preferably Barolo)
- 3 cloves
- 2 pieces lemon zest
- $^3/_4$-inch/2-cm stick cinnamon (optional)

Preheat the oven to 350°F/180°C/gas 4. • Peel the pears carefully, leaving them whole with the stalk still attached. • Transfer to a

Beat the Ricotta, sugar, cream, and lemon juice in a medium bowl with an electric mixer at high speed until creamy. • Cut the pineapple into eight thick slices. • Sauté the pineapple in the butter in a large skillet (frying pan) over high heat, turning often, for 10–15 minutes or until caramelized. • Transfer to serving plates and drop a tablespoon of the Ricotta cream in the center of each slice. Dust with the cinnamon and serve.

## Lemon cream dessert

*Serves: 4–6*
*Preparation: 15 minutes + 2 hours to chill*
*Cooking: 10 minutes*
*Recipe grading: easy*

- $^1/_2$ cup/100 g sugar
- $^3/_4$ cup/125 g all-purpose/plain flour
- grated zest of 2 lemons
- 1 quart/1 liter milk

Stir together the sugar, flour, and zest of 1 lemon in a medium saucepan. • Gradually pour in the milk, making sure that no lumps form. • Place over medium-low heat and bring to a boil, stirring constantly. • Boil for 1 minute, then remove from heat. • Pour into a pudding mold and let cool completely. • Refrigerate for at least 2 hours. • Serve cold, sprinkled with the remaining grated lemon zest.

## Zabaglione

*Serves: 4*
*Preparation: 15 minutes*
*Cooking: 10–15 minutes*
*Recipe grading: easy*

- 4 egg yolks
- $^1/_3$ cup/70 g sugar
- scant $^1/_2$ cup/100 ml dry Marsala or sherry

Beat the egg yolks and sugar in a double boiler (not yet on the heat) until pale and thick. • Add the Marsala gradually, beating constantly. • Place the pan over barely simmering water and cook, beating constantly with a whisk, until the mixture thickens. • Keep the heat extremely low so that the zabaglione does not boil or it will curdle. • Serve warm or cold. If serving cold, cover with plastic wrap (cling film) so that it is touching the surface to prevent a skin from forming as the mixture cools.

Sautéed pineapple slices with Ricotta cream

beating until just blended. • Stir in the rum. • Pour the mixture into the prepared mold. • Bake for 30–35 minutes, or until lightly browned. • Cool the cake for 15 minutes in the pan. • Turn out onto a serving plate and serve warm.

## Ginger and banana loaf

*Serves: 4*
*Preparation: 25 minutes*
*Cooking: 55–60 minutes*
*Recipe grading: easy*

- $^3/_4$ cup/135 g golden raisins/sultanas, soaked in warm water for 10 minutes and drained
- $^3/_4$ cup/75 g candied ginger, cut into small cubes
- 1 cup/150 g all-purpose/plain flour
- $^1/_3$ cup/50 g whole-wheat/wholemeal flour
- $^1/_2$ teaspoon baking powder
- $^3/_4$ cup/180 g butter, softened
- 1$^1/_3$ cups/200 g confectioners'/icing sugar
- 2 eggs + 4 egg yolks
- 1 tablespoon dark rum
- $^1/_2$ teaspoon vanilla extract/essence
- $^1/_8$ teaspoon salt
- grated zest of 1 lemon
- 1 large ripe banana, mashed

Preheat the oven to 350°F/180°C/gas 4. • Butter a 9 x 5-inch (23 x 13-cm) loaf pan. Line with aluminum foil, letting the edges overhang. • Sprinkle the raisins and ginger with enough flour to cover lightly, about 1–2 tablespoons. • Sift the remaining flours and baking powder into a large bowl. • Beat the butter and confectioners' sugar in a large bowl with an electric mixer

## Rice pudding with raisins and candied peel

*Serves: 6*
*Preparation: 20 minutes*
*Cooking: 30–35 minutes*
*Recipe grading: easy*

- $^3/_4$ cup/150 g short-grain rice, such as Italian Arborio
- 1 quart/1 liter milk
- 1 vanilla pod
- $^1/_2$ cup/100 g sugar
- $^1/_2$ cup/90 g golden raisins/sultanas
- 2 tablespoons finely chopped candied peel
- $^1/_8$ teaspoon salt
- 1 teaspoon butter
- 2 eggs + 2 egg yolks
- $^1/_2$ cup/125 ml dark rum

Preheat the oven to 350°F/180°C/gas 4. • Butter a turban ring mold and sprinkle with bread crumbs. • Bring the rice, milk, and vanilla pod to a boil and simmer for 10 minutes. • Discard the vanilla pod. • Add the sugar, raisins, candied peel, salt, and butter. Remove from heat and let cool completely. • Add the eggs and egg yolks,

at high speed until creamy. • With mixer at medium speed, add the eggs and egg yolks one at a time, beating until just blended after each addition. • Beat in the rum, vanilla, salt, and lemon zest. • With mixer at low speed, gradually beat in the dry ingredients, followed by the raisins, ginger, and banana. • Spoon the batter into the prepared pan, smoothing the top. • Bake for 55–60 minutes, or until a toothpick inserted into the center comes out clean. • Cool the loaf completely in the pan. • Turn out onto a rack and remove the foil.

## Almond and pistachio cake

*Serves: 8*

*Preparation: 30 minutes + 1 hour 30 minutes to
    cool*

*Cooking: 40–45 minutes*

*Recipe grading: easy*

- 1¹/₄ cups/250 g sugar
- ²/₃ cup/150 ml water
- ¹/₃ cup/50 g almonds, shelled
- 2 cups/200 g finely chopped almonds
- 1 cup/100 g finely chopped pistachios
- 6 tablespoons butter
- ²/₃ cup/150 ml milk
- grated zest of 1 orange
- 1 teaspoon ground cinnamon
- 1 teaspoon honey
- 2 rolls fresh short-crust pastry
- 1 egg yolk, lightly beaten

Preheat the oven to 350°F/180°C/gas 4. • Butter and flour a 10-inch (26-cm) baking pan. • Bring the sugar and water to a boil in a heavy-bottomed saucepan over high heat. • Reduce the heat and cook for 15 minutes, or until the sugar begins to caramelize. • Remove from heat and stir in ¹/₄ cup (40 g) of whole almonds, the finely chopped almonds, ¹/₂ cup (50 g) of pistachios, the butter, milk, orange zest, and cinnamon. • Return the saucepan to low heat and cook, stirring constantly, for 15 minutes, or until the mixture thickens. • Add the honey and remove from heat. • Pour the mixture into a large bowl and let cool for 30 minutes, stirring occasionally. •

Unfold or unroll the pastry on a lightly floured surface. • Fit the pastry into the bottom of the prepared pan, trimming the edges to fit. • Spoon the nut mixture over the top, spreading it out. • Cover with a second pastry layer, trimming the edges to fit. Moisten the edges and seal well. Prick all over with a fork and make a small incision in the top of the pastry to allow air to escape during baking. • Brush with the beaten egg yolk and sprinkle with the remaining pistachios and almonds. • Bake for 40–45 minutes, or until firm to the touch. • Cool the cake in the pan for 1 hour.

## Golden raisin focaccia

*Serves: 10*
*Preparation: 1 hour + 3 hours 30 minutes to rest the dough*
*Cooking: 35–40 minutes*
*Recipe grading: complicated*

- 1 oz/30 g fresh yeast or 2 packages (¼ oz/7 g) active dry yeast
- 1 cup/250 ml warm milk
- ⅛ teaspoon salt
- 2⅓ cups/350 g all-purpose/plain flour
- 1 cup/150 g whole-wheat/wholemeal flour
- 8 tablespoons butter, melted
- 2 Golden Delicious apples, peeled and cut into thin slices
- ½ cup/90 g golden raisins/sultanas
- 2 oz/60 g semisweet/plain chocolate, cut into shavings
- 2 tablespoons pine nuts
- 2 teaspoons light brown sugar
- 1 tablespoon sugar crystals

Mix the yeast, ⅔ cup (150 ml) of milk, and salt in a small bowl. Set aside for 5 minutes, or until foamy. • Sift the flours into a large bowl and make a well in the center. • Stir in 6 tablespoons of butter, the yeast mixture, and remaining milk to obtain a smooth dough. • Knead for 5–7 minutes, or until smooth and elastic. • Place in an oiled bowl, cover with a clean cloth, and let rise for 3 hours. • Butter and flour a 10-inch (25-cm) baking pan. • Sauté the apples in the butter in a skillet (frying pan) until lightly browned. • Turn the dough out onto a lightly floured surface. Roll out to a ¼-inch (5-mm) thick. • Sprinkle with the raisins, chocolate, sautéed apples, pine nuts, and brown sugar. • Shape into a large roll and cut into 2-inch (5-mm) slices. • Place the slices in the prepared pan, fitting them closely together. • Cover with a clean cloth and let rise for 30 minutes more. • Sprinkle with the sugar crystals. • Bake for 35–40 minutes, or until lightly browned and risen. • Cool the focaccia in the pan for 15 minutes. • Serve warm.

## Yellow cornmeal and candied fruits cake

*Serves: 6*
*Preparation: 1 hour + 15 minutes to stand*
*Cooking: 1 hour*
*Recipe grading: fairly easy*

- $^2/_3$ cup/60 g coarsely chopped almonds
- $^1/_3$ cup/30 g finely chopped candied peel and cherries
- 2 tablespoons finely chopped dried figs
- 3 tablespoons raisins
- 1 teaspoon fennel seeds
- 5 tablespoons grappa or eau-de-vie
- 1 quart/1 liter milk
- 2 cups/300 g finely ground yellow cornmeal/very fine polenta
- $^2/_3$ cup/100 g all-purpose/plain flour
- 6 tablespoons butter
- 6 tablespoons shortening/lard
- $^1/_2$ cup/100 g sugar
- $^1/_8$ teaspoon salt

Preheat the oven to 350°F/180°C/gas 4. • Butter and flour a 10-inch (25-cm) baking pan. • Stir together the almonds, candied peel and cherries, figs, raisins, fennel seeds, and grappa in a large bowl. Let stand for 15 minutes. • Bring the milk to a boil in a large saucepan. • Gradually add the cornmeal and flour, stirring constantly with a wooden spoon over low heat. Cook for 15 minutes, stirring constantly. • Add the butter, shortening, sugar, and salt and cook for 10 minutes more. • Remove from heat and add the fruit mixture. • Pour the batter into the prepared pan, tapping the pan on the work bench to settle the batter. • Bake for 30 minutes. Remove from the oven and cover with aluminum foil. • Bake for 25–30 minutes more, or until firm to the touch. • Cool the cake in the pan for 15 minutes. • Turn out onto a serving plate and serve warm.

Golden raisin focaccia

## Frosted lemon cake

*Serves: 6–8*
*Preparation: 30 minutes*
*Cooking: 55–60 minutes*
*Recipe grading: easy*

- $1^1/_4$ cups/180 g potato flour
- 2 cups/300 g all-purpose/plain flour
- 2 teaspoons baking powder
- 1 cup/250 g butter, softened
- $1^1/_4$ cups/250 g sugar
- finely grated zest and juice of 1 lemon
- 4 eggs
- $1^1/_2$ cups/225 g confectioners'/icing sugar

Preheat the oven to 350°F/180°C/gas 4. • Butter and flour a 9 x 5-inch (23 x 13-cm) loaf pan. • Sift the flours and baking powder into a large bowl. • Beat the butter and sugar in a large bowl with an electric mixer at medium speed until creamy. Add the lemon zest and eggs, beating until just blended. • With mixer at low speed, gradually add the dry ingredients. • Pour the batter into the prepared pan. • Bake for 55–60 minutes, or until a toothpick inserted into the center comes out clean. • Cool the cake in the pan for 15 minutes. • Turn out onto a rack and let cool completely. • Beat the confectioners' sugar with enough lemon juice to make a thick frosting. • Spread over the top of the cake and serve.

## Polenta and lemon cake

*Serves: 6–8*
*Preparation: 20 minutes*
*Cooking: 35–40 minutes*
*Recipe grading: easy*

- 1 cup/250 g butter, softened
- $2^1/_2$ cups/375 g confectioners'/icing sugar
- 3 eggs + 6 egg yolks
- 2 tablespoons lemon liqueur
- 1 cup/100 g finely ground almonds
- $1^3/_4$ cups/275 g finely ground yellow cornmeal/very fine polenta
- 1 cup/150 g all-purpose/plain flour
- finely grated zest of 1 lemon
- 1 teaspoon baking powder
- $^1/_2$ teaspoon vanilla extract/essence

Preheat the oven to 375°F/190°C/gas 5. • Butter and flour a 9-inch (23-cm) fluted tube pan. • Beat the butter and confectioners' sugar in a large bowl with an electric mixer at high speed until creamy. • With mixer at medium speed, add the eggs and egg yolks, beating until just blended. • Stir in the lemon liqueur, almonds, cornmeal, flour, lemon zest, baking powder, and vanilla. • Spoon the batter into the prepared pan. • Bake for 35–40 minutes, or until a toothpick inserted into the center comes out clean. • Cool the cake in the pan for 15 minutes. • Turn out onto a rack and let cool completely.

*Like all nuts, almonds are high in protein and healthy oils. Almonds are widely available as whole nuts or in various prepared forms, from finely ground to unblanched Their distinctive flavor adds aroma and interest to a wide range of dishes, from candies and desserts to salads and starters.*

## Almond nougat

*Serves: 4*
*Preparation: 10 minutes*
*Recipe grading: easy*

- 1 cup/200 g sugar
- 2 cups/300 g unpeeled almonds
- 1 teaspoon vanilla extract/essence
- 2 tablespoons almond oil

Place the sugar in a large heavy-bottomed saucepan over medium-low heat. Stir in the almonds and vanilla. • Cook, stirring constantly with a wooden spoon, until the sugar begins to stick to the almonds. The mixture should become semi-liquid and the almonds will begin to stick together. • Grease a marble surface with the almond oil. • Pour the mixture onto the surface and let cool to warm. • Use a metal spatula to work the mixture until it is about $^1/_2$-inch (1-cm) thick. • Leave until almost, but not completely, cool. • Use a long sharp knife to cut the nougat into bars. • Set aside for 12 hours in a cool place before serving.

## Mountain snow dessert

*Serves: 4–6*
*Preparation: 20 minutes + 4 hours to stand*

*Cooking: 10–15 minutes*
*Recipe grading: easy*

- 3 eggs
- 1$^2/_3$ cups/250 g all-purpose/plain flour
- $^1/_2$ cup/125 g butter, softened
- $^1/_4$ teaspoon salt
- 3 tablespoons brandy
- 2$^2/_3$ cups/400 g confectioners'/icing sugar
- 4 teaspoons fresh lemon juice

Preheat the oven to 350°F/180°C/gas 4. • Butter a large baking sheet. • Separate two eggs and place the whites in a large bowl. Set aside. • Sift the flour into a large bowl and make a well in the center. • Add the remaining egg and egg yolks, the butter, salt, and brandy. • Use your hands to work the ingredients into the flour until the dough is smooth and elastic. • Divide the dough into 4 or 5 portions and roll each into a long cylinder. Cut into slices about $^1/_2$-inch (1-cm) thick. • Place on the prepared baking sheet. • Bake for 10–15 minutes, or until lightly browned. • Cool the cookies completely on the baking sheet. • Beat the egg whites, confectioners' sugar, and lemon juice in a medium bowl with an electric mixer at high speed until smooth. • Set aside 7 tablespoons of the frosting in a small bowl. • Working fast (so that the frosting doesn't have time to set), add the

cookies to the frosting in the large bowl and stir until well coated. • Divide the mixture into 4–6 portions and heap it up on confectioners' or ice cream wafers, cut into squares or disks. • Spoon some of the extra frosting over each one. • Let stand for at least 4 hours before serving.

## Chocolate dream squares

*Serves: 6*
*Preparation: 15 minutes*
*Cooking: 20–25 minutes*
*Recipe grading: easy*

- 8 oz/250 g semisweet/dark chocolate
- $^1/_2$ cup/125 g butter
- 1$^1/_4$ cups/250 g sugar
- $^1/_4$ cup/30 g all-purpose/plain flour
- 4 egg whites
- $^1/_8$ teaspoon salt
- 1 cup/250 ml heavy/double cream

Preheat the oven to 300°F/150°C/gas 2. • Butter a 10-inch (25-cm) pie pan. • Melt the chocolate and butter in a double boiler over barely simmering water. • Remove from heat and add the sugar, followed by the flour. • Beat the egg whites and salt in a large bowl with an electric mixer at high speed until stiff peaks form. • Use a large rubber spatula to fold them into the chocolate mixture. • Spoon the mixture into the prepared pan. • Bake for 20–25 minutes, or until the cake has a slight crust, but is still soft inside. • Cool the cake completely in the pan. • Turn out onto a serving plate. • With mixer at high speed, beat the cream in a medium bowl until stiff. Spread over the cake and serve.

Almond nougat

DESSERTS

# INDEX